Travel and Transport Agency

Travel and Transport Agency

V K Mandal

CYBER TECH PUBLICATIONS
4264/3, Ansari Road, Daryaganj N.Delhi - 110002
Phone : 011-43559448, Fax : 011-23280028
Email : cybertechpublications@gmail.com

CYBER TECH PUBLICATIONS
4264/3, Ansari Road, Daryaganj
New Delhi - 110002 (India)
Phone : 011-23244078, 011-43559448,
Fax : 011-23280028
E-mail : cybertechpublications@gmail.com
Website : www.cybertechpublications.com

Travel and Transport Agency

Published : 2026

ISBN 978-81-7884-374-2

Printed at :

New Green Print Solutions, New Delhi 110078

Preface

The travel agency industry depends upon commissions for a majority of its revenue. When these commissions decrease or stop the industry must change the means in which revenue is made. The Internet has caused a significant reduction in airline ticket sales and therefore has caused travel agencies to change. In addition travel agencies have reduced commissions paid to airlines thus causing more changes. There were four categories of travel agencies discussed in the article along with their adaptation styles. These types include the independent operator of a small travel agency with very limited resources, the normal agency with 2 or 3 agents which does a substantial business, the larger agency that is high-tech and high touch and depends on automation and the Web to some extent (innovators), agencies that are Web based with very little automation otherwise and who were technologically adaptable and saw opportunity in the Web. This book examines how agencies have adapted and prospered through this transitional period.

The objective of this book is to identify a generalizable factor model of job satisfaction for the lodging industry. A model specifying generalizable facets of satisfaction could provide a research base to further study the components of job satisfaction, and in turn job satisfaction's relationship with turnover, absenteeism, and job performance. Rather than building and testing a fixed number of scales developed a priori, a questionnaire was designed incorporating a broad range of items from the Job Descriptive Index.

I hope that this book will produce the real picture of the trade, and its problems what ever it is facing.

—*Author*

Contents

1

INTRODUCTION

LAND TRANSPORT

Although, there are different modes of transport such as surface transport, water transport and air transport. Among these modes of transport, the air transport is most leading transport.

Like the printing press, a transport system is extremely productive and the economies of scale appear in its case at the initial stages of production. The result is a better use of transport fleets leading to reduced fares, especially for leisure and holiday travel.

TOURISM AND TRAVEL

Tourism cannot be differentiated from travel. The types of travel condition the size of the tourism market. Till the steamships and horse carnages were in vogue, holiday travel was limited. The advent of the railways in 1830s made it feasible for mostly people to travel with comfort and speed. There were apprehensions too. On seeing the first train, the Duke of Wellington said, "Progress be damned! All this will do is to allow the lower classes to move around unnecessarily." 'time accordance, the railways became the best economic, comfortable, and fast mode of travel.

The changes in travel technology have been dramatic since World War II. Aeroplane technology developed during the war was brought to commercial usage and has since overtaken individually all other means of travel for international tourism with the US leading the way. The number of Americans who travelled to Europe in 1950 was 2,86,000. The number in 1996 was about 10 million according to US Department of Transportation.

MODES OF TRAVELLING

The starting modes of surface travel are: automobile, bus, rail, and sea. Their importance, however, changes according to the technological advancement, affluence and resources of a country. While the railways are the predominant means of travel in India, China and to a lesser extent in Japan, the automobile has stolen a march on rail in the United States, Canada, Europe and Australia. long route overseas travel is predominantly by air. The old superliner ships are no longer used for tourist transportation. They are now utilised for sea cruises in warm waters for a growing number of affluent holiday makers.

Coach or bus travel remains the cheapest mode of travel anywhere in the world.

The introduction of recent technology in the railways is speedly eroding the speed advantage of the air services, especially on short domestic routes. Speeding up of TVG in France covering 400 kms an hour has caused panic among airlines which had 90 per cent of short-haul traffic with them on some routes.

The relaxation and amusement on a voyage by sea appears to make up for the speed for all those who have time and money for comfortable travel.

New technology has also led to the development of new forms of water-bome transportation, i.e., vessels like Hovercrafts and Hydrofoils. Technically, hovercrafts are like an aircraft because they move a few feet above the surface of the water. It has its derivativesùthe jetfoil and twin-hulled jet cat. These too, have provided speedy transportation over short sea routes and over difficult terrain. People still enjoy travel over water. That has led to new tourist developmentsùyacht mannas, self-driven motor-craft, dingy sailing in the Mediterranean and canal barge holidays in Great Britain.

Fascination with steam engines has led to the reintroduction of lake steamers, in England and paddle steamers in USA.

The automobile is the most liked mode of transport, specially in the developed countries. Railways and coach services are the most used forms of transport in countries like India and China. The air services are normally used for long destination travel though the low cost of air travel in USA has also brought it within the reach of most Americans for domestic short-haul trips.

Automobiles

Automobile is the most famous mode of travel ill over the world, specially in North America and Europe. Within Lurope, the automobile acts a specific role in international travel because it works out to be more economical if one travels in a car with the family. Developing countries too are witnessing a boom in lomestic travel with the increasing number of people being in a òosition to own a car. The successful launching of small Maruti (Suzuki) in India has led to numerous families in cities looking for places away from home for a holiday. The recent count of domestic tourists in India is 100 million.

The growth in private car ownership has done more to change travel habits than any other factor in tourism. It has given the families a new source of freedom of movement. They saw the prices of motoring falling, though ignoring the indirect costs of depreciation, wear and tear. This perception of low cost coupled with more flexibility led to great growth in motoring holidays everywhereùindividually short distance holidays.

Most travel in the world, both domestic and international, takes place in the family car. Over the years, the promotion of world travel is pointed by the passenger car registrations. One of the better ways to forecast world travel is to project the world's passenger cars registrations.

Between 1970 and 1989, the world passenger car registration grew by an yearly rate of 4.4 per cent. This is also a good signal of development of world tourism which also has been in that range. Car ownership in the world today is evaluated to be 600 million. In 1989, car registrations in the USA accounted for 34 per cent of the world's total passenger cars. There were a total of 424.4 million cars registered worldwide. Europe comprising erstwhile USSR and Eastern Bloc countries had more cars than USA. While Europe had 4.9 people per car, in USA there was one car for 1.7 persons only. The significant number of cars in Europe in 1989 were in West Germany (30.1 million). Italy for the first time surpassed France in the ownership of cars ù 24.3 million compared to 23 million in France and 21.8 million in the United Kingdom. Russia came next with 12 million cars. The evaluated growth since 1989 till 1995 is 25 per cent worldwide.

In West Germany, there was one car for two people, in Russia one for 25.

Americans continue to drive more every year clocking 2.1 billion passenger miles (a passenger mile is one passenger carried one mile) on highways in 1991. Travel by car accounts for more than four out of five inter-city passenger miles. According to American Automobile Association (AAA) study, the cost to drive a new car went up from 30.6 cents per mile in 1989 to 33 cents in 1990. The reason was the higher sticker prices of new cars and higher insurance. Americans spent 12 % of their total personal consumption expenditure on transportation alone in 1990, most of it on their cars.

The British took approximately 75% of their holiday trips on automobile, according to a 1990 survey. It is up from 25 per cent thirty years ago. According to official calculation, the number of motor vehicles registered in India went up 25 times, from about 6,00,000 in 1950 to 25 million in 1995. The buyers of these automobiles, especially the government employees, have been subsidised through low interest loans.

The effect of this change on the travel industry of India has been significant. The hotel and catering industry responded by providing required facilities on the roadsùwayside motels, transit hotels, roadside cafes and restaurants to serve the travellers. Hotels at remote places welcomed the business generated by the new road travellers. Hills and beach resorts came within easy reach.

A household receives a ear in the first place for personal use; taking children to school or to go to work. Once the car is taken for this objective, the owner feels that it is also economical to take the family in car for a holiday.

AMERICAN WAY OF LIFE

Henry Ford and good roads have supported make automobile the symbol of American way of life which has now been considered by the people elsewhere. For an average person living in non-congested suburbs of cities, it is the most convenient way to go to work. Originally, the speed was 50 kins an hour. Now there are speed ranges which permit over 100 kms an hour and there are no speed zone highways in Germany.

In India, speed is prohibited to 45 kms an hour in most cities and 60 to 65 kms an hour on highways. But, the speed limits are seldom followed and the number of fatal accidents on Indian roads jumped from 4,500 in 1960 to 75,000 in 1995 ù more than those in the USA where density of cars is 100 times more than in India. Refferring the chaos on Indian roads, William K.

Stevens of New York Times wrote in 1975 that India has roughly half the number of traffic deaths as in the United States which has nearly forty times more vehicles. He adds, "Four times as several people die in traffic accidents in Delhi than are murdered. Five times as many die on India's roads as are killed in the religious strife that seems to be endemic here. Twenty times more people die in traffic accidents than are killed in an average year during the floods that are the scourge of rural India." Some of these are:

Pedestrians

They "cross wherever and whenever they want, as if there has been no change from the days of slower and more benign traffic."

Vehicle Drivers

"Routinely cross the centre line and drive the wrong lane. Sometimes two whole lanes of traffic travel on the wrong side of the undivided roadways. Cars and heavy vehicles routinely barrel through the centre of village at high speed relying on people and animals to scatter and save themselves."

Scooter Riders: "These are particularly vulnerable, and the danger is often compounded when a whole family father, mother, and perhaps two three children zips through traffic on a single twowheeler."

The automobile is not an unmixed blessing. It is sounded and pollutes the air and environment. It takes up large areas of land for parking. It is also a dangerous instrument in the hands of man.

INDIAN ROAD TOURISM

There are a number of cars are running on the Indian roads, road tourism has become a way of life with middle class Indian families. The Haryana Government was first to notice the change and they did the pioneering the work then by developing roadside complexes. They developed man made lakes at some places in the state and put up neat hotels and motels on the Grand Trunk Road. Other states followed Haryana's example and now India has same facilities in different states and union territories encouraging motorists to use their car for a holiday. Driving is no longer drab and dreary as in the past, motorists can break journey en-route at pleasant locations. Private sector including major hotel chains have newely evinced interest in setting up same facilities.

Recreation Vehicles (RVs)

Automobile in its wake, brought recreation vehicles (RV)s-motor homes, travel trailers, park trailers, campers, folding camping trailers and vans conversion. In USA, 300,000 recreational vehicles of costing over US $ 8 billion are sold yearly. Twenty nine million Americans use such vehicles for holidays every per year spending on an average 23 days in the vehicle.

The market is not so vast in Europe for RVs but camping is actually common.

According to David J. Humphreys, Chairman of the Recreation Vehicles Industry Association, there are almost 8.5 million RVs in the US that are privately owned and about 25 million people continuously use their RVs. In Canada, there are estimated 850,00 privately-owned RVs.

Of increasing economic significance is the rental segment of RV market. Two national companies conduct about 400 rental locations for RVs across the USA. Another 300 independent dealers have entered the rental business of RVs.

The recent surge of foreign tourists to USA has givena fillip to the rental market. In 1995, over half a million foreign tourists rented RVs for travel within the USA.

A University of Michigan survey revealed that one out often vehicle owning family had atleast one recreational vehicle. The inspection reported that 44 per cent of RV owners were 55 and above; 39 per cent 35 to 54. The rest were owned by persons below 35. The people above 55 had more leisure time.

The price of RV vary widely. A luxury motor home would cost US $ 60,000. With smaller models available from US $ 25,000 and above. A travel trailer may be about US $ 13,000. A folding camp trailer starts at US $ 4000.

The increase in RV and camping markets has generated its problems and opportunities. The public camping grounds can no longer accommodate all the cars that queue up for permits. The result is that at times camping grounds became as congested as the areas from where the motorists came all the way for a quiet holiday. Environmentalists, public officials and property owners were alarmed by the hordes of campers bringing with them toys of plastic and metal. The rules became flexible creating problems to the travellers.

Realising the opportunity, entrepreneurs have set up private camping grounds all over North America to satisfy increasing demands of the campers.

A private membership ofRV camp ground lodging sector has also developed. It has a membership of about half a million.

RV vehicles are also popular in Europe but the number is not even 10 per cent of USA ownership.

An Indian company has recently developed a motor home in India. It is yet to see how many takers will be pulled towards. The role of self-driven car hire companies in travel is becoming more important. The car rental industry has been developing at a cost equal to or even faster than the airlines industry. The business worldwide was worth US dollars 13 billion in 1995. You can book your car in New York and it will be ready for ybu when you reach Beij ing airport in China.

There were evaluated 850,000 rental ears available in the USA in 1995 according to Hertz Corporation. The general service life of a rental vehicle changes from 10 to 16 months, after which it is sold as a used car. The largest car rental company in the United States is Hertz Corporation.

Hertz is also the largest in the world ù 5,500 locations and 400,000 cars; followed by AVIS 5,000 locations and 420,000 cars. National 4,600 locations and 276,000 cars and the Budget

3,477 locations and 250,000 cars. Source: Corporate Travel Magazine.

The car rental companies, about 5000 in number, have 26,000 locations in the USA. The big tour companiesùHertz, Avis, Budget and Nationalùcontrol 90 per cent of the airport business and 70% of the overall car rental business in the USA. Other small companies handle the rest.

There has been ownership change in major car rental companies during the last four years, financed mainly by auto-manufacturers. Auto manufacturers are the motivated parties as car-rental companies are their major bulk customers. All the four leading car rental companies are now owned by the three leading car manufacturers of USA. Hertz, Avis, National and Budget have multinational network. Avis, Hertz and National have registered their presence in India too. In Europe, the two major car rental companies, apart from American car rental multinationals, are Eurocar and Godfrey-Davis.

The combined group operates about 34,000 cars in Europe. The international operation of US Car Rental Companies has led to criticism in UK and some other European countries. George Young, author of Tourism-Bliss or Blight wrote, "Car Rental is an important part of UK's travel industry and one which is developing fast. It provides an example of how business and profit created by tourism to UK are increasingly going to non-UK firmsùtwo of the three large car hire firms in UK are American owned."

Although most cars are hired by business travellers, the car rental companies encourage their use by leisure travellers because they keep these cars longer than the business travellers and use them on weekends when businessmen go home.

Famous car rental companies are incessantly trying to modify their product ù and servicesùto beat the competition. You can hire a car with mobile telephone also. Glen R. Femandez, Director Hertz Corporation of USA, told the PATA Annual Conference in 1992 at Hong Kong, "Hertz Gold service customers are taken to a specific rented facility in 29 US airports. When reaching at the rental area, customers will see their name in lights on an electronic display board explaining where their car is locatedùunder a sheltered canopy to shield it from inclement weather.

The trunk will open, the engine running with either the heater or air-conditioner on. Customers merely put their luggage inside the car, present their driving licence at the security check-point and they are on the way." He revealed that Hertz's most famous customer service product was their computerised driving direction terminals located at airports and down-town locations in the USA and Europe. The American version supported six different languages while the European version supported nine. The product, he added, was wholy self-service using the latest touchscreen technology to guide customers along their way to hundreds of business and tourist-destinations. Detailed driving directions are printed, pointing specific distances and travel time.

The product, he continued, is embellished by a satellite based video-mapping feature which provides Customers with an overview of their locale and zoom in features to a 10 block radius.

The Hertz, he informed, was located at over 2000 airports in over 120 countries serving customers with a fleet of 4,20,000 cars.

AUTOMOBILE ASSOCIATIONS AND CLUBS

To serve motoring fraternity and to assist members, the Automobile Associations and Clubs in many countries are of great help. If your car has a breakdown and you are held up on a highway, go to the nearest phone booth and their mechanic for the maintenance vehicle will come rushing and move your car. If you want a road itinerary to reach a tourist centre 500 kilometres away, they will provide you reach a route map or detailed literature. Some Automobile Association have their own driving institute. The Automobile Association in New Delhi has a simulator to teach members how to drive their vehicles safely in adverse driving conditions.

The world's largest Automobile Association, naturally, is in America. It is called Automobile Association of America or triple A (AAA). It is also the largest single membership travel group. It is one of the largest travel agencies in the world. Its membership exceeds 25 million. Members who buy travel service from this organisation are entitled to different advantages.

It operates worldwide travel service like those provided by travel agencies and tour operators. Travel services give it a matchloess colour and provide a good source of profit. It also sells insurance.

The AAA publishes maps and tour books which explain tourist attraction, their history, points of interest, accommodations, resorts, motels-almost anything which the motorist may require to know. Information is periodically checked through visit by its field officers. An international organisation of expanded geographical membership is the World Touring and Automobile Organisation with headuarters in London.

There is one more similar organisationùthe Internationl Federation of Automobile Federation with headquarters in Paris. India's Automobile Associations are authorised to the Paris organisation.

INTEREST OF THE OIL COMPANIES

Oil companies have vested interest in developing automobile tourism and some of them provide information and routing services through their various outlets. An example of these service is a publication called Mobil Travel Guide which lists 20,000 hotels, motels and restaurants in the USA giving them one to five-star rankings.

In India, attempts by the Department of Tourism, Government of India to persuade the oil companies to get available road information on road-side facilities for motorists have not been very successful.

World Gasoline Prices and Taxation

Country	Total price per gallon	Tax % of price(US Dollars)
France	3.85	77
Italy	5.00	75
Germany	3.85	71
Spain	3.75	69
Britain	3.69	69
Japan	3.75	47
United States	1.19	28
India	3.00	(NA)

Source: International Energy Agency

Indian Automobile Associations: There is a Federation of Indian Automobile Associations (FIAA) in India. It was oranised in 1959, with its head office in Bombay, at the office of Western India Automobile Association. The following are the objectives of this Federation:

1. To adjust with the problems of general interest affecting the motoring community as a whole and the member of automobile associations especially.
2. To excite and develop automobile movement in India.
3. To study the question of national touring and vehicle movement in India and to promote growth and effect reforms suggested by such studies.
4. To collect and disseminate information on touring and motoring cast.
5. To show the members of the Federation at international meetings, conventions, discussions impressing the motoring public.
6. To encourage the development of international touring and movements in all their aspects in the East and with specific reference to India.
7. To study problems affecting motorists in regarding the use of roads by motor transport, taxation, road safety, the tourist trade and other ancillary and incidental problems and to make efforts through constitutional means for the emelioration of the conditions for motorists regarding all matters.
8. To develop mutual cooperation, reciprocity and settlement amongst the member automobile associations in India, for rendering efficient and maximum service to the motoring public.
9. To get, by mutual understanding, discussion and help, the coordination of activities of different automobile associations in India from an all-India point of view.
10. Develop mutual relations with kindred institutions in other countries.

The Federation of Automobile Associations is registered to the "Federation International De l" Automobile, Paris, the controlling body for motor sports in the world. It excites motor sports activities in the country on coordinated and healthy lines.

Automobile Association of Eastern India (AAEI) The Automobile Association of Eastern India was founded in 1904 and is the oldest in the country. It was established at the time when there were only fifty cars in Calcutta. The membership at present increases 25 thousands.

Western India Automobile Association: This association was organised in 1919 which is the biggest association in India at present. Now there are 40,000 members of this association.

The Automobile Association of Southern India (AASI): Founded in 1911, the Association has a membership of 25,000. It branches are situated at Bangalore, Coimbatore, Emakulam, Guntur, Kozhikode, Maduraf, Ootacamnd, Secunderabad and Trivandrum.

The Automobile Association of Upper India (AAUl): The Automobile Association of Upper India gives expandise service to its members. It was established in 1950 with the merger of the Automobile Association of Northern India and the Automobile Association of Delhi.

U.P. Automobile Association (UPAA): The Association was founded in 1927 with head office at Allahabad. The Association serves the requirements of motorists all over Uttar Pradesh. It has branch offices at Agra, Kanpur, Lucknow, Meerut and Varanasi.

In spite of predictions from specialists that automobile tourism may decline due to increasing costs of motor travel and due to the dwindling resources of petroleum, it continues to develop. The oil shortage of 1973 had created doubts about the future of road tourism by personal car. The personal car, it was believed, may be changed by more efficient and economical public carriers avoiding also car related pollution and over-crowding. Although cars may dominate the holiday scene for a few more decades, the future undoubtedly is with the coach and rail services.

'Leave the Driving Tours' was the slogan of Greyhound Bus Company in USA in the seventies. It did not work. In future, more and more people will leave the driving either to coach drivers or to the Railways ù with or without their drivers. Driverless trains are on the horizon in future.

MOTOR COACH SERVICES

Bus and coach operators all over the world across the world offer a expanded range of tourist services to the public, both directly and through other sectors of industry. These services can be classified under the following general headings:

1. Regular tours, sight-seeing and excursions.
2. Express Coach Routes which can be within a country as well as international.
3. Transfer services from airport to town.
4. Hire Services to private parties for touristic movements.

Bus Tours

Buses and coaches gives the most inexpensive and safe mode of transport.

Motor coach travel is a major part of the travel industry in North America and Europe. Coach travel in US has the Credit of budget travel patronised by relatively low-income ranges and senior citizens. Nevertheless, it is still a popular mode of travel linking 15,000 communities in the USA compared to only 500 by Amtrak, the rail company, and 700 by all the airlines of the USA.

The two major coach companies in the USA are the Greyhound and Trailways. Both are under the same management.

The majority of Indian holiday travellers to USA buy the popular Visit America Bus Travel Pass providing unlimited travel within the USA on a marked price and during a given period. It is an excellent buy to move within the USA for people on budgets.

According to the US Department of Transportation, there were 638,000 buses registered in USA in 1992. different companies owning buses are in the business of operating motor coach tours. Over 22,000 such motor coaches are n^w on the road for coach tours.An inspection of this industry conducted by SEA Tourism/ Travel Research reported that in 1990 some 60.7 million motor coach passengers spent $ 13.8 billion on group tours in North America. About 77 % of the passengers carried on these coaches were on day trips. In other words, one-third of the population of USA takes group tour of one kind or the other by coach.

The American Bus Association is the country's national body representing some 450 bus companies conducting in the USA and Canada. These companies, in close cooperation with their travel industry counterparts like Hotel and Motel chains. Food Service Organisations, Charming and Theme Parks, Local, State and divisional Tourist Promotional Bodies offer package tours. It is a big business.

Apart from the American Bus Association, the country has another non-profit organisation called the National Tour Association (NTA) which works with authorised tour operators to develop packages and market tours within North America. This again is a big business.

The motor coach tours represent a sizeable market for the nation's hotels and travel attractions.

In Europe, coach services do not have the negative image of a poor man's transport. Long distance coach services are immensely famous with international travellers and are patronised by young people under 35. Coach services are also patronised by budget travellers from Asia and Africa.

In the case of India scene most communities are connected by buses than the rails and air services. The motor vehicle population including buses and trucks in 1950-51 was just 34,000. The number in 1995 increased 25 million including two-wheelers. Road transport in India was individually nationalised in 1950. The State Transport Corporations functioning in various states of India operate a fleet of 1,50,000 vehicles carrying 6.50 crore passengers per day more than the population of many countries in Europe. 60% of road transport is operated in the private sector.

The total road network in India in 1990 was 16,20,600 kilometres of which national highways were 33,700 kilometres.

In the field of Indian tourism, a new development is the introduction of that are popularly described as "luxury" tourist buses. These buses are used for the promotion of domestic tourism by Tourism Development Corporations of different states of India. A few State Tourism Development Corporations generally offer complete scheme comprising accommodation and meals enroute. Private tour operators also operate same tours. The term 'luxury' buses is a misnomer. These are comparatively new buses with better seating facility ù no luxury really. Occasionally, air-conditioning is added for a price which seldom works.

The 21st century will see the booming of automobile and coach tourism inmost countries of the world, provided fuel costs do not become exorbitant. The requirement for motoring holidays will remain buoyant in the nineties and beyond. The development of motoring has brought and will accentuate the problems of over-crowding of highways and pollution. Holiday resorts around scenic pulls cannot be expanded to meet the demand for additional parking space as has happened in USA and Japan. This is bound to destroy the beauty which tourists are seeking to enjoy.

Places such as Kullu, Shimla or Nainital in the Himalayas take the form of packed parking lots during peak summer months. The scenic highways have become danger zones due to congestion. Driving on Kalka-Shimla highways, one of the finest in India, is now a traffic hazard due to congestion on the road. If tourism is expected to play a beneficial role, the Governments have to take a deep look at emerging situations and take equal measures. In many resorts of Europe, cars are left outside the resorts and the tourists are hoped to proceed further by public transport. Same is true of Wild-life Parks. As the world's economy develops and more people move up the income ladder, the stress on our roads will be heavier. This is a problem to which there are no ready answers.

Railways

Railways play an important role in travel and tourism all over the worldùexcept in the United States. Railways in the USA never taken themselves to the needs of travellers. Till the thirties, 70 per cent of traffic within the United States was taken by railways. With the development of alternate and more promoting modes of travel, the railways were relegated to the position of freight carriers. Now they carry only about 1 % of the total passenger traffic in the USA. The fast development of automobile and airlines has replaced the travel scene in the USA.

Airlines are one of the few industries of the twentieth century which have consistently reduced the price of a seat in the plane till the increase in oil prices in the mid-seventies because of oil producing countries making a cartel of their own. In the past, low price of gasoline in USA had excited people to travel long distances by automobile with their families taking them away from the rail-road.

The following table gives the performance of diverse modes af transport (Please note the poor performance of US rail network sailed Amtrak).

In USA Profile of Domestic Trip

(Base-1275 million person ù trips to places 100 miles away from home on domestic travel. Average distance for trip 839 miles)

Auto-Truck RV	17%
Airlines	79%
Buses	2%
Trains	1%
Others	1%
Total	100%

Source: US Travel Data Centre.

The rail transport was reached to its peak value in 1920 during the efforts of the rail deptt. The only surviving system Amtrak is now subsidised by the Government. It would compact but for the Government monetary support. Endeavours to divert traffic to Amtrak for intercity movement have not been very successful, though it is promoting. An idea of insignificance of the part of passenger rail-roads in the country can be had from the reality that Amtrak has only 2,000 cars operating over 20,000 mile network while much smaller countries such as France and Germany have 20,000 cars each proving the service approximately the same number of miles. Japan has over 30,000 cars for a 13,000-miles route. It may be pointed out that in India railways subsidise passenger traffic and make money from freight.

Railways both in the USA and in Europe work relativily with travel agents and pay them the normal service of 10%. In Japan, one can buy rail tickets at major offices of Japan Travel Bureau a mega travel agency with over 300 offices all-over Japan.

In Western Europe, the rail journey is now ahnost as smooth and fast as an Airlines even. On fast European trains, one can safely keep a cup of coffee on a side rack without spilling. For international trips to adjacent countries in Europe, one can save time by using trains as a traveller does not have to commute long distances to catch a plane from busy, airports. Rail-road stations are normally situated in the heart of the European cities. In 1981, when the world's fastest train ù TRES-GRANT VITESSE (TGV-very high speed) was introduced in France (now.commuting at 400 kms an hour), Air-Inter, the popular, less fair French Domestic carrier, lost about three-fourths of its one million annual Paris-Lyon. passengers to the new train. To overcome the disadvantage of time-consuming trip to the airport, Air-Inter has made a consortium to make a new rail link to Orly Airport and Paris so that the passengers can commute to the airport as fast as to the railway station and switch back to flying.

The railways are now in far better performance in Europe. The enhanced profit has been produced largely by the Community of European Railways (CER) representing the 12 European Community States plus Switzerland and Austria. CER plans to co-operate European proposals for fast trains into a continent-wide network. Investment of 75 billion US dollars is contemplated. The First stage to be completed by A.D. 2005 can be sufficiently alarming for the airlines. Except for Greece, Italy and Austria, all other sountries have modified their rail-lines and introduced point-to-point services. Some of these services were available in 1995. European politicians see the development in railroad transportation as symbol of a new unified Europe which is taking shape. The new channel tunnel has made the task easier.

In order not to hurt each other, there are plans to coordinate the two systems of rail transportation in Europe. Journey time is crucial. Some of the cities proposed to be linked under the CER plan are London-Paris, London-Brussels, Brussels-Cologne, Amsterdam-Cologne ù and the list can be continuous.

The Euro-Tunnel

Communications in Europe have undergone a revolutionary changes with the completion ofEuro-Funnel, linking England and France.

It was formally opened in May 1994 jointly by Queen Elizabeth of England and the French President, the late Francois Mitterrand. The official starting crowned six years of work which claimed lives often workers and cost more than US $ 17.50 billion. It has linked Paris and London with 291 km per hour under-water trains cutting drastically time between the two countries.

It came more than two centuries after a French Engineer, Nicolos Desmarets, first put forward a proposal for making a tunnel in 1751.

Eurail Pass

To make train travel attractive for foreign tourists, European Railways have supported to sell the entire system in the shape of Common Eurail Pass placing at the disposal of travellers more than 200,000 kilometres of the rail lines in 17 European countries. The Eurail Pass is very attractively priced ùUS dollars 498 for 15 days, US dollars 648 for 21 days and US dollars 798 for one month in second class. There are other passes available for two and three months also. Besides, there are different variations of Eurail Pass ù Youth Pass for people below 26 in second class is US dollar 398 for 15 days (1995 prices).

Such passes can also be bought separately for each country. For instance, the French Railways offer all of France for US dollars 99 for 4 days and the British Railways have a similar discount pass for their rail network.

Most foreigners can tour France in four days.

The Eurails World

From	To	Distance (Miles)	Shortest travel time
1. Barcelona	Madrid	430	6¾ hours
2. Berne	Zurich	81	1¾ hours
3. Amsterdam	Cologne	162	6 Hours
4. Frankfurt	Munich	287	3¾ hours
5. Brussels	Paris	195	2½ hours
6. Geneva	Paris	391	3½ hours
7. Lisbon	Madrid	404	10 hours
8. Paris	Lyon	265	2 hours
9. Rome	Florence	198	2¼ hours
10. Stockholm	Goteborg	285	4 hours

There is no confusion that travellers will flock back to trains in Europe to avoid congestion on the roads created by too many automobiles and chaotic conditions at the airports.

SITUATION IN INDIA

In India, the railways which carry some 11 million passengers perday, almost equal to the population of Australia ù are the preferred mode of travel. Indian Railways yearly lose about rupees 1,300 crore on passenger traffic due to low fares. In other words, passenger traffic is decreased by Government-owned Railways as its social liability. In the 1990 budget, passenger fares were enhanced particularly for first class passengers to meet a part of the annual loss on passenger traffic. There was some more increase in the 1994-95 budget and in 1997. The subsidies over the years have put tremendous strain on the Railways and the major casualty has been the track which has deteriorated over the decades endangering safety.

There are a number of accidents following outmoded rolling stock. The Indian Railways which include the principal mode of managed transportation in the country, are the nation's single largest undertaking with a capital investment ofRs. 10,000 crore, staff strength of 1.62 millions and a route length of 61,985 kilometres. Over 11000 trains criss-cross the country per day (1995 statistics). It is the largest public sector corporation in the world ù one of the three largest rail-networks in the world, the other two being Russia and China.

The Indian Railways operate on three gauges ù the broad gauge (1.67 metres), the trunk line, the metre gauge (1.00 metre) roling mainly as feeder lines. And, the third is the narrow gauge (0.762 metre and 0.610 metre) on definite sections in difficult terrain. The Indian Railways still use some steam engines-which have gone out of use in most countriesùattracting some tourists to India whA wish to experience the nostalgia of trains hauled by steam engines.

The Indian Railways are working overtime to convert the metre gauge lines into broad gauge.

Making a small beginning in 1853 when the first ever railway train in India commenced its journey from Bombay to Thane is a distance of 34 kilometres and the Indian Railways have emerged as Asia's the largest. The Indian Railways have 12,500 kms of electrified system ù the second longest in the world after USSR. More electrification is on the cards.The Railways have also moved into an era of computerisation in reservation and freight management. More fast trains have been introduced in latest years years. For peaceful management, the Indian Railways are categorised into nine zones with a General Manager in charge of each. At the corporate headoffice in New Delhi, the Railways are managed by a six-member Railwdy Board, comprising its Chairman. The Board is accountable to the Minister of Railways. Two more zones were added in 1997 railway budget.

The Government-owned Railways have a distinct budget which is presented yearly to the Parliament ù separately from the general budget. The Railways, however, distribute to the general revenue through payment of annual dividends. Dividend rate paid since 1980 stands at 6.5 per cent on capital invested.

Indrail Pass

Indian Railways have a limited number of appointed agents but agents are paid no service charge. They are allowed to add a service charge to customers they serve. However, the Railways pay 10 per cent commission on Indrail Passes sold by Travel Agents against foreign exchange. The Indrail Passes ù on the lines ofEurail Pass ù are available in all categories and are properly priced. For instance, a First Class Pass for one week is only US dollars 80 which comprises sleepers.

Indrail Passes are available for all classesù7,15,21,30,60 and 90 days of unlimited travel. To encourage sale of these passes, the Railways have appointed GSAs or General Sales Agents in some countries like UK, Germany, Thailand, Singapore and Japan. The Pass has not yet caught the imagination of tourists to India. Once the reservation system is entirely computerised, Indrail Pass may become a more famous moc of travel especially for the young foreigners.

Palace on Wheels

The Palace on Wheels ù a train introduced in starting eighties and comprising of state carriages of the former Maharajas and the special saloons used for travel by the Viceroys of India ù has become fairly popular with foreign travellers. Since these coaches will have soon outlived their life, the Indian Railways have made another train with modem facilities ùthe proper replica of old coaches to give a nostalgic touch to luxury travel in older times.

The New Palace on Wheels is a famous 14-coach weekly train operating from October to April each year, starting from Delhi and reaching Jaipur, Jodhpur, Jaisalmer, Bharatpur, Agra and back to Delhi. The ambience is that of royal living with liveried waiters dressed in 18th century Rajasthani costumes, at the beck and call of the passengers. Indians pay a little less. Catering is done by the Rajasthan Tourism Development Corporation. The new train is fully air-conditioned ù the old train was not.

The train has become famous with foreign tourists and the booking is done months in advance. The all-inclusive charges including food areUS $ 300 per day per person (1996).

The Palace on Wheels, already ranked as one of the ten best rail journeys in the world, has changed over from metre gauge to broad gauge. The new train is completely air-conditioned with vestibule links to all the coaches and every cabin has an adjacent toilet.

(The older train which plied on metre gauge has been diverted to Gujarat and is called the Royal Orient.)

During its year of operation, the Palace-on-Wheels has played host to over 20,000 tourists; 95 per cent among them were foreigners. Its foreign exchange earnings exceeded US dollar 2.5 million.

The Indian Railways have determined to start 8 more trains like the Palace-on-Wheels in many parts of India for tourists. The private sector is expected to finance these trains while the Indian Railways will conduct them.

The following are the eight circuits identified for this purpose:

BROAD GAUGE

1. Mumbai-Pune-Aurangabad-Nanded-Secunderabad-Hyderabad-Bombay.
2. Delhi Cantt-Jaipur-Jodhpur-Jaisalmer-Bharatpur-Agra-Sawai Madhopur-Delhi Cantt (Palace on Wheels already operational).

3. Howrah-Gaya-Varanasi-Gorakhpur-Bhubaneswar-Puri-Howrah.
4. Bangalore-Mysore-Madras-Kodai Road-Kanyakumari-Thiruvananthapuram-Cochin-Mettupalayam-Bangalore.
5. Goa (Madgaon)-Mangalore-Mysore-Hospet-Bangalore-Goa.
6. Delhi-Jaipur-Agra-Gwalior-Jhansi-Varanasi-Lucknow-Delhi.

METER GAUGE

1. Delhi Cantt-Jaipur-Udaipur-Ahmedabad-Veraval-Palitana-Delhi Cantt-already in operation (The Royal Orient already operational).
8. Madras-Eginore-Pondicherry-Karraikal-Velankanni-Trichy-Madurai-Rameshwaram-Thanjavur Chidambaram-Madras-Egmore.

If it works, tourists to India will have an alternate to travel in India extensively by unique trains in utmost comfortùrelieving pressure on airlines.

International Tourism through Train Travel Train travel is important for international tourism. It is a convenient and promoting way of travel for budget tourists in Western Europe. It provides fast, prominent and economical intercity links in the continent of Europe. The Europeans, undoubtedly, run good train services at fair prices on well arranged rolling stock.

In North America, Mexico City in Mexico is connected by rail to Texas and California, providing international services. And, Los Angeles has been connected to Miami ù journey time 58 hours. Trains of some of the countries are international heartpull by themselves. Canada, for instance, provides spectrus scenery with good accommodation in Trans-Continental trains. These trains are favoured by US'tourists to Canada.

India is now wooing affluent foreign tourists on its now famous Palace on Wheels trains. Another train-The Great Indian Rover was involved to attract Buddhist tourists. But, it was holdfor lack of patronage.

Another Palace on Wheels built earlier for narrow gauge operations has been diverted to the Gujarat region. And it costs US $ 200 a night. It is known as the Royal Orient.

Thailand and Malaysia have a good train link, providing an option for to air journey.

New Zealand and Australia provide attractive scenic train services. Australia's chief attraction is a 4-day journey across the Australian outback from Sydney to Perth, on board the Indian Express. It provides a fantastic vista. The trains in Switzerland are famous with foreign tourists ù they can reach everywhere by train in the small country. These trains are also an epitome of efficiency and regularity designed to meet the requirements of the tourists. The Swiss rail-roads offer improper extras to travellers like cycles on rent at all stations.

Some of the trains offer special half-coach for children where seats are lifted up so that the children look out from the windows while parents keep a watch from the nearby dining area. The children's room is full of toys to play with.

Japan and France are two other countries known for their high-tech and prominant train services which attract many foreign tourists.

France has one of the fastest trains in the world ù TVG ù which runs at a speed of about 400 kms an hour. Japanese Bullet Trains, travelling at speeds reaching 300 kms an hour, are normally used by foreign tourists for an experience. They link Tokyo with other metropolitan areas of the country. Their regularity is unmatched.

Japan has already pioneered a new 'Megalav' (Magnetic levictalion) train which runs at a speed of 260 kms a hour.

In Russia, the Trans-Siberian rail/road ù the longest in the world (5, 787 miles) ù is a tourist attraction. It links Siberian industrial area with the core area of European Russia.

Orient Express, Europe's Historical Train The Orient Express, Europe's most exciting train, was originally prepared in 1883. It operated from Paris to Constantinopole ù now Istanbul in Turkey ù covering a distance of 2,600 kms.

The train has hosted kings, presidents, prime ministers, spies and smugglers-creating history and romance.

A few years ago, it ran into financial problem and finally was sold to the highest bidder in 1977. Later, an American Tycoon, James Sherwood, re-assembled the cars and restarted the Orient

Express in 1982. Now, some 35,000 tourists experience the impression of the great Orient Express every year.

OCEAN LINERS AND CRUISING

Today, there are some passenger shipping lines in the world offering transport on port-to-port basis. After their bright period in the late forties and early fifties, these services are almost extinct. The chief shipping lines like P&O and Cunard holded their long established routes from UK to Far East or to America as air transport became cheaper than the surface transport. Many of their vessels were sold and cost of changing and operating them appeared restrictive due to shortage of patronage. Since the fifties, the passenger shipping industry steadily shifted its emphasis from line voyages to cruises. Initially, they had their problems.

Vessels were too old, too large and too expensive to run for cruising purposes. Their large size limited the number of ports they could enter. These ships were made for speed rather than leisure cruising. An ideal cruise ship is 18,000-22,000 tons with a passenger ability of less than 1,000.

The shipping industry, therefore, have since adjusted to the needs of new cruise holiday market. The largest number of cruise patrons live in the United States ù 3.5 million in 1989 and 5 million in 1995 and their number is developing every year. Now, some of the shipping companies are extending their capacity for individual demands in certain areas. The Royal Caribbean Cruise Line has involved its 2,282-passenger ship-Sovereign of the Sea. It is the biggest ship to serve in the Caribbean. The company has ordered two more similar ships.

The Carnival Cruises have built a 2,600-passenger ship Fantasy which will make three to four night cruises to Bahamas. Princess Cruises have introduced 1500-passenger ship Star Princess while two more 1600-passenger ships are based on order. Some shipping companies are ordering smaller ships to meet the needs of several markets.

North America is responsible for 81 % of the cruise market for cruises of 3 days or more. The total world spending on cruises in 1995 was evaluated to be about US dollar 11 billion.

It has been evaluated that there are about 190 ships.in deep water cruise business ù 36 belong to Russia or some of the erstwhile members of the USSR.

Four leading companies dominate the cruise industry ù Carnival, Royal Caribbean, Princess and Norwegian.

The dominance of American travellers in the cruise market has resulted in hard standards of hygiene and safety put on all foreign flag cruise ships operating out of the US ports. They have also been contracted against financial collapse. These hard regulations have driven old vessels out of the cruise market.

CURRENT SITUATION

In recent years, the cruise travel has received a momentum from certain innovative marketing valuation introduced by operators during the sixties and seventies ù like Fly-Cruises promote in Great Britain in late sixties. This involved basing of a cruise ship, say in a Mediterranean port, and flying the holiday makers to that port from where they cruise to the warmer climates. This saved the passengers long ship journeys to reach warmer climates. In the starting, the cruise travellers were older people who wanted to avoid flying. The new Fly-Cruise concept attracted younger travellers to a cruising holiday and extended the market. The concept has caught on and now even the Europeans fly to Miami in the USA to catch a cruise ship to the Caribbeans and the Americans fly to Mediterranean ports. The third most popular cruise destination is Australia with cruises to Pacific Islands like Fiji.

The composition of cruise market has changed in dramatic manner Passengers are younger, the average length of cruises is shorter and fierce competition has created in a price war. The fastest developing part of the business is 3-4 day and 6-8 day cruises. An imp9rtant source of income of cruise ships are the Casinos and duty-free shoping available on board.

Referring to the booming cruise markets, Joel M. Abel, Editor of The Travel Trade in New York commented in 1992, "While it is true, even at this level of the travel game, a mere 5 % of the US population has ever taken a cruise, the numbers are developing. Today, 3.5 million annual passenger volume is hoped to rise to 10 million a year by the year 2000."

India and Indian Ocean do not figure anywhere in major cruise itineraries. By chance, a luxury cruise ship on its round the world journey may touch an Indian port like Cochin, Madras or Bombay ù seldom more than five days.

Some of the cruise passengers take off to Delhi or Agra to have a brief look at India. By basing a cruise ship in the Indian Ocean, say Bombay, and taking the passengers to the nearby Goa, Andamans, Sri Lanka or Malaysia, India could develop a new cruise market. The developing Indian middle-class too will patronise opportunities for cruising holidays. The Travel Corporation of India (TCI) has plans to get a cruise ship for this aim.

Some observers feel cruise liners are of not much support to the economies of small islands where they often stop. No expenditure is charged on accommodation, entertainment, etc. The ships are self contained-the guests get all lunches and dinners on board followed by different entertainment during the evening.

Their schedules are full and the travellers get very short time to shop around and see the city they land. An idea of what is available on a given day in the terms of food alone may be seen from the following programme in a cruise ship:

6 a.m	Roll and coffee
7 a.m	3 0-foot buffet
8 a.m	Sit-down breakfast
10 a.m	Mid-moming bouillon break
Noon	Formal lunch or burgers and tacos on deck
4 p.m	Ice-cream sundaes
5 p.m	Hot hors d'oeuvres
8.15 p.m	Five-course dinner

PROSPECTS

As we explained earlier, travel by cruise ships has a bright future. USA alone has some 25 million potential travellers with economy and time.

The markets in Europe, Japan and South America offer good potential for growth.

Cruise services are sold mainly through travel agents. Therefore, cruise lines do not have to retain large marketing staff to sell their product. To make the most of their limited sales staff, they centralises on key travel agencies expertising in cruise passengers. They try to reach them by telemarketing, travel trade exhibits, and direct mail.

They make more use of newspaper advertising to reach the potential travellers and advise them to contact their travel agents. Travel agents get 10 % to 15 % service charge a major source of their income. Addressing the 1992.PATA annual conference in Hong Kong, Robert Perry, Vice-President of Princess Cruise gave some interesting statistics to connote the growth of cruise market, "Since 1970, an estimated 40 million passengers have taken a cruise.

The number of passengers has increased from 1.6 million in 1981 to just over 4 million in 1991. The industry load factor has stabled at the range of 85 to 90 per cent." The leading cruise markets were Caribbean 57 per cent, Europe 9 %, Western Mexico 7 %, Alaska 7 %, and Transcanal 4 per cent. The Pacific Asia marketùHawaii and South Pacific ù was 5 %.

The Ferry Services

The boom in automobile travel has led to short sea voyages within Europe to transport cars. From Great Britain alone, 4 million cars out of 10 million individually owned cars are transported annually to Europe for a car-bome holiday. The ferry companies are also helping with increasing number of coach operators who provide infra-Europeans long distance services by transporting their trainers to the continent from Great Britain.

While the busiest seasons for ferries are June-August, the ferry companies have kept themselves well-used during off-seasons by offering attractive off-season prices. With the availability of economical tariff during off-season, the travellers now tranship their cars to neighbouring countries even for 2-3 day holidaysùa new trend.

Hovercrafts and Hydrofoils

Hovercrafts and Hydrofoils have given another attraction over the water transport. Hovercrafts are lifted by propeller induced pressure and run over a cushion of airù 8,feet above the water.

They can speed up to 125 kilometres an hour. Hydrofoils pulled up by foil action through the water can run even faster. Today, these are utilised extensively in Europe making intra-European travel easy.

There are hydrofoils between Copenhagen (Denmark) and Malmio (Sweden). Naples and Capri in Italy, Spain and Morocco are also connected by similar services. In the USA, hydrofoil services operate between Miami and Port Landerdale and between many Hawaiian Islands.

In Asia, these services operate every thirty minutes between Hong Kong and Macau. Goa tourism is also planning to introduce hovercrafts.

Inland Waterways

Inland waterways ù lakes, rivers and canals ù in any country are a source of an unique water-borne holiday. It can take the form of day excursions and even bigger cruises on the lakes or rivers. The lake steamer is a familiar sight and an important tourist attraction in areas such as Scottish Locks in United Kingdom, in the US-Canadian Great Lakes or in the Swiss or South German Lakes.

The big rivers of the world also provide interesting cruising services ù some of which have been schemed for international travellers. Among these are paddle steamers on the Mississippi River, cruise along the Rhine, the boats in China's Yangtse River, and on the Amazon River which is modifibable even for the ocean-going vessels.

India has resources, 52,000 kilometres of major rivers and only 1,700 kilometres are utilised for modiication. Besides, India has 4,300 kilometres of canals only 485 kilometres are used for mechanised crafts. India has not yet made any use of its inland waterways for tourism purpose.

Cruises on the Ganges, Brahmaputra or Hoogly could be a gainin gtourist attraction. Recently, an element of adventure travel has been involved with white water river rafting in the Ganges and a few other Indian rivers.

Of the tourists who come to India, 97 % of them travel by air. Some ten per cent of foreign tourists came by road from Europe to India via Turkey, Iran, Afghanistan and Pakistan using the Asian Highway till 1975.

The pattern has since changed due to momentary in Iran and Afghanistan. Now, road traffic has been decreased to a trickle, less than 2 per cent. Once, there were continuous coach services between London and Delhi in the sixties. Coach travel was very inexpensive.

If conditions on the Asian Highway improve, India would be a popular destination for road travellers with good motorable highways throughout the length and breadth of the country.

Since India started developing international tourism, attempts have been prepared to provide tourists ears and coaches which they are used to in their own countries, authorised transporters were allowed by the Department of Tourism to buy foreign cars sold by the leaving diplomats for use of the tourists. Loans were also made avialiable to them.

Indian Tourism Development Corporation (ITDC) pioneered the theory of deluxe imported tourist cars and trainers in the late seventies. They also set up some 16 transport unitsùnow 12 onlyùat major tourist centres providing educated, well mannered liveried drivers.

While ITDC pioneered good service, major tour operators all over India now have a image of good foreign and Indian cars with uniformed drivers. Tourist taxis have special number plates ù in Delhi ù DLZ or DLY.

International car rental companies like Hertz, Avis and National and Budget have started business in big cities with Indian partners. But self-driven cars are still not properly available. It works economical with the driver.

Recent liberalisation of economy has made it possible for tour operators, travel agents and hoteliers to directly import cars for use of overseas tourists using a part of their foreign currency earnings.

Although, India manufactures good trainers, it is proposed also to import specific air-conditioned coaches from abroad for the use of tourists.

AIRLINES

While we have already explained three major arteries of tourism ù car, rail and sea transport, airlines are the most important for international tourism. Airlines have changed the travel figure in the passed fifty years.

This chapter discusses arteries of tourism-rail, road and sea transportation. Sea transportation includes ocean cruises. Each has its own importance and caters to the needs of definite part of travel market.

By far, travel by automobile is the most liked mode of holiday specially in the developed countries. 75 per cent of domestic holiday travel in developed countries is done by automobile which combine Recreation Vehicles (RVs). It is convenient and economical for the whole family.

Automobile will remain the most important means of travel for holiday for some more decades, but it is likely to see a declining trend due to diminishing resources of oil and hiking costs adding to pollution level. Automobile is now coming up in developing councils where more people are becoming part of the emerging middle class. Coach travel comes nextùanother very economical mode of travel individually in the developing societies.

In well established societies, specially in the USA, prosperous do not patronise bus and coach travel as it has an image of poor man's transport. It is patronised by budget travellers ù students and the senior citizens. In developing countries such as India, bus travel is the most general mode of travel. In India, about 7 crores people hire inter-city travel by bus annually.

As road travelling being most crowded and accidental, the charm of this mode of travelling is decreasing. Railways which had been relegated to a back seat in well established societies are re-gain ing their hold once again, with traffic congestion on the roads. Railways are giving the airlines a run for their money as they move up their speed and quality.

A train in France travels at a speed of about 400 kms an hour and one airline lost a million airlines customers to the train. Trains normally save time that is spent on reaching the airport through congested highways. Japan's Bullet Trains cruise at a speed of up to 300 kilometre an hour linking major cities. In developing countries, like India, railways are still the most liked mode of travel.

The Indian Railways carry some 12 million passengers daily, almost equal to the population of Australia. Presently the fastest train in India is Shatabdi which covers a distance of 410 kms from New Delhi to Lucknow, in four hours. A number of Shatabdi trains have been introduced for making inter-city travel more comfortable and fast.

These trains are also patronised by foreigners. The Indian Railways operating one of the biggest rail network in the world are taking interest in developing tourism. Their luxury train, Palace on Wheels, has been very famous with foreign tourists. Now, they have decided to add 8 more similar trains in various regions of India. These trains will be in operation in three years. Cruise-lines offering luxurious holidays on the sea are a US dollar 11 billion industry. They catered to 5 million passengers in 1995, the calculated potential is 10 million by A.D. 2000.

Basically patronised by old travellers, the image of cruise holidays has now changed as younger people also have started travelling by ships by using fly-cruise packages offered by the industry. The three modes of holiday travel ù automobile, rail and sea cruisesùall have their separate benefits and separate markets. None of these three modes of transportation face danger of stagnation. Growing marketing should keep them strong and complementary to each other.

In a boon to travellers and the tourism industry, the government has increased the rate of abatement for levy of service tax by 35% for tour operators. The service tax exemption that applies to package tours which is 40% at present has been increased to 75%.

At present, tour operators providing package tours, which include provision of transportation, accommodation, tourist guides, entry to monuments amongst other overheads, is liable to pay service tax on 40% of the gross amount charged for such tour. This has now been reduced to 25%.

The decision was taken after tourism minister Ambika Soni raised the issue with FM P Chidambaram. The move is expected to benefit tour operators and the travel industry who are increasingly being turfed out by internet travel sites.

In a related move to promote domestic tourism, the government intends to promote Hampi in Karnataka to make it equivalent to Taj Mahal in terms of tourist destination. Responding to a Lok Sabha question, Soni said Hampi was the "agenda number one" in terms of development and enormous amount of money had been earmarked for it.

Noting that the government had taken a number of steps to promote tourism, she said inflow of foreign tourists was growing by leaps and bounds and about five million travellers were expected this year.

2

Modern Travel Agencies

A travel agency is a business that sells travel related products and services, particularly package tours, to end-user customers on behalf of third party travel suppliers, such as airlines, hotels, tour companies, and cruise lines. In addition to dealing with ordinary tourists, most travel agents have a special department devoted to travel arrangements for business travellers, while some agencies specialise in commercial and business travellers. Some agencies also serve as general service agents for foreign travel companies in different countries.

The British company, Cox & Kings is sometimes said to be the oldest travel agent in the world, but this rests upon services that the original bank (established in 1758) supplied to its wealthy clients. However, the modern travel agent first appeared in the second half of the nineteenth century.

Thomas Cook, in addition to developing the package tour, established a chain of agencies in the last quarter of the nineteenth century, in association with the Midland Railway. These not only sold their own tours to the public, but represented other tour companies. Other British pioneer agencies were Dean and Dawson, the Polytechnic Touring Association, and the Co-operative Wholesale Society.

Travel agencies became more commonplace with the development of commercial aviation starting in the 1920s. Originally, the agencies largely catered to middle-class customers, but the post-war boom in mass-market package holidays resulted in travel agencies on the main streets of most British towns, catering to a working class clientèle looking for a cheap overseas beach holiday.

FUNCTIONS

As the name implies, their main function is to act as an agent, that is to say selling travel products and services on behalf of a supplier. Consequently, unlike other retail businesses, they do not keep a stock in hand. A package holiday or a ticket is not purchased from a supplier unless a customer requests that purchase. The holiday or ticket is supplied to them at a discount. Thus, the agent's profit is the difference between the supplier's price and the price at which the product is advertised or sold to the customer. This profit is called the agency commission, and varies a great deal. In Britain, 12% would be considered a good commission. Other commercial operations are undertaken, especially by the larger chains. These can include the sale of in-house insurance, travel guides and timetables, car rental, and the services of an on-site bureau de change dealing in the most popular holiday currencies.

The majority of travel agents have felt the need to protect themselves and their clients against the possibilities of commercial failure, either their own or a supplier. They will advertise the fact that they are bonded (posting a financial bond with an organisation). In the case of a failure, the customers are guaranteed either an equivalent holiday to that which they have lost, or (if they prefer) a refund. Many British agencies (and tour companies too) are bonded with IATA for those who issue their own tickets, ATOL for those who order tickets in, or ABTA for those who sell package holidays on behalf of a tour company.

Of course, a travel agent is supposed to offer impartial travel advice to the customer. This function almost disappeared with the mass-market package holiday, and some agency chains seemed to develop a 'holiday supermarket' concept, in which customers chose their holiday from brochures on racks and then booked it from a counter. However, a variety of social and economic changes have now contrived to bring this aspect to the fore once more, particularly the advent of multiple no-frills airlines.

THE CLASSIFICATION

There are three different types of agencies: these are Multiples, Miniples and Independent Agencies. The former comprise a number of national chains, often owned by international conglomerates

(Thomson Holidays is now a subsidiary of TUI, the German multinational). It is now quite common for the large mass-market tour companies to purchase a controlling interest in a chain of travel agencies, in order to control the distribution of their product.

The smaller chains are often based in particular regions or districts. Independent Agencies usually cater for a special or niche market. Some cater to the needs of residents in an upmarket commuter town or suburb, or concentrate upon a particular area or group (catering to the travel needs of Polish expatriates, perhaps), or an activity such as sports(servicing the needs of football supporters).

Travel agencies have been accused of employing a number of restrictive practices, the chief of which is known as 'racking'. This is the practice of only displaying the brochures of those travel companies whose holidays they wish to sell, the ones that pay them the most commission. Of course, the average customer tends to think that these are the only holidays on offer, and are unaware of possible alternatives.

Generally speaking, small or specialist tour companies do not sell their product through travel agents, since they could not afford to pay the rates of commission that would be demanded. There are a few exceptions to this rule. Independent agents might sell or take bookings for local tour companies (such as coach companies) or tour companies offering specialist holidays that fit into their target market. Consequently, even before the advent of the internet, small niche tour companies ignored travel agents and sold direct to their customers.

THE THREAT

With the advent of general public access to the internet, many airlines and other travel companies began to sell directly to passengers. As a consequence, airlines no longer needed to pay the commissions to travel agents on each ticket sold. Since 1997, travel agencies gradually became victims of disintermediation, the reduction in costs caused by removing layers from the package holiday distribution network.

Many travel agencies have developed an internet presence by posting a website, with detailed travel information. Full travel booking sites are often complex, and require the assistance of outside travel technology solutions providers such as Travelocity, Patheo and Open Fares. These companies use travel service distribution companies who operate Global Distribution Systems (GDS), such as Sabre Holdings, Amadeus, Abaccus, Galileo and Worldspan, to provide up to the minute, detailed data on tens of thousands of flight, hotel, and car rental vacancies.

Some on-line travel sites allow visitors to compare hotel and flight rates with multiple companies for free. They often allow visitors to sort the travel packages by amenities, price, and or proximity to a city or landmark.

Travel agents have applied dynamic packaging tools to provide fully bonded (full financial protection) travel at prices equal to or lower than a member of the public can book on-line. As such, the agencies' financial assets are protected in addition to professional travel agency advice. All travel sites that sell hotels on-line work together with numerous outside travel agents. Once the travel site sells a hotel, one of the supplying travel agents is contacted and will try to get a confirmation for this hotel. Once confirmed or not, the customer is contacted with the result. This means, that booking a hotel on a travel website will not get you an instant answer. Only some of the hotels on a travel website can be confirmed instantly (which is normally marked as such on each site). As different travel websites work with different suppliers together, each site has different hotels that it can confirm instantly. Some examples of such on-line travel websites that sell hotel rooms are Expedia, Travelocity, Tripadvisor, Excelloz, Travel Tickets Plus and Venere.

With the many people switching to self service internet websites, the number of available jobs as travel agents is decreasing. Most jobs that become available are from older travel agents retiring. Counteracting the decrease in jobs due to internet services is the increase in the number of people travelling. Since 1995, many travel agents have exited the industry, and relatively few young people have entered the field due to less competitive salaries. However, others have abandoned the "brick and mortar" agency for a home-based business to reduce overheads, and those who remain have managed to survive by promoting other travel products such as cruise lines and train excursions, or by promoting their ability to aggressively research and assemble complex travel packages on a moment's notice (essentially acting as a very advanced concierge).

There are the Wholesalers and Retailers among travel agents. The wholesalers develop package tours for different places and sell them either directly to travellers, or through retail travel agents-small travel agencies running in each country. Retailers get a 10% percent commission from wholesalers for every tour package sold. The retailers need not make any arrangement for their customers themselvesùthat is the responsibility of the wholesalers iwho are in touch with hotels and travel agencies overseas, if it is an overseas package, or within the country if it is a domestic package, for making what in travel agents' terminology is called 'ground arrangements'. The tour operators who receive tourists and handle arrangements in that country are called 'Inbound tour operators'.

They service the inbound travellers from foreign countries. Those who promote tours to foreign destinations are called 'Outbound tour operators'. The tour operators who provide these services provide only within their own country, are called 'Domestic tour operators'. Several of them provide both types of services. Tour operation is a complicated businessùwheels within wheels, each doing its job to make travel trouble-free for the tourists. There is a thin line between the diverse sorts of travel agenciesùbig travel agencies often combine all the functions including retail selling. They have several branches in a country. Sometimes they act as wholesalers and allow other travel agencies also to retail their tour packages.

Whole-selling is a popular business in countries like the USA where one company may move more than half a million people in a year. In India, it is not so common Generally, wholesalers have their retail outlets as well. With the taking over of large scale like Sita World Travel by Kuonis, a multinational travel company, Whole-selling may be a big business in future. Infact, there are two types of travel agencies: the general travel agency and the specialised travel agency. The general travel agency is a small scale (One to ten employees) that deals with almost all types of travel and offers about every kind of travel-related services. The specialised travel agency is really large operation and may specialise in one form of travel, or travel service to a group or a community.

The most travel agencies in India belong to the category of general travel agencies. The specialised travel agenciesùnot general in Indiaù may specialise in corporate and commercial accounts, exclusively dealing with business travel, organising air tickets, arranging hotel accommodation, car rentals, etc., for corporate executives. The other areas of particularly are ship or cruise travel, outbound travel, specially in packaging and marketing overseas holidays, organising and promoting conferences and conventions, and creating and catering to an incentive travel market, etc. Some travel agencies confine their business to developing and marketing domestic tours only. This is an unique business in developed countries and is now this business is very advantageous in India too.

RELATED COMMISSIONS

Most travel agencies do not charge anything from their clients for their professional services. They depend on commission given by their principals, i.e., airlines, hotels, motels, railways, car rental companies, bus and insurance companies, etc. Where they do not get commissions, they but a service charge. For instance, the Indian Railways do not give commissions to travel agents. So, a travel agency will add its service charge if a client wants them to buy train-ticket. However, Indian Railways makes an exception.

They allow 10% commission to travel agents selling Indian rail Passes to foreign tourists against foreign currency. They also offer the same commission on sale of Palace on Wheels' tickets. Commissions to travel agents vary from country to country, depending on the competitive situation. For example, commissions increases upto 15% and more in the USA where the international airlines are free to offer any commission to make a sale.

There is infact no boundation on payment of commission due to the policy of deregulation followed by the US Government. But now the airlines are getting wiser and some of them have put a boundation or 'Prohibition' as they call it. It has made travel agencies less profitable. The scene is changing during the economic situation of airlines. In India, we follow the IATA normsù7%

commission on international tickets. Recently, Indian Airlines followed their own rules. They had the monopoly and paid a less 4% commission. With the entry of private airlines are paying. Now Indian Airlines pays five per cent commission which is same as the private airlines. Now, the Government has added its 10% tax on the total value of the domestic air ticket, which is collected by travel agents No commission is paid to him by the Government for this service. Tax is deposited to the government officers.

Membership of IATA

Although one may find all travel shops calling themselves travel agencies, a dependent travel agency is one displaying the logo of IATA (International Air Transport Association) appointed agent for representing their symbol. An IATA appointed travel agency is reliable, because such a company has been approved by this international organisation, after standard proper scrutiny of their professional competence and financial reliability. Such agencies have to provide financial guarantees to the airlines against default. The agencies which are not IATA members, may not be trustworthy because they buy tickets from other registered IATA agents, or the general sales agents of airlines and resell these to their clients, sharing a part of the commission with their clients. Their gain is so small that they cannot give good service. Until a travel agency is approved by IATA, it cannot get commissions directly from an international airline. IATA approval does not automatically make an agency eligible for commission from Indian Airlines or private domestic airlines. The IATA approval helps. Airlines, to make their own rules, follow up and yardsticks for approval.

INDIAN ASSOCIATION OF TRAVEL AGENTS (IATA)

Most IATA approved travel agents in India, are also members of a national organisation called Travel Agents Association of India (TAAI). Its membership is further proof of their reliability. The TAAI logo can be displayedin such travel agencies which have ISI mark, indicating professionalism and reliability. TAAI makes a close scrutiny before accepting new members and expects all its members to follow a code of conduct.

The head ofice TAAI, is in Mumbai and the organisation has seven branches in major cities of India. The objectives of TAAI are to protect the genuine, and legitimate interests of the professional travel agency members. TAAI membership includes not only travel agencies domestic and international airlines, hotels, motels, resorts, etc. At the annual conference of TAAI, called the Indian Travel Congress, they discuss their general problems. TAAI was established in 1950 by a group of eight travel agents led by late Nari. J. Katgara. Now Membership get increased more than two hundred.

Indian Federation of Travel Agents

Travel Agents Federation of India (TAFI), is yet another organisation of India for claiming to represent travel agents. The head office of TAAT was started in Mumbai had special rules for its membeship It is now really large and both the organisationùTAAI and TAFI-try to work together to protect the interests of travel agents and touroperators.

Indian Association of Tour Operators

Delhi-based IATO (Indian Association of Tour Operators) is the representing organisation of tour operators handling inbound tourism. It is a new and active organisation and has among its members, all those involved in tourism industry, including hotels, transporters, state tourism department and airlines. It holds annual conventions to deliberate over its problems.

UNIVERSAL ASSOCIATIONS

At the world level, there is the Universal Federation of Travel Agents Associations (UFTAA). There are more than hundred and twenty one countries including India in the Universal fedeation of Travel Agens Association (UFTAA) Travel agency membership exceeds forty-eight thousand. The world body represents the interests and main points of travel agents all over the world, vis-a-vis organisations like IATA and IHRA (International Hotels and Restaurant Association). UFTAAalso provides training opportunities to travel agents who are members of this organisation.

There are about one thousand five hundred LATA-appointed agencies in India, Some of them have a dozen or more offices all over the country and provide employment to a large number of qualified young people. A travel agent tries to give perfect service to his clientsùprepares their itineraries, issues tickets after necessary reservations, arranges passports and visas for international travellers, books hotels at the place or places to be visited by his clients, sells travel insurance and if required, arranges cars on arrival at the destination. In fact, there is hardly anything which a travel agent cannot do for his client at the other end of the journey, provided the client is in the hands of an experienced travel agency.

ASTA

ASTA (American Society of Travel Agents) is another famous international travel organisation of travel agents. Due to the global nature of travel business, ASTA's agenda is according to international requirement. It permits travel agents from all countries of the world to become its members. While the American members are active members, others are called allied members. Its annual conventions is called World Travel Congressùis attended by seven thousand to eight thousand travel agents each year. It is held one year in the USA and in the alternative year in a foreign country. The participation is so large that a country like India does not have sufficient hotel rooms in one city, to be able to invite ASTA conference. Till now ASTA conference is not held in India.

Setting up of an Agency

To start a new travel agency, the first important step is to select a proper location. The selection of the location can play an important role for the success. There should be special care of diverse areas with high potential for development and profits. While opening the location, the agency owner must choose an area which is appealing and accessible to the types of client he wishes to attract. It must be an expanding area or a new development with possibilities of growth. It must be convenient to businessmen enroute to or returning from work. The owner should also take care ofcompitability preferably, there should be less competition in the type of business he wishes to attract.

As for budget, the rule of thumb is that rent and uses should not exceed ten per cent of the tamed budget. A travel agency office must be well-designed, neat and attractive. Outdoor signs and window displays are necessary features of a good travel agency. Telex, fax and photocopying machines have become necessary part of office equipment. Computer terminals from airlines will have to be rented once business starts growing. More successful travel agencies have back-room computerisation tooùfor accounting, billing and to follow-up on outstanding payments. A new agency is not immediately approved by IATA. It has to function successfully for one year, giving business to airlines. During the first year, the agency does not get the commission, but after getting approved, the commission earned in the past year is paid back.

Promotion

Since travel agency business is highly competitive, the management of the agency must have a expanded marketing plan to make easy. sale of its services. Under the broad term 'marketing', promotion means all the activities undertaken to promote a business and its products and services. It comprises the projection of a proper sigh of the agency and creation of demands for the services of the travel agency. It can be done by personal contacts, through a sales force and advertising.A travel agent sells his services. Sometimes, there may be some malfunctioning somewhere in the long chain of travel, not essentially because of the mistake of the agent. It may be the mistake of an airline which did not operate a service at time, or of the hotel which did not honour a reservation because of overbooking. But, the travel agent is blamed from his clients. Hence this business has a lot of tension also.

There is an interesting story of a travel agent who died and was face to face with St. Peter. He was trembling and expecting to be confined to hell since he never had time to pray in his lifetime. St. Peter asked,

"What was your profession on earth?"

"A travel agent, sir."

St. Peter gave a benevolent smile and ordered, "Let him go to heaven. The poor fellow had faced more than of hell on the earth at the hands of his clients."

Role of Travel Agencies

Travel agencies play a important role in developing international tourism. In India, only 25% of incoming business is handled by set up travel agenciesùmostly groups. Other tourists make independent arrangements. But they should have a large share and should be helped by the Government to handle more inbound business. The travel agents of India have a good efficiency overseas and are known for their quality, reliability and hospitality. The National Committee on Tourism established by the Government of India, realised the importance of travel agencies in marketing Indian tourism overseas. The Committee said:

Considering that the travel trade industry is an important link in the total tourism chain, we recommend that the industry should be expanded suitable bonus to help improve its performance. We believe that the activities of the travel trade are in the nature of export services, earning foreign exchange as they do. As such, the industry requires to be given selected fiscal and instant incentives which are already available to the export industry.

Some deductions were extended to travel agents earning foreign exchange in the budget presented by Dr. Manmohan Singh, for the year 1992-93. More deduction have been added by the Finance Minister in 1997 and later in 2000.

The Committee suggested that travel agents should get the same concessions for earning foreign exchange as the hotel industry. The plants and machinery of the travel agents are cars, coaches, camping, sports and skiing equipment..less customs duty on these equipment should be levied as for project imports. In accordance with an American Express Travel Agency Survey in India, corporate business for travel agents in India is increasing at'the rate often per cent annually (American Express Survey, 1996). No wonder, therefore, the rate ofIATA approved travel agencies folding up in India is one of the lowest, in fact, negligible.

CURRENT TRENDS OF TRAVEL AGENCIES

The development of Travel Agencies are seen as the scale of he development of the country in the developed countries as USA, followed by many other countries, brought in a plethora of reduced airfares and tempting commission structures. Lower airfares resulted in expanded business and higher commissions for travel agents. Business has never been so good. In the USA, membership of IATA is no longer essential to charge commission from IATA or other scheduled carriers. America has set up its own Air

Transport Association (ATA) which works closed with IATA. Agent members ofATCùa division of ATA of Americaù are as good as IATA agents and IATA has supported them.

Several Govemments comprising those of the Japan UK, USA, and Singapore, have enacted legislation regulating the working of travel agencies to protect the Customers. The regulations emphasis that new travel agencies will have trained staff, minimum capitalisation and consumer protection insurance, etc. There have been examples oflargejtravel agencies declaring bankruptcies, while hundreds of their client? were travelling in many countriesùleaving them high and dry as airlines refused to honour their tickets. In India, there is no legislation regulating travel agencies or protecting travellers. The newly developed of Consumers Forums can, however, take note of complaints against travel agents.

Attracted by new opportunities in expanding travel business, the number ofIATA-recognised travel agencies has doubled in ten years, from thirty thousand in 1980 to over sixty thousand in 2000, according to an IATA report.

Statistics related to the travel agency business in the USA are mind-exciting. In 1995, travel agencies in the USA wrote a record US$45 billion in airlines ticketing and the amount of commission paid wasùcommission payments amounted to US$4 billion. In India, statistics related to legal payment in the shape of commissions are seldom availableù airlines are secretive about it as part of it is generally paid under the table. The Indian Airlines which has no reason to be secretive about commission is also not eager to part with this information in an endeavour to expand their area of direct sales at the cost of travel agents. Overall, approved Indian travel agents sell more than sixty per cent of domestic and seventy-five per cent of international tickets.

The rest of the selling is done either directly by the Airlines or through their General Sales Agents (GSAs), which have mushroomed everywhere. GSAs are generally appointed by an airline at a place where there are no IATA agents. A GSA sells tickets of only one airline which represents and operates his office as the Airlines' own office, making him to a higher commission. Over the years, GSAs in India have become an outlet for price-cutting by airlines to beat the competition. They have become experts in cross-border sellingùselling across the area of their jurisdiction. Air India, the national carrier, has its GSA in New Delhi where there are more than a score of IATA agents, not setting a very good example for foreign carriers. IATA agents are generally hostile to the institution of GSAs since they know that this is a way of taking away their legitimate business from them, by their own rulesùthe international airlines.

Suppliers and Travel Agents

Suppliers and Travel Agent based services can be given in the table format as following.

USA Estimated percentage of business booked by travel agents-wholesalers

Airlines	60 per cent (Domestic)
	70 per cent (International)
Hotels	25 per cent (Domestic)
	75 per cent (International)
Bus	10 per cent
Rail	30 per cent
Rental Car	50 per cent
Packaged Tours	90 per cent

Source: Travel Industry World Year Book.

In India, the suppliers' dependence on travel agents is a little less.

Current Developments

Deregulation of airlines in the USA in the eighties, made able airlines to offer any fare to travel agents or customersit has done to two new developments in the travel agency distribution system. One is the emergence of Consolidators-(business organisations) which buy airlines and cruise tickets in bulk at special rates from the principals and give for offer these at discount rate to travel agents. The other is Consortium or Co-ops. A Consortium is composed of affiliated travel agencies whose objective is to enhance the volume sales' profits of independently-owned travel agencies. This is done by means of group advertising, production of promotional material, educational opportunities, consulting resources, suppliers' discounts and other grants. This development has occurred to meet the competition of mega-travel agencies which have a greater bargaining power with the suppliers.

At present development is an arrangement arrived at between North-Western Airlines, Thomas Cook, which is a mega-travel agency, and Ford Motors whereby Ford personnel are hoped to travel by North-Western through Thomas Cook only. North-Western in turn gives a better rate to Ford travellers and a higher commission to Thomas Cook. The consortium concept seeks to achieve the same bargaining position for small travel agencies.

These concepts have also slowed down to other countries during the first decade of the new millennium. In India, Thomas Cook has introduced their bid or buy.com site which offers last minute rate settlementsales of international tickets as well as holidaysùboth domestic and international.different products are on sale. Outbound travellers from India reached four million mark during 2000 which was only 1.9 million in 1991. Till the mid eighties, Indiansùespecially the leisure travellers were discouraged to go foreign and foreign exchange was not released in their favour, if they declared their objective as leisure. Foreign exchange was only released to travellers declaring their mission as business promotion, official or by chance medical treatment in the foreign The bureaucrats and politicians utilised the release of foreign exchange as patronage.

At one time, Indian travellers could take only US$20 with' them if they were on any mission other than business or official. How did they manage with this paltry sum in countries where even the taxi fare from airport to city costs more?

Well, either they were sponsored by their friends or relatives abroad or they cheatedùcollecting US dollars from an intermediate point where they had parked their dollar accounts clandestively, or buying it in black market paying more rupees. It was a matchless philosophy of the Government to save foreign exchange. They encouraged their citizens to cheat. Overseas, Indian travellers were not respected as they acted like beggars. The scene changed a little when in the late seventies, the Government of India allowed US$300 for leisure travellers, later raised to US$500 in three years and some travel agents in India started marketing tours with this amount on shoestring budgets. It became possible as air ticket could be bought in Indian rupees and for sightseeing purposes, buses and trains were used abroad which were relatively less expensive.

However, India decided to liberalise its economy in the starting of 1990s. The country gained an average growth rate of 4.5 per cent annually during this decade, with an accelerated growth in the later part of the decade. Allied to a strong economic growth, demand for international travel increased Until 1996, basic travel quota allowed by the Governmentù(BTQ) remained at US $500. It was increased to US $3000 per year per person in June 2000 and later on an further get increased to US $3000 a year. Now, it is US $5000 a year per person. For business orientedtravellers and for those attending conferences or those going for medical treatment, the foreign exchange quota was get increased to US $25,000ùup from US $15,000. The system was further simplified as the release of foreign exchange was administered by designated commercial banks, as a matter of routine and the people did not have to get prior clearance from the Reserve Bank of India or the Government, for foreign exchange quota to travel overseas. It acted as a major stimulus for overseas travel.

GLOBAL ECONOMY

The liberalisation of economy has resulted in greater scale to the international business community and increased travel among the middle classes, who could afford travelling. There were other factors tooùpopularity of colour TV in Indiaùwith almost every other household having one or two colour TVs at their homes in urban areas. Indian films were shot in far-off foreign destinations like Switzerland, New Zealand and other European countries thereby twelve creating interest in these foreign destinations.

Now the market is big enough to attract twelve foreign government Tourist Boards to open their representative offices in India, to lure Indian citizens to their respective destinations including Great Australia, and Britain. The departures from India in the year 2000 were 3,996600ùsmall for the size of a country like India but growing at a fast rate specially in the leisure part. The outbound travellers were 3.5 million in 1995 and 3>8 million in 1998. And, about 4 million in 2000.

PATA Report

The increase in outbound travellers, especially the leisure travellers from India, made Pacific Asia Travel Association (PATA) sit up and to take note. They asked Travel Research on International level a research organisation based in UK, to conduct a survey of India's outbound market for its members. This hundred-page study is a comprehensive survey of the current expansion spread of outbound travel from India and its future caliber. The first of its kind, it is an attempt on the part of an international organisation to do such a research on its own. The report, a rated publication, was publisher in January 2001 and examines India's present status as an international outbound market, its potential for the future and reasons that deter its faster growth.

So far, the focus of the Ministry of Tourism, Government of India, has always been on inbound tourism by which India gets, foreign exchange more than US 75 million dollars to lure foreign travellers to this country anually, not very successfully. In less than a decade, outbound market has left the inbound far behind with the number of foreign inbound travellers pegged at less than 2.6 million in 2000 and outbound reaching four million. India's balance of trade in tourism is now in the red. Indian travellers abroad are respected as their average spending is more than that of citizens of affluent countries. According to official statistics of Singapore, the average Indian spending in that country exceeds that of the US tourists.

Famous Foreign Destinations

PATA Report estimated that out of the four million outbound travellers, 35% were leisure travellers which includes a sizeable chunk who fall in the category of Visiting Friends and Relatives (VFR). And among the VFRs, the USA and UK have the largest part. Other popular destinations are nearer homeùSingapore, Thailand, UAE, Nepal and Hong Kong, in that order. One reason for Indians opting for foreign destinations nearer home is possibily the high price tag of air tickets for domestic air travel. The Government of India, for reasons of its own, keeps the price of air tickets for travel in India high to an extent that it is now cheaper for Indian citizens to travel to Singapore or Bangkok from Delhi, than from Delhi to Cochin or Chennai. generally, they prefer foreign destinations. Tickets to these destinations are cheaper due to intense competition among foreign carriers.

TOUR OBJECTIVE

Perfect outbound leisure tourism in India is still in its infancy but it has grown out of all approval compared with ten years ago and continuing to increase at a rate of fifteen to 20% annually. According to an International Passenger Survey done on behalf of the Government of India in 1996-97, thirty per cent of the outbound tourists were travelling for business-related purpose, twenty per cent were visiting friend&and relatives, 13% were joining their families, 13% for employment and only 13% declared their objectives as pure leisure. India being a vast country, purpose also varies from region to region depending on the nature of the people.

Most leisure travellers came from metro cities but the share of smaller towns was not insignificant. The impact of liberalisation of the economy is spread all over the country. PATA report estimates that at present some twenty-five million Indians are affluent enough to be able to afford overseas holidays. With only four million Indians travelling abroad, the potential is six times more and it is rising with levels of incomes Increasing in the country.

Within the broad spectrum of outbound travel, the composition of the outbound market has changed radically in current years. Business based travelling has changed from being a market composed basically of businessmen and entrepreneurs pursuing business opportunities within the region, to encompass bonus und conference travel, as well as long-haul trips for increasing number of Indian companies with offices overseas on the one hand and multinational companies based in India on the other. Indian and as multinational companies sponsor bonus travel holidays for their good workers or salesmen, or hold seminars and training programmes for their staff abroad.

Travel Corporation of India (TCI), one of the biggest travel outfits in India, reported sending eight thousand Indians per year, representing white goods manufacturers of automobile and pharmaceutical sectors. Air India reported that such groups could vary from two hundred to UK, to five hundred to Singapore.

American Express has estimated that business travel out of India is worth more than US $1 billion a year business on the Net will soar to US $9 billion but the overall travel business in the USA may well be nearer to 800 billion US $. Thus the business on the Net is only 1.2 per cent of the total travel business, leaving the rest to travel agency playersùenough for everyone to have his share of the cake.

Role and Significance of Internet

In the present marketplace, it is necessary to talk about internet deals as a channel of distribution. It makes direct selling from suppliers to the customers easy and hassle-free. The internet is an evolving communications tool with greater caliber than any of its predecessors. Information technology is beneficial 10 every major principles like airlines, hotel chains who can do marketing their products worldwide on their websites; the tour operators can market their destinations. National Tourist Organisations can have their websites to expose tourist attractions of their countries; individual travel agents can showcase their productsùfair chance to all the players.

But it is only the travel agent who can get added the value and pleasure to the product. We were, therefore, not surprised to read a research paper which revealed that for every person ecstatic about booking on the Net, there were many more who were frustrated by the vast data and bewildering information which their head could not accept. Another IATA research further tells us that of the five passengers who book globally, four come through travel agentsùnot very different than what was happening thirty years ago. Again, only one in five explores the surf for informationùbut only one in ten actually books.

E-commerce is coming of age; Whch is developing very rapidly which 33.33% per month. Creating this growth are supplier' websites and internet booking services such as Microsoft Expedia, Sabre's Travelocity, Internet Travel Network, Preview Travel, American Express and Travel Web, etc. These are full service mega sites doing business in millions. Most airlines too have mega sites but they only give their schedules and rates. They do not give comparative prices. This difficulty is overcome by sites like, www.travelocity.com, which gives comparative prices as well as airline schedules. There are different other websites offering same services. Although the impact of internet on travel agency business is going to affect it adversely in the long run, the travel agent will not be out of business. European budget hotels are some of the best benefits of the internet revolutionùreceiving bookings from all over the world from travellers required economical accommodation.

According to Cyrus Gazdar, former President of the Travel Agents Association of India and a leading expert on new technology, by 2005 the revenue of travel agents from travel agency commissions will come down by fifty per cent.

India is one of that country where IATA discipline still holds. Therefore the price war has left no standard tariffs settledall airlines are offering large discounts to sell their seats including those with excellent reputation as dependable carriers. Another innovation in the Indian market is the emergence of consolidators, appointed by airlines to offer cut-throat prices. Consolidators are bulk-buyers of airlines seat who then retail it to individuals as well as travel agents, keeping a small margin for themselves. Another new institution to reappear in India will be travel agent Co-ops or Consortia as in USA. It may be in the offing as the industry reshapes.

The number of LATA-affiliated travel agencies in India has not declined, in fact it was thousand and two hundred Just before two years but now increased to one thousand and five hundred at present. Travel business in India is increasing at a good rate 12.5% annually. Outbound business is even better, the shortage of airlines seats make travel agents kind of indispensable.

Adi Katgara, Director TCI, expressed his anguish at airlines policy to introduce consolidators, throwing away their seats to beat each other in preference to regular IATA travel agents who worked for them for small commissions. Now, they end up paying higher commissions unprecedented in the history of Indian travel industry. secondly development in Indian travel industry is the mix up of large Indian travel outfits with much larger multinationals. The trend was started by Airfreight Ltd. with Carlson, followed by Sita Travels joining the Kuonis. This is a significant of the shape of things to come and we can predict more mergers, but it is good for the travel industry of India. Both our inbound and outbound tourism will grow up.

ABOVE ALL CONCLUSION

TCI of India

The Travel Corporation of India with its headquarters in Mumbai, is the largest travel agency of India the financial turnover, offices in India and abroad, and the staff employed. July 1961 was a watershed year for the travel trade in India. It marked the merger of three leading Indian travel agencies, Jeena & Co., Lee & Muirhead (India) Pvt. Ltd. and N. Jamnadas & Co., to form the Travel (corporation (India) Ltd. Since that time, TCI has pioneered new areas in tourism and helped thousands of tourists to discover India and other parts of the world. Along the way, they have earned on behalf of the Indian exchequer, millions of dollars in foreign exchange, collected several prestigious tourism awards and secured a global reputation as successful travel agents. It has won the Government of India's National Tourism Award around fourteen times.

Complete Travel Shop

TCIs provides the different services such range from international as domestic ticketing to travel, documentation and hotel reservations. Their exclusive "Speedotel" service assures instant room reservations at over seventy hotels all over India. TCI has its own fleet of the latest air-conditioned and non-air-conditioned deluxe coaches and limousines. TCI are agents for India's wide rail network, Indrail passes. They are also special representatives of Eurail, Japan Rail, Amtrak, Greyhound and Cosmos in India. TCI has an annual turnover of Rs. 2500 million.

It has more than thousand professionals in its twenty-seven offices in India and twelve sales offices in London, Paris, Frankfurt, Milan, Madrid, Barcelona, New York, Seoul, Sydney, Tokyo and Toronto and Beunos Aires. TCI has achieved international approval and is a member of almost all major international travel trade associations. It represents more than a thousand international tour operators. TCI has achieved specialisation through its innovative endeavours. It was often first with new travel ideas, such as exploring and developing new areas for tourism such as Bhutan, Sikkim, Islands, Lakshadweep, Ladakh, and Andaman promoting India as a conference destination and pioneering cruises in the Indian Ocean; introducing air charters and developing incentive and particular interest tours to India. TCI was the first association for ofering scuba-diving facilities in India at its Andaman Beach Resort, achieving the position of an reputated leader in its field. because of their large volume of business with hotels and airlines, TCI is in a position to get better rates for their clients.

INBOUND BUSINESS

In promoting inbound business, TCI has been very innovative. For instant, they were one of the first agencies to introduce special interest tours. A large number of special interest tours offered offered. Among these are:

1. Anthropology	Yoga
2. Archaeology	Angling
3. Architecture	Biking
4. Astrology	Desert Safari
5. Buddhism	Golf
6. Cuisines	Hang Gliding
7. Fairs and Festivals	Hell-skiing
8. Horticulture	Rock Climbing
9. India by Rail	Scuba Diving
10. Museums	Skiing
11. Ornithology	Trekking and Mountaineering
12. Palaces	Water Sports
13. Photography	White-water-rafting
14. Gems and Jewellery	Wild-life
15. Shopping.	

TRAVEL BONUS

Another area of their specialisation is bonus travel to India. bonus travel tours are luxurious travel programmes offered by major international companies as rewards to their best workers. TCI designs their programme in India with great care and imagination, adding special reaches like the flowers and sandalwood welcome, elephant and camel rides, mock Indian weddings, folk and classical dances, palmistry, magic shows, juggling and other folk entertainment. Lavish banquets and theme parties are organised in chanceller. It ballrooms of Maharajas' palaces and royal gardens. Sometimes, desert camps are organised for guests. Hospitality for each group is different. Bazars and fashion shows are also organised. Special souvenirs, video films and photo albums pertaining to their visit are gifted to clients.

WORLD CONFERENCES

International conferences are also an area where TCI has done a good job. They tteve to establish special conference management cell to undertake the handling of international and national conferences with precision. Their services include selection of conference venues, hotel and airline reservations, local transportation, sightseeing, pre-and post-conference tours and all the supporting services required for the smooth operation of an international or national conference.

Air Charters and Cruise Ships

TCI has pioneered the development of tourist air charters to India. With the liberalisation of the Government of India's regulations on charter movement, TCI is now handling tourist charters from Scandinavia Germany and UK.

Similarly, TCI handles ground arrangements for many luxury liners calling on Indian ports, looking after their tour and travel arrangements while these ships berth in Chennai Goa, Cochin, Mumbaior ports.

Searching New Spots

Discovering new areas for tourism has been a tradition with TCI. That was the first agency to discover the potential of both Andaman as well as the Lakshadweep Islands. TCI built the Andaman Beach Resort, the first deluxe resort in Port Blair in 1978, opening up the area for international tourism. It was the first to introduce cruises in the Indian Ocean in 1974. They have ambitious plans to develop more cruises to South-East Asia, Africa, Mauritius and the Seychelles. Ladakh was yet another area which TCI promoted and brought on the international tourist map.

Outbound of India

TCI is a major promoter of overseas holidays, tailored for Indians and is one of the biggest outbound tour operators of the country. TCI's "Funtours" are carefully planned and include accommodation at grand hotels, offering Indian vegetarian and non-vegetarian meals, transportation by deluxe coaches and sightseeing with knowledgeable local guides. Every tour is accompanied by a trained and experienced TCI tour escort. Destinations include Europe, UK, USA, South-East Asia, South-East Africa, Mauritius, Maldives, Nepal, Turkey, Greece, Egypt, Dubai and Australia. Every year thousands ofjindians make use of their services for overseas holidays.

INDIAN TOURISM

TCI is also active in domestic tourism, though it is not their most strong area.

Specially designed for the Indian holiday market, the TCI's "24 Carat Indian Holidays" are flexible and economical offer to popular holiday destinations like Goa, Shimla, Kulu-Manali, Darjeeling, Bangalore, Mysore, Ooty, Kodaikanal, Kerala, Andaman Islands, Lakshadweep Islands, Mahabalipuram and Delhi-Agra-Jaipur etc. During the four decades of its existence, TCI has grown from strength to strength during its creative marketing approach to tourism. For the development international tourism in India, TCI has several firsts to its credit. It was the first Indian travel agency to open offices overseas. It responded to the needs of the market and wherever it found caliber, it opened an office. For instance, it opened its office in Tokyo immediately after the Japanese started travelling overseas in the mid-sixties. Now, it has opened an office in Beuros Aires to tap the tourist potential from South America.

TCI is also one of the first to introduce automation in its operations and put up its website: www.tcindia.com to market tourism services worldwide. The success of any modern travel agency depends upon its ability to respond to the needs of customersùTCI seems to follow that best rule. To summarise most leisure travel business at present revolves around travel agents and tour operators. They promote and sell all sorts of travel and travel-related services to the public. The travel agency business is not very old. The first travel agency was established by Thomas Cook in the year 1845, as he discovered Occasionally that packaging of travel services could be a profitable business. He also introduced travellers' cheques and hotel vouchers, eliminating the need of cash in travel.

Today, there are over sixty thousand travel agencies appointed by IATA and perhaps the same number which do not have the official approval. In India, there are only one thousand five hundred IATA-appointed travel agencies, but many of them have more than one office. Travel agencies are^of two kinds: one, the general services travel agency which undertakes all kinds of travel and travel-related business and two, specialised travel agencies specialising in business travel, conventions and conferences, incentive travel, outbound or inbound travel. Travel agencies can be further sub-divided into wholesalers and retailers, but several of them combine both functions. Among the services provided by travel agencies are airlines, rail and cruise reservations, booking of hotels and rent-a-car vehicles at the other end of the journey, developing and marketing overseas and domestic package holidays, arranging conferences/conventions, entertainments/sports, developing bonus tours, insurance, etc.

Their main source of advantages is from the commissions earned from their principals such as airlines, hotels, steamship companies, car rental companies and railways. To open a new travel agency, it is important to select a location, which is easily accessible to the type of customers whom it wishes to attract towards itself.

To make it profitable, the owner has to get IATA and other authorities in the starting year of its operation. Only then is an agency entitled to get commissions from international airlines. New technologies like the computerised Central Reservation System (CRS) has made the committment of travel agencies easier and more profitable. With a touch of a few buttons, they can hand over the whole itinerary to a client duly printed. But a recent technology-communications through internet opens new horizons. It may support travel agents further but it also threatens their very being.

Any person owning a personal computer can access any travel information through internet, make reservations and is already in a position to pay by fibre cash. There are at present five million internet connections in India but within the next few years there may be several million. Payment done by internet internet may take more time to reach India but Lufthansa Guman Airlines has announced that a potential traveller could do any travel transaction with the help of their 'Smart Card' through internet on all their flights andthe flights of seven hundred other airlines through their Reservation System. Other airlines are not far behind. Because recent liberalisation of the Indian economy, and relaxation of foreign exchange restrictions, Indians are travelling overseas in large numbers.

The outbound business at present is more than inbound which is four million against 2.6 million inbound.

The balance of trade in tourism is no longer in India's favour. It helps Indian trade, industry, exports and expands educational horizons. Many foreign government have started their tourist offices in India to lure Indians to travel to their landsùa healthy competition. We should welcome that. PATA has done a survey on India's outbound tourism. In accordance with its estimates, twenty-five million Indians are today in a position to afford foreign travel. Only four million are travelling, leaving a big potential untapped.

TRAVEL AGENT

Consumer is the last tourist who purchases the package tour as offered by the wholesaler through the retailer.

Retailer is one who is in actual contact with the consumer. There are two types of retailers:

(a) Captive retailers who gets contacts with customes and sell only his tour programmes, who belong to the whole seller

(b) Independent retailers who will sell tour programmes of various wholesalers. These retailers display brochures of tour programmes and sell such programmes through limited advertising, direct mail (which means sending letters and brochures to identified prospective consumers) and through personal selling. These retailers receive commissions from the wholesaler of 10-20% of the total cost of the programme.

Wholesaler is often referred to as Tour Operator. The wholesaler puts together a tour programme after negotiating prices with principals like the airlines for airlines seats, hotels for rooms and meals and surface transporters who operate taxi and tourist coach facilities from airport to hotel and back and travel to other destinations in the city and outside.

He may approach these principals either directly or through travel agents. He invests money in printing and distributing brochures to various destinations and undertakes trade or consumer advertising. He may sell tour programmes through his own retail outlets or through independent outlets. The risk in his business is high, but returns of success are phenomenal.

The travel agent operates in the local market and have necessary licences to represent the important domestic carriers such as airlines, railways, steamship and road transport. He may be the official ground handling agent at a destination for the wholesaler who appoints him for negotiation of prices on his behalf with principals such as hotels, domestic airlines and surface transporters. The travel agent earns his revenue through commissions received from the principals and a mark-up on prices quoted to the wholesaler. Most travel agents act as wholesalers in the domestic market for outbound tours. They are also in cargo business.

Principals

These are institutions in the tourism infrastructure which own independent businesses. Principals are international airlines, hotels, domestic airlines and surface transporters. Surface transporters could be taxi/tourist coach agencies, railways and shippers. Principals give commissions to travel agents who get them business.

DUTIES OF TRAVEL AGENT

1. To receive intimation from wholesale operators for planning itineraries both for groups and particularly in his country.
2. Negotiation with road transport to provide taxis/coaches for transport from airport to hotel, sightseeing tours or intercity transportation.

3. Negotiation with hotels for reasonable prices for room, meal and for other services.
4. The arrange cheap and best transportation services.
5. Negotiation with histoical and cultural places for the entertainment.
6. Coordinate with various tourist centres for sightseeing tours.
7. Cost all points 2 to 6 above and offer a package price to a wholesaler.

Travel agents also advise on luggage insurance, the best season for travel, cloth ing'required, local foreign exchange rules and help in preparing travel documents like visas, health, passport, etc.

In the role of a wholesaler to the local domestic market, they will deal with all principals developing fantastick tour packages nationally and abroad for realised part reputated in the market. They take the responsibility to promote these tour packages through advertisements, e-mail or personal selling.

To determine that clients gets satisfactory reputated, travel agents have also gone into transportation which makes them part principals in their own right.

Travel agents undertake on a day-to-day basis to book/make reservation on behalf of clients' seats on airlines, railways, steamship and taxies/coaches on a commission basis.

3

Tour Organisation

INTRODUCTON

A great sharing factor in growth of air travel holiday tourism has been the development of the 'inclusive tour'. By means of a package for a holiday. This has been the result of a dramatic growth of tourist traffic to the Mediterranean countries from Europe in the last thirty years. The idea of buying a package of travel, accommodation and possibly some ancillary services such as amusement, etc., became an establishment in Western Europe in the 1960s.Necessarily, an 'inclusive tour' is a package of transport and accommodation and probably some other services, which is sold as a single holiday for an all inclusive price.

This inclusive price is generally significantly lower than could be gained by conventioilal methods of booking transport and accommodation separately from specific hotel and transport tariffs. The main feature of the inclusive tour is that the tourist may buy for a single price a holiday which is cheaper than would be feasible for the holiday maker if he brought the parts of his holiday separately and directly from individual hotels and from transport companies or from a retail travel agent.

TOUR OPERATOR

The main important part of the 'Tour organisation is' "tour operator" The tour operator buys different requirements for the tourist such as aircraft seat, hotel beds and other facilities like road transport, entertainment articles and makes up packages. Historically, the tour operator has mostly emerged from retail travel agency.

However, today a travel agent and a tour operator is different from each other. The latter, the retail travel agent, undertakes to sell the travel services of his principal, i.e., airline companies and other transport undertakings, hotel groups, shipping lines and the provision of such ancillary services as traveller's cheques, insurance, etc. The tour operator is a producer of a tourism product unlike the travel agent who is the retailer of the tourism products. He plans, organises and sells tours.

The tour packages operator makes all the important arrangementsùtransport, accommodation, sight-seeing, insurance, entertainment and other matters and sells this 'package' for an all inclusive price. A package tour is preparedto fit a special group of travellers. There may be special interest tours, i.e., trekking, wildlife tours, etc., and can be escorted. An escorted tour generally includes transportation, meals, sight-seeing, accommodation, etc. It is. the "escort" or the "group leader" who is accountable for maintaining the schedule of the tour and for looking after all the arrangements.

PACKAGES OF TOUR

Group Inclusive Tour (GIT)

This is the most famous form of tour in this category in which people travel in groups of 15 or more persons. These tours are available for any destination. The terms and conditions for group inclusive tours are decided by IATA. The escort for such groups generally travels free as the airline gives him with free passage and accommodation. The Foreign Inclusive Tour (FIT), on the other hand, is an unescorted package tour. The FIT tours are relatively more adjustable. The traveller can buy a pre-decided package with arrangements for sight-seeing, hotels and particular meals, where essential. He does not tour with a group. He can make his own arrangements and programmes according to his desire. The inclusive tour is one of the many devices which enable tourists to enjoy the lower price.

The Group Inclusive Tour (GIT) programme made up of a series of integrated travel services. Each of the travel services like seat in a aircraft, a hotel room, etc., is purchased by a tour operator in bulk and resold to his retailers or customers directly as part of a. package at an all-inclusive price. The product generally referred to as a 'package tour are single destination holidays'. In other words, a customer would buy a package holiday from a tour operator or a wholesaler to any single destination, for instance, a tour operator in a individual country will sell a package at a particular price for a cultural holiday in India, a beach holiday in Bali, a wildlife adventure trip in Kenya or a shopping holiday in Singapore, etc. However, some packages comprise two or more destinations. Now, twin destination packages have become quite popular as with little more price one can visit more than one country. These tours are quite common and popular in Europe.

PRICE ADVANTAGES

The success of the package tours depend upon the cheaper and reasonable services for the negotiation, purchased by tour operators for the tourists This lower price of the package tour or inclusive tour is made possible by obtaining the air travel and the hotel accommodation in bulk. As tour operating today has become a highly competitive business its success mainly depends upon the operator maintaining the lowest possible prices while continuing to give to its customers a 'value for money'.

Because of the bulk purchase, tour operators are able to procure substantial discounts from carriers, hoteliers, etc., and offer their package deals at much lower rates. The profits of the tour operator and the success of his operations, however, depend mostly on the achieving of very high load factors for the aircraft and high occupancy rates for the hotel. In this way unit costs can be maintained lowest to enable the tour operator to offer his package at a price which is often lower than the cheapest available fare alone. A breakthrough in the business of tour operation came when airlines realised that tour operation could fill the empty seats, and introduced special fares for use exclusively by tour operators for combining into an inclusive tour.

The tour operator has thus emerged as the main facturer of the tourist product. The product is the inclusive tour, packaged, standardised and mass produced. The tour operator may sell this product directly to the public or through the channels of the retail travel agencies. It can be marketed successfully in the tourist-generating countries to a mass market just because if is standardised, packaged and quality controlled.

The product is, therefore, susceptible to the similar marketing techniques that are applied to the marketing of consumer goods.

Package Tour Marketing (Discounts)

In the competitive world market, there is several choices of the package tours for the different destination, in that situation tour operators have to take careful decision for the promotion of the marketing of the tour packages After considering various alternatives, a tour operator has to narrow down the choice to few potential destinations. A realistic appraisal of the potential of the selected destinations is to be made.

Selection of a potential destination by a tour operator is to be based on different factors; some of these factors include the:

(i) presently, number of tourist attracted by the individual areas;

(ii) growth rate in tourist arrivals in these areas;

(iii) share of the competing companies;

(iv) evaluation of expected share of the market by a company in the next few years of the operation.

(v) availability of suitable and convenient relation to a destination;

(vi) negotiations with principals like the airlines and hotels; and

(vii) negotiations with local conducting agents at the destinations, etc.

PAMPHLET FOR TOUR

Once all the above factors have been considered, when a tour operator arrange a package of tour and incorporate it in a brochure called"tour brochure". A brochure is a document bound in the form of a booklet. It is a voluminous publication with special stress on the quality of a paper, the graphic design of the cover and the layout of pages. The tour operators brochure is the most important marketing tool for selling his product.

Since tourism is an intangible product which cannot be pretested by the prospective customer prior to the purchase, the brochure becomes the important channel of informing a customer about the product and also exciting him to buy the product. The brochure contains a comprehensive and detailed information about a destination including cruises, bus tours, safaris, charter vacations, etc., with colour photographs with regard to all the destinations which a company is developing. Comprehensive information about hotels, weather conditions, frontier formalities, etc., is also given. The price of various tours is invariably mentioned along with the dates when tours take place. Several tour operators take great care with production of their brochures. There are, however, no travel industry standards or guidelines or the production of brochures. Established tour operating companies take great care for designing their tour brochures. The following are some important areas which require to be taken care of while getting the tour brochure printed:

(i) Layout
(ii) Quality of paper
(iii) Photography
(iv) Quality of printing
(v) Special features
(vi) Detailed itineraries
(vii) Weather conditions
(viii) Maps of areas
(ix) Hotel information
(x) Terms and conditions of tour.

Many large tour operating companies get their brochures designed and printed in their own advertising departments. Some get the brochures printed in relation with the design studio of their advertising agency, who in turn negotiate with the printer to get the best quotation and ensure that the print deadlines are adhered to. Adhering to the print deadline is very important as the company has to introduce the brochure at a predecided date, coinciding in most matters with travel trade and consumer holiday fairs. The introduction of a brochure at these events both to travel trade and consumer is decisive for marketing a package.

Tour Brochure

Two diverse versions of a tour brochure printed by two different companies are exhibited in the following pages. Brochure-

I is printed by one of the progressive tour operating companies having a worldwide network of its branches. A four-colour brochure printed on glazed art paper contains different programmes in the form of packages which the company is developing through its brochure.

However, only a few programmes of the company related to India/Nepal have been shown to give to the reader an idea as to how these are packaged. In the brochure, different programmes have been offered for their clients. These have been appropriately titled to motivate the client. For example. Programme-titled 'Indian Experience' is a nine-day classical tour covering Delhi-Agra-Jaipur-Delhi. From day one which is a departure day from USA to India till the ninth day with departure from India to USA, each of the days' details have been worked out. The client can also take extension of one week's holidays to Goa to relax on a beach or go to look for a tiger at one of the many game parks. Most of the tour operators offer extension programmes beyond the planned itineraries. A client has basically to pay a printed price for a basic programme and an additional price in case he takes an extension. The brochure gives both departure and return dates of the programme.

Programme-II entitled "Splendours of the North" covers two weeks' programme covering in addition to Delhi-Agra-Jaipur, places like Varanasi, Gwalior and Udaipur. Programme III is a special programme of 18 days entitled "Forts and Palaces". This programme has been specially put together for those clients who have interest in arts and architecture covering forts and palaces. Programme-IV is twin destination programme spread over India and Nepal. A 22-day programme takes a client first to Nepal and then to India. Titled as "Classical Journey" it covers places associated with religion, culture, legends and mysteries. Travelling at a leisurely pace a tourist can get the grand sights and saviour the unique flavour in both Nepal and India. Programme-V is again a special interest programme for those interested in nature and wildlife. An 18-day programme takes a client prosperous rich tropical jungles, extensive grasslands, temperate forests of India which are reserves of wildlife and some of the world's most stunning national parks. Programme-VI is a 19-day programme to South India entitled "Southern Trader" spread over golden beaches and temples in the region.

Programme-VII is a 17-day tour entitled "Culinary Feast" covering both North and South India and tailor prepared for those who have interest in Indian cuisine. Similarly Programme-VIII again is a twin destination programme covering India and the Maldives. An special interest programme of 16 days covers the finest beaches in the Southern coast as also the Maldives. The programme in India covers some of the famous trade routes searched by the Arabs, Greek, Roman, Portuguese, Dutch, French and British traders. A sample of the brochure may be seen in the following pages.

In signing this reservation form, I/we accept the Conditions as set forth in the brochure on behalf of all those listed above. I/we all declare that I/we have been offered trip cancellation/ baggage insurance and that I/we will not hold travel agent nor its agents responsible for any expenses incurred.

Travel/Agency Stamp/ Signed...............................

Client Address's Date.................................

Day 13. The Maldives

Day of leisure, taking rest on some of the finest beaches the world has to offer, enjoying the tranquillity of the island, resting in hammocks, swimming or snorkeling.

Day 14. The Maldives

Take a cruise out to sea to visit some of the neighbouring atolls, enjoying a picnic lunch and a magical sunset as you return to your island retreat.

Day 15. To Male

Morning for leisure. Afternoon return by boat to Male in time to catch your return flight to the USA which departs very early the next morning.

Day 16. To USA: Early morning flight to the USA.

	OUT		RTN
26	Jan	10	Feb
30	Mar	14	Apr
5	Oct	20	Oct
16	Nov	1	Dec

A tour operating company, in addition to printing programmes, also gives description about package prices, booking conditions and an information sheet for the advice of the clients. The information sheet is an important document for the client as it gives important details about flights, national travel, transfers, surface transport, visa and health requirements of a destination. This practical information comes very handy for a tourist. All these information can be part of a tour brochure or can be printed separately as in the case of company whose programmes have been discussed. This separate printed form which is also a Passenger Reservation Form for booking a programme is shared together with the brochure. An example of the same is as follows:

CONDITIONS OF BOOKING

Booking Procedures

'Firstly we get the information about holiday tour package then we make a contract for a tour package and we deposit the fee and we get signed booking from the travelage at.

Payment

An appropriate deposit for each tour chosen will be your only obligation until eight weeks prior to move. The balance of the tour cost must be paid eight weeks before you travel. If the final balance is not received on time we reserve the right to treat the booking as cancelled by you and to levy cancellation charges. If you book your tour within eight weeks of departure, the full amount of the tour must be paid at the time of booking.

Insurance Advice

You will be automatically billed for and nominated in our travel insurance programme. Should you not require this insurance you must indicate so at time of booking. After receipt of your booking you will be sent a complete brochure on your coverage.

Alterations by a Client

If you request any amendments to your travel arrangements once we have confirmed a booking, telex charges and other charges will be payable by you together with an amendment fee of $50 per alteration. If, after the commencement of your tour, you request for any amendment to your arrangements or accommodation we will do our best to implement it, but we cannot guarantee that it will be possible. In the event of such an amendment being made, you will be responsible for any cancellation/retention expenses that may be levied for the previously booked service and for any costs incurred by us or our agents in efforts to secure any revised arrangement.

Cancellation by a Client: If you want to cancel your tour then you will have to give the notification detailed about the reason ofconcellation as you may be covered by your insurance policy. If noification of cancellation is received more than six weeks before departure you will only lose your deposit. For notification received within six weeks of departure, cancellation charges are as follows:

Day before departure	Total tour cost lost
42 to 29	25%
28 to 16	75%
15to 1	85%
Day of Departure	100%

Cancellations received on Fridays for tour departures that weekend (Saturday, Sunday and Monday) will be treated as no-shows.

We cannot give any allowance or refund for meals, rooms, excursions, etc., not taken when these are {incorporated in the price of the tour and no refund can be made on lost, mislaid or destroyed travel tickets or vouchers.

Cancellations by Tour Operator

All holidays in our brochure are based on group airfares and hotel rates including a given minimum number of passengers. If this minimum is not reached we reserve the right to cancel the departure and offer an substitute date, or the same date with a supplementary charge, or at your option, a refund of all sums paid by you. Such cancellation will not take place after the date at which the final balance becomes due. We may be obliged to cancel your tour because situations beyond our control. These may be for reason of force majeure (cancellations of international and domestic scheduled services, technical problems with transportation, closure of airports, warùwhether declared or notùthreat of war, riots, civil disturbances, disasters, strikes, terrorist activities of threat of such, alteration of international and domestic scheduled services). In such cases we shall inform agents and direct clients without being late and shall offer clients, the choice of a substitute holiday of comparable standard, if available, or a prompt and full refund'of all monies paid.

Changes Made to the Scheduled Programme

Our holidays are planned before several months and changes may be unavoidable because of conditions amounting to force majeure or similar reasons beyond our control, delays in departures on travel arrangements caused by technical problems, weather conditions, overbooking or closure of a hotel, strikes, riots, decisions by state governments or tourist organisations altering the itinerary, the duration of time spent in a city or even omitting a city or part of the itinerary because of the local situation. In such cases we will provide comparable alternative arrangements or You will have an option of full refund of money paid by you.

If any of the situations listed above occur during the course of the tour, we reserve the right to change the scheduled itinerary accordingly and no compensation will be paid. If your tour must be curtailed due to circumstances amounting to force majeure, reparation costs will be met out of unused accommodation costs. No compensation will be made out of accommodation costs. We will make every scietable effort to give you with the booked tour arrangements but subtle changes may occur. If they are importance we shall, if it is feasible, before your departure, inform you or your travel agent. Again, we will offer comparable alternative arrangements or at your choice to make a full refund of all money paid, by where such our control you will be entitled booked tour arrangements but minor changes may occur.

Price

Any like in the original tour price will be notified to you at least eight weeks before departure. If you make your booking within eight weeks of departure the surcharge will be added in your voice. The company will acquire an amount equivalent to 2 per cent of the holiday price. Any surcharge will not exceed 10 per cent of the listed tour price. If you settle the final balance by the due date we will absorb any price increases after that due date. In return for this commitment, we are unable to make any refund or deduct any other costs should the value of the US dollar improve against the currencies used.

ADVICES FOR TRAVELLERS

The company are of the view that a good holiday is based not on luck but on decision. We have, therefore, compiled the following traveller's service to outline the nature of travel in the Indian sub-continent and to help you prepare for your holiday. During our un matured experience some problems are created by chance. While our ground staff are always' ready to correct such an occurrence we do request that you have a patient and broad approach to travelling in the subcontinent.

GLOBAL FLIGHTS

International flights to and from India, Pakistan, Nepal, Sri Lanka and Bhutan are not added in the tour cost as marked on the Tour Prices sheet. We would be pleased by giving support to you in making international flight bookings from your departure city in North America to the arrival city for the tour that you have booked.

The departure dates listed on the brochure indicate the date that you would leave North America to arrive at your destination city in time to join the first organised programme on your tour. We have prebooked hotel for the immediate arrangement at the arrival time for you. Should your flight connections bring you to the arrival city earlier than listed on the itinerary we would be pleased to make additional hotel bookings as required.

INLAND TRAVEL

All flights within the country or countries visited as part of the tour are included in your tour price. Group reservations are made in economy class and all tickets will be tackled by your Tour Director. We regret that we are unable to accept seating requests for internal flights as the domestic airlines generally assign seating only at time of check-in. Additional information on baggage allowance and security regulations will be included in your documents sent to you at the time of booking.

THE TRANSFERS

All the expenses such as airport, road transport, hotel, etc. described in the tour pakcage are included in the amount paid for the package You will met at the airport by a company representative after clearing both immigration and customs and transferred in a private car to your hotel. If you have booked your own international flights you must advise us of your arrival and departure details and any subsequent change to these details so that we may be able to meet you upon your arrival.

TRAVEL BY ROAD

Most cars are used of local construction, and while they may appear to be antique they are comfortable and ideally suitable to the local road conditions, with spare parts readily available. Coaches are also principally locally made and while not of the standard of an American touring coach they are comfortable and well maintained. Most of our coaches are air conditioned exception of some coaches of southern cities of India.

TRAVEL BY TRAIN

On the tours that feature travel by train we always try to reserve first class air-conditioned carriages, but these cannot always be reserved ahead of time and do not exist on all routes. Please contact our tour consultants to discuss the facilities available on the route you would like.

REQUIREMENTS FOR VISA

US citizens require a passport with at least 6 months of validity from the date of entry into the country/countries included on your tour. Visas are required for entry into India, Nepal, Tibet, Bhutan, Jordan and Syria. At this time US citizens do not require visas for entry into Sri Lanka, Pakistan and Israel.

At the time that you make your booking we will mail you a visa kit outlining the visa required necessarily for the tour that you are booked on. This visa kit will include visa forms and an information sheet outlining the visa requirements and procedures. All of the visa handling is done through our visa service.

Please note that the above information and service is valid only for US citizens.

MEASURES OF HEALTH

At the time of printing, the countries specification in our tours do not have any compulsory inoculation requirements for entry with the exception of those travellers having been to a country infected with yellow fever within five days of their arrival. However, it is generally recommended that travellers to India have current tetanus inoculations, and gamma globulin injections to protect against hepatitis.

If you are travelling in South India or in other jungle areas malaria precautions are advised. For further medical information we advise you to contact your local physician. If you need any special medication we advise carrying sufficient supply. Additionally you should carry diarrhoea antidotes and upset stomach medication. Sun lotions, lip balms and sun glasses are highly recommended. Recommendations and advice on food and drink within the country countries visited will be supplied at the time of booking.

In all countries it is mainly recommended to drink only packed mineral water or other bottled beverages. These are generally available in all the hotels that you will be staying at. It is not necessary to purchase destination currency prior to your arrival in India or another country featured on your tour. There are foreign exchange counters in the hotels which ive the same exchange rate as banks. It is, therefore, not essential or recommended to purchase local currency at the airport. However, it is recommended to purchase small denominations for use as tips or for small purchases.

All major credit cards are accepted at the city hotels you will be staying at. Smaller hotels and wildlife park lodging accept cash in local currency only.

Airport Departure Taxes

In the cost of our tour packages the airport departure taxes are not included. It is, therefore, essential for you to pay these locally and in local currency. Foreign currency is not accepted. The taxes vary in each country and will be advised to you before your departure from the USA. These taxes arc subject to change and if they do your tour leader or our ground staff will advise you on site.

Tipping

Tipping for porterage and all significant sightseeing is incorporated. Tipping is not added for services besides these such as meals not included, optional sightseeing, etc. In addition, some members of the groups may want to collectively pick the bus driver or local guide.

This is not needed and is completely at your discretion. Please ask your tour leader any question you may have about this. Our Tour Directors do not accept tips.

Cuisine

In the city hotels, restaurants give the serving of Continental as well as Indian and Oriental cuisine. In the more remote areas and smaller hotels and places the food is basic and mainly Indian. We suggest that in these areas you request vegetarian food since this tends to decrease the risk of stomach upsets.

The hotels that we use are keenly aware of the Western visitor's reaction to Indian food and they take great care in the area of hygiene. While health problems can occur, these are generally minor and often result in the change of diet and time zones.

Insurance

We percept that no one likes to consider the unexpected problems that interrupt holiday plans. Unfortunately, difficulties by chance do arise, despite the most careful planning. So, to offer you peace of mind the company offers a comprehensive Passenger Protection Programme exclusively for our passengers.

The Passenger Protection Programme is not just cancellation insurance. Yes, it does give reimbursement for penalties that may be assessed due to cancellation for acquired reasons, but it also provides much more. Momentary, the programme offers medical expense reimbursement for covered accidents overseas, particularly significant since Medicare, and different private insurance policies, restrict coverage of medical expenses incurred abroad.

We strongly recommend that all passengers participate in the Passenger Protection Programme. A full description of coverage will be sent to you or your travel agent automatically with your bill. For your convenience the cost of the programme is automatically included to your bill and may be purchased with your initial deposit or prior to final payment but cannot be added at a later date.

This is only a concise description of the plan. For full terms, conditions, exclusions and pre-existing limitations, refer to the description of coverage which should be reviewed thoroughly before purchasing.

Travel Insurance Coverage

Trip Cancellation/Interruption	Total Tour Cost
Baggage/Personal Effects	$ 1,000
Acćident Medical Expense	$3,000
In-Hospital Idemnity (Sickness Only)	$3,000
Emergency evacuation	$2,0000
Worldwide Emergency Assistance	24 Hours
Travel Insurance Rates	
Tour up to $2,000	$99
Tours between $ 2,000 and $ 3,500	$169
Tours between $ 3,501 and $ 5,000	$259
Tours between $ 5,001 and $ 6,000	$299
Tours between $ 6,001 and $ 7,500	$359

Brochure II has a different presentation form while all other elements remain the same. In this brochure most of the programmes are multi-destinational. A client has a option of more than one destination in a individual region.

The tour operator developing these programmes specialises in East Asia. Although the basic programmes cover India, the tour operator however does not take his clients there first. Tour No. 1 entitled 'Asian Highlights' is a 20 days trip starting in USA and covers Hong Kong, India, Nepal and Thailand. A client returns home from Bangkok. In this programme, the client also has a option of an extension in India and the orient as per his requirements.

Tour No. 2 is a 15-18 days tour covering India and Nepal. Tour No. 3 is entitled "Magnificent India and Nepal" and covers both these destinations in 18 days. Tour No. 4 is again a twin destination tour named "Essence of India and Nepal" and is of 12 days duration with possible extensions.

Unlike in Brochure No. 1, the price of the tours', start dates and terms and conditions of the tour form part of the main brochure. No separate sheet is printed as in the case of Brochure I. The brochure is printed in four colours using glazed art paper. Use of colour pictures in the brochure is another important element which projects the destination.

Each of the programmes shows a colour representation of an important monument, event or an activity covering the itinerary. The following pages show the sample of the brochure discussed above.

Not Incorporated in Quoted Tour Price

Costs of getting passports; visas unless otherwise specified in particular itinerary; extra baggage charges; travel insurance; personal expenses such as laundry; room service in excess of your meal allotment; gratuities and road transport to/from lestaurants for a la carte meals; gratuities to escort, staff and crew of Eastern & Oriental Express, Road to Mandalay or Yanzi Princess; communication charges; meals, beverages or sightseeing; not included in the itinerary any airfares.

Luggage

Tour prices included the handling of two pieces of baggage per person. Baggage and personal effect are at owner's risk throughout the tour. Check with the airline for baggage prohibition applicable to your international flights.

Passport and Visas

Valid passport are required for travelling to the destinations in this brochure; check with your travel agent or ask the latest requirement and support.

Registration

A deposit of $ 500 per person is required at the time you book, at which time you will get your invoice and pre-tour documentation. The reminder of the price of your trip is due 60 days prior to your departure date. If your reservation is done within 60 days of departure, the entire price of the trip must be paid at the time of confirmation. When your reservation is initiated within 30 days of your departure, a non-refundable "rush booking" fee of $ 50 per booking will be charged.

Cancellations

Cancellations received up to 60 days before departure, $100 per person cancellation fee per tour or extension; 59-45 days, 10 per cent of tour price; 44-15 days, 20 per cent of tour price; 14 days or less 100 per cent of tour price.

Claims and Refunds

All claims for days missed while on tour should be made in writing within 30 days of the cancellation of the tour. This claim should be accompanied by a statement from the Tour Operating Company approving the claim.

Refunds are based on the actual prices of service involved and not on a per claim basis. Refunds will not be done for unused sightseeing trips or meals. The company will not accept any responsibility for any claims which are not received within 30 days of the termination of your tour.

Arrangements

Quoted tour prices included planning, handling and operational charges, and are based on the current rates of exchange and tariffs as of July, 1995. In the event of a pointed change in foreign exchange rates, fuel costs or tariff rates, tour costs are subject to revision.

Responsibility

The company purchases transportation, hotel accommodation, restaurant services and other services from diverse independent suppliers that are not subject to its control.

The Company, cannot, therefore, be liable for any personal risk or property damage, which may take place due to (1) any act of Commission of such a supplier or (2) defects in or failures of any aircraft, vessel, automotive vehicle or other type of transportation that is not under its control.

The company reserves the right to adjust US dollar prices without information, to reflect fluctuations in the Foreign

Exchange Markets. The Company also reserves the right to cancel a tour or any part of it, to make such alternations in the itinerary as appears necessary or desirable, to refuse to accept or to retain as a member of the tour any person at any time, and to pass on to tour members any expenditures or losses caused by delays or events beyond its control.

Air Transportation

We will arrange the most reasonable airfare available in the different categories you request at the time of your booking. Sample air prices are shown in this brochure. Should you cancel or change your air reservation before or after departure, cancellation penalties may apply.

Airlines concerned are not to be held accountable for any act, omission or event during the time passengers are not on board their planes or conveyances, These tours may use the services of any IATA carrier. The passage contract in use by these companies when issued shall organise the sole contract between the companies and the purchaser of these tours and/or passage.

Components in a Tour Brochure

The description of the tour brochure of the two companies shows how diverse elements of a programme are carefully planned to comprise "all required information to make a holiday comfortable. The essential elements of a good programme in a brochure can be divided into two parts, e.g.

(i) 'pre-visit' and

(ii) 'on arrival'.

Pre-visit details would include the following:

(a) destination information

(b) cost of a tour

(c) departure dates

(d) hotel information

(e) visa requirements

(f) medical fitness

(g) insurance advice

"On arrival" details would include the following:

(i) transfers
(ii) guide service
(iii) day today itinerary
(iv) currency exchange
(v) shopping
(vi) entertainment/cultural programmes
(vii) emergency services
(viii) customs to be observed
(ix) cuisine
(x) airport departure taxes

All the elements in a programme of a big tour operator are tailor-made to develop particular interest and need of a client. A tour operator, after carefully considering different alternatives available and based on the market research packages, offers different programmes for including in his tour brochure.

NETWORK OF DISTRIBUTION

The tour operator has thus emerged as the true producer of the inclusive tour product packaged, standardised and quality controlled. The inclusive tour product can be marketed successfully by a tour operator in the tourist producing countries to a mass market, either directly or through travel agents.

A large majority of tour operators sell their tour packages through a network of several hundred agents who are the members of the Association of Travel Agents in a particular country. For instance, if a tour operator happens to be USA based he would sell his product through ASTA, (American Society of Travel Agents) in UK, through ABTA (Association of British Travel Agents) in Australia, through AFTA (Australian Federation of Travel Agents) etc. A large percentage of tour packages are marketed in this manner.

Some tour operators resort are directly selling the tour package through the network of their branches For instance, in Switzerland, the largest tour operating company 'KUONF' Sells its product through 85 of their own Kuoni retail sales offices as also through 765 appointed retail agents who are the members of FASV, the Swiss association of travel agents. Thomas Cook is well known as a travel retailer of its own product in addition to being a major tour operator of package tours. Most of their package tours are sold through an expanded network of their own retail sales offices.

Direct sale of the holiday scheme is however resorted to by large tour operating companies having retail sales agencies of their own within a destination where these are situated or in other neighbouring destinations.

On the other hand, small tour operating companies not having retail sales outside will either Centralised on selling their product or will support a select few travel agencies in important areas spread over the country. However, unlike sales of a tour operator programmes through travel agencies, direct selling engages higher fixed costs in advertising, direct mail development and similar other aspects. Direct selling also requires strong and efficient administrative back-up to deal smoothly with consumer and trade enquiries and sales,

Agreements of Sales

A tour operator who decides to sell his tours through a network of travel agents, has to get in some form of an agreement with them. A formal contract with the travel agents they appoint is to be drawn up to facilitate the agents to sell the services on behalf of a tour operator.

The contract inter alia specify the various terms and conditions of sale including issues like quantum of commission to be paid to the agents. It also makes clear if the travel agent is to be a cash or credit agency as also the dates by which the operator is likely to settle his'accounts. Another potent condition of the contractor relates to a sale price of a tour. Most tour operators impose on an agent the condition in the contracts that their tours shall not be sold at a lower price than that published in the brochure.

Brochure Marketing

Printing of a tour brochure is very expensive. A brochure is a voluminous publication with special pressure on the quality of paper, the reproduction of illustrations, graphic design of the cover and the layout of the pages. To be an attractive sales tool, it has to be printed on glazed art paper in four colours.

Special pressure is laid on the quality of papers and printing, as its main objective is to inform the prospective tourist about the attractions and facilities of a programme being developed by a tour operator. Considering all the above aspects, a tour operator has to spend reasonable amount of money on printing of a tour brochure. Some of the tour brochures of large companies contain different programmes running into many hundred pages.

Each of the particular programme in a brochure is to be marketed to percept a sale of that programme, different programmes contained in a brochure are to be marketed both by the tour operator and the agents at a destination to get actual bookings for a individual programme.

Marketing and promotion of a special programme in a tour brochure involves many elements starting first with the contribution of a brochure to travel agents situated throughout the country. In case a tour operator had retail sales offices of his own, the brochure is also to be contributed to them.

The quantity will depend on the size of the agency as also its location. It will also depend on the volume of business generated by the agent during the past few years. Launching a press conference is another important element in developing a holiday programme printed in a brochure. A special advertising campaign is necessary to be launched in specifiedcustomer newspapers in the generating market featuring tour programmes.

The selection of the customer newspapers should be based on factors like the area to be covered, the type of.audience to be reached, the appeals to be used, etc.

The consumer newspapers are selected due to of their wider reach. Window display campaign is another important and effective way of developing a tour programme of a brochure. Specially prepared window display materials featuring tour programmes of a company for a special destination can be used in retail sales office locations.

The visual appeal of displaying motivation of a prospective tourist to enter the office and ask for more details. Simultaneous launching of a press conference and window display campaign gives added profit in that it registers a message about a destination more forcefully. Trade education is another important element in promoting the sale of a holiday package. The sales staff of a tour operating company should be given orientation concerning the tour programme they are to promote through their outlets. This could be handled by planning specialist of the tour operating company.

A similar trade education programme can be organised for retail agents. All appointed retail sales agencies should be engaged in this programme. Press and public relations activities of the company developing a programme play a vital role. A large tour operating company has a separate press and public relation department which create special press releases on their various tour programmes. The text of these press releases is given to select consumer newspapers throughout the country.

4

INTERNATIONAL TOURISM

According to current reports in the media, travelling to outer space should become possible for everyone by the beginning of the next century. In April 1998, the newspaper Berlin Morgenpost reported that the international Hilton Hotel corporation is planning the construction of a 5-star hotel, the "Lunar Hilton," on the Moon. A team of British architects was commissioned to develop plans for the gigantic building project. The luxury hotel with 5000 beds and a height of 325 metres provides its own beach at its private "ocean," and should be equipped with all the amenities one can expect from a first class hotel.

However, the short-term realisation of this utopian project of the Hilton Group will most likely take a little more time, and for the first half of the 21st century it must be regarded as pure science fiction. Apart from the technical feasibility of some of the construction plans, economic analyses performed by DLR and the Technical University of Berlin show that the transportation of humans and building materials to the Moon would be extraordinarily expensive, even if very optimistic economic conditions in space operations are assumed [LAssMANN94, REICHERT97a]. With the announcement of its spectacular project, the Hilton Corporation competes with three Japanese corporations, Shimizu, the construction firm Nishimatsu, and Obayashi, all of which have already invested millions into futuristic colonising concepts for the moon.

Life-cycle cost analyses performed in [ESA99, REICHERT97b/c/d] for the planet Mars indicate, that the transportation of humans would require ticket prices in the range of hundreds of millions of dollars, even if very favourable economic conditions in space operations are assumed. In addition, one must consider that after the successful completion of the Apollo program no transportation infrastructure is currently available that would allow humans to be transported beyond the Earth orbital. The creation of such a new infrastructure would require investments of billions of dollars. The Moon and Mars are therefore not likely to play a role in international tourism in the first half of the next century, although Mars represents one of the most promising travel destination because of its many similarities to Earth and its potential of possible former life forms.

Therefore future space tourism will focus for a long time on Earth orbit which can be reached more easily. Figure 2 shows the expected roadmap for space tourism for the next decades with its four sub-scenarios. It is likely, that the space tourism business is initiated by very short suborbital flights, followed by short Earth orbital tourism in advanced, reusable spacecraft which allow several orbits around Earth. Before extended stays in space hotels will become a reality in the far future, touristic trips to existing orbital facilities (e.g. the international space station) might represent an intermediate step.

Already since the mid-sixties, several important analyses of Earth orbital space tourism have been carried out [EHRICKE67]. Various scenarios of transportation and accommodation of tourists in space have been analysed in the frame of industrial research in Japan, increasingly over the last 10 years [COLLINS97, MATSUMOTO97]. In the United States, NASA and the American "Space Transportation Association " have completed a study of the feasibility of space tourism with some promising results [O'NEIL97] in 1998. Furthermore, DASA (DaimlerChrysler Aerospace) investigates touristic spacecraft and space hotel concepts and supported the first international symposium on space tourism in the spring of 1997, which took place in Bremen (Germany) and attracted more than 100 experts from around the world. The symposium also found a significant echo in the media. Moreover, in 1998/99, the general feasibility and economics of space tourism played also a considerable role in an ESA study under the lead of DLR [ESA98, ESA99, REICHERT98]. All of these activities indicate that space tourism is gaining more and more attention and significance. Today, it is already possible to book atmospheric parabolic flights in aeroplanes for the short-term simulation of zerogravity, and to reserve future passenger flights into suborbital space, even though the technology for the latter has not been developed yet.

INDUSTRIAL SIGNIFICANCE

According to an estimate of the World Travel Tourism Council, annual global expenditures in the terrestrial tourism sector amount to about 3400 billion US dollars for the year 1995. Tourism thus globally represents one of the largest industries. If it would be possible to shift only a few percent of the world-wide terrestrial tourist expenditures to a future space tourism market, this could double the civil space budgets to 60 billion dollars. This would create up to half a million new jobs also in the high technology space industry, if it is assumed that a sales volume of $50000 to $250000 creates one job.

If a space tourism business can be established in the future, the scientific and operational know-how-globally gained after decades of research and experience in manned space flight (e.g. by astronaut training centers or institutions of aerospace medicine)-could be applied to the space flight preparation and medical supervision of future space tourists.

Furthermore, touristic spaceflights could be planned, controlled and monitored by existing space operation centers in Europe, the USA or Russia. As soon as a space tourism market is established, large commercially oriented industrial conglomerates will cooperate in strategic alliances to operate and expand the space tourism business comparable to the terrestrial tourism and telecommunications industries. The main motivation for an industrial investment in the space tourism sector will be the potential of very high achievable profits, which can be expected due to multi-billion dollar market potential.

THE MARKET FOR SPACE TOURISM

As soon as the "space ticket" can be purchased for some $10000-in the best of all cases a ticket price comparable to that of a transatlantic flight with the Concorde-one can expect that a global space tourism market will be established. This has been confirmed by first national and international polls and market analyses (e.g. in the US, Japan, Europe) which indicate that a remarkable segment of clients would be already willing to make considerable financial commitments for short trips into space. For example, 4.3% of all Germans are willing to pay several $10000-which is roughly comparable to an annual income-for a space trip.

This could be a ticket price which might be achievable with future generations of spacecraft, and it is comparable to the cost of a vacation on a cruise ship which already attracts a steady clientele. Figure 4 shows the expected number of passengers for a space trip as a function of the ticket costs according to international polls performed in the US, Japan, and Europe. With current costs of several ten million dollars to transport a human into space, space tourism is not affordable and finds no acceptance in the public.

However, with declining space travel ticket prices the situation will change. Once a ticket price of $ 1000 is obtainable, a passenger volume of about 20 million is expected, and even with a ticket price of $ 50000 a passenger rate of 1 million per year can be expected.. Nevertheless, the above mentioned polls have to be critically assessed with respect to their accuracy and credibility. Therefore, more detailed and representative polls and market research in this area have to be carried out.

Generally, any average person in good health and with appropriate preparation is able to go on a space trip. NASA, for example, just recently decided to send 77-year old former astronaut and Senator John Glenn into space with the Space Shuttle. He took part in important medical research experiments from which especially the older generation will profit.

THE FASCINATION OF SPACE TRAVEL

The fact, that a significant portion of the public is willing to spend a lot of money on space trips proofs that these are regarded as very promising and fascinating. The confrontation with the high technology of space missions, the heroic myth of astronauts, and the possibility of orbiting planet Earth in just a little more than 80 minutes with a speed of about 30000 kilometres per hour (compared to the 80 days needed a hundred years ago) will represent for each tourist an unforgettable adventure and event. Furthermore, for the first time in his life, the tourist in a space hotel will experience an entirely different environment. Depending on the rotational velocity of the Space Hotel Berlin various levels of artificial gravity can be obtained, ranging from customary terrestrial gravity (1G) to Mars gravity (1/3 G) and even Lunar gravity (1/6 G), i.e. a human being will weigh only one sixth of his or her earthly weight.

In the central node of the Space Hotel Berlin there will be nearly zero gravity. Here the tourist can experience weightlessness. How does one behave if one can not get from A to B in a normal way and "above" or "below" are without meaning. Many of the questions that astronauts were asked-how they manage eating, sleeping, and personal hygiene-can be explored by tourists themselves. The zerogravity area also offers fascinating opportunities for entirely new sorts of entertainment, games and sports.

For example a ball game in zero-gravity and three-dimensional space. Or one can imagine a swimming pool. The water would not be in a basin, but would float as wobbly water bubbles in space, some of which are several meters in diameter, and one can swim and dive through them. One can imagine that some tourists may want to use the zero-gravity zones for future medical therapies: This could represent a first step towards a future space hospital. Furthermore, the Coriolis force, which only appears within rotating systems, will baffle the tourist, since it will push him, like a magic force, into a certain direction, depending on his direction of movement. Probably, the predominant part of the vacation will be spent with the breathtaking view each tourist will have from the panoramic window of each apartment onto the blue home planet from a distance of 400 kilometres. Even if initially concentrating on his home city and country, soon the tourist will discover earth with its thin and precious atmosphere and a wide variety of picturesque structures on its surface as a totality without national borders. On the other hand, the view of the infinite expanse of outer space will dramatically symbolise that we owe our human existence, history and future a singular, beautiful, tiny "grain of sand" which we call Earth.

After returning to Earth, the consciousness of many tourists may have changed; it will be expanded and globalised with many potentially positive social consequences, which could help, for example, to lower the dangers for environmental pollution, local conflicts, and war. Once space tourism is affordable to the broad public, space activities-especially manned space programs-will develop and increase in a way that is hardly imaginable today. A wide variety of space station concepts have been investigated for decades and first concepts for gigantic, circular cities in orbit are available. Perhaps many humans increasingly will harbour the wish to visit the more remote planetary worlds of Mars and of the Earth's Moon some day, according to the Russian space pioneer Ziolkowksy who proclaimed around the year 1900: "Earth is the cradle of humanity, but one cannot always remain in the cradle."

INTERNATIONAL TOURISM CHARTER

The Charter Ethos

At the broadest level, the natural and cultural heritage belongs to all people. We each have a right and responsibility to understand, appreciate and conserve its universal values.

Heritage is a broad concept and includes the natural as well as the cultural environment. It encompasses landscapes, historic places, sites and built environments, as well as bio-diversity, collections, past and continuing cultural practices, knowledge and living experiences. It records and expresses the long processes of historic development, forming the essence of diverse national, regional, indigenous and local identities and is an integral part of modern life. It is a dynamic reference point and positive instrument for growth and change.

The particular heritage and collective memory of each locality or community is irreplaceable and an important foundation for development, both now and into the future. At a time of increasing globalisation, the protection, conservation, interpretation and presentation of the heritage and cultural diversity of any particular place or region is an important challenge for people everywhere. However, management of that heritage, within a framework of internationally recognised and appropriately applied standards, is usually the responsibility of the particular community or custodian group.

A primary objective for managing heritage is to communicate its significance and need for its conservation to its host community and to visitors. Reasonable and well managed physical, intellectual and/or emotive access to heritage and cultural development is both a right and a privilege. It brings with it a duty of respect for the heritage values, interests and equity of the present-day host community, indigenous custodians or owners of historic property and for the landscapes and cultures from which that heritage evolved.

Dynamic Interaction Between Tourism and Cultural Heritage

Domestic and international tourism continues to be among the foremost vehicles for cultural exchange, providing a personal experience, not only of that which has survived from the past, but of the contemporary life and society of others. It is increasingly appreciated as a positive force for natural and cultural conservation. Tourism can capture the economic characteristics of the heritage and harness these for conservation by generating funding, educating the community and influencing policy.

It is an essential part of many national and regional economies and can be an important factor in development, when managed successfully. Tourism itself has become an increasingly complex phenomenon, with political, economic, social, cultural, educational, bio-physical, ecological and aesthetic dimensions. The achievement of a beneficial inter-action between the potentially conflicting expectations and aspirations of visitors and host or local communities, presents many challenges and opportunities. The natural and cultural heritage, diversities and living cultures are major tourism attractions. Excessive or poorly-managed tourism and tourism related development can threaten their physical nature, integrity and significant characteristics. The ecological setting, culture and lifestyles of host communities may also be degraded, along with the visitor's experience of the place.

Tourism should bring benefits to host communities and provide an important means and motivation for them to care for and maintain their heritage and cultural practices. The involvement and co-operation of local and/or indigenous community representatives, conservationists, tourism operators, property owners, policy makers, those preparing national development plans and site managers is necessary to achieve a sustainable tourism industry and enhance the protection of heritage resources for future generations. ICOMOS, the International Council on Monuments and Sites, as the author of this Charter, other international organisations and the tourism industry, are dedicated to this challenge.

Objectives

The Objectives of the International Cultural Tourism Charter are:

- o To facilitate and encourage those involved with heritage conservation and management to make the significance of that heritage accessible to the host community and visitors.
- o To facilitate and encourage the tourism industry to promote and manage tourism in ways that respect and enhance the heritage and living cultures of host communities.
- o To facilitate and encourage a dialogue between conservation interests and the tourism industry about the importance and fragile nature of heritage places, collections and living cultures, including the need to achieve a sustainable future for them.
- o To encourage those formulating plans and policies to develop detailed, measurable goals and strategies relating to the presentation and interpretation of heritage places and cultural activities, in the context of their preservation and conservation.

In addition,

- o The Charter supports wider initiatives by ICOMOS, other international bodies and the tourism industry in maintaining the integrity of heritage management and conservation.
- o The Charter encourages the involvement of all those with relevant or at times conflicting interests, responsibilities and obligations to join in achieving its objectives.
- o The Charter encourages the formulation of detailed guidelines by interested parties, facilitating the implementation of the Principles to their specific circumstances or the requirements of particular organisations and communities.

Principles

Principle 1

Since domestic and international tourism is among the foremost vehicles for cultural exchange, conservation should provide responsible and well managed opportunities for members of the host community and visitors to experience and understand that community's heritage and culture at first hand.

The natural and cultural heritage is a material and spiritual resource, providing a narrative of historical development. It has an important role in modern life and should be made physically, intellectually and/or emotively accessible to the general public. Programmes for the protection and conservation of the physical attributes, intangible aspects, contemporary cultural expressions and broad context, should facilitate an understanding and appreciation of the heritage significance by the host community and the visitor, in an equitable and affordable manner.

Individual aspects of natural and cultural heritage have differing levels of significance, some with universal values, others of national, regional or local importance. Interpretation programmes should present that significance in a relevant and accessible manner to the host community and the visitor, with appropriate, stimulating and contemporary forms of education, media, technology and personal explanation of historical, environmental and cultural information.

Interpretation and presentation programmes should facilitate and encourage the high level of public awareness and support necessary for the long term survival of the natural and cultural heritage. Interpretation programmes should present the significance of heritage places, traditions and cultural practices within the past experience and present diversities of the area and the host community, including that of minority cultural or linguistic groups. The visitor should always be informed of the differing cultural values that may be ascribed to a particular heritage resource.

Principle 2

The relationship between Heritage Places and Tourism is dynamic and may involve conflicting values. It should be managed in a sustainable way for present and future generations.

Places of heritage significance have an intrinsic value for all people as an important basis for cultural diversity and social development. The long term protection and conservation of living cultures, heritage places, collections, their physical and ecological integrity and their environmental context, should be an essential component of social, economic, political, legislative, cultural and tourism development policies.

The interaction between heritage resources or values and tourism is dynamic and ever changing, generating both opportunities and challenges, as well as potential conflicts. Tourism projects, activities and developments should achieve positive outcomes and minimise adverse impacts on the heritage and lifestyles of the host community, while responding to the needs and aspirations of the visitor.

Conservation, interpretation and tourism development programmes should be based on a comprehensive understanding of the specific, but often complex or conflicting aspects of heritage significance of the particular place. Continuing research and consultation are important to furthering the evolving understanding and appreciation of that significance.

The retention of the authenticity of heritage places and collections is important. It is an essential element of their cultural significance, as expressed in the physical material, collected memory and intangible traditions that remain from the past. Programmes should present and interpret the authenticity of places and cultural experiences to enhance the appreciation and understanding of that cultural heritage.

Tourism development and infrastructure projects should take account of the aesthetic, social and cultural dimensions, natural and cultural landscapes, bio-diversity characteristics and the broader visual context of heritage places. Preference should be given to using local materials and take account of local architectural styles or vernacular traditions.

Before heritage places are promoted or developed for increased tourism, management plans should assess the natural and cultural values of the resource. They should then establish appropriate limits of acceptable change, particularly in relation to the impact of visitor numbers on the physical characteristics, integrity, ecology and biodiversity of the place, local access and transportation systems and the social, economic and cultural well being of the host community. If the likely level of change is unacceptable the development proposal should be modified.

There should be on-going programmes of evaluation to assess the progressive impacts of tourism activities and development on the particular place or community.

Principle 3

Conservation and Tourism Planning for Heritage Places should ensure that the Visitor Experience will be worthwhile, satisfying and enjoyable.

Conservation and tourism programmes should present high quality information to optimise the visitor's understanding of the significant heritage characteristics and of the need for their protection, enabling the visitor to enjoy the place in an appropriate manner.

Visitors should be able to experience the heritage place at their own pace, if they so choose. Specific circulation routes may be necessary to minimise impacts on the integrity and physical fabric of a place, its natural and cultural characteristics.

Respect for the sanctity of spiritual places, practices and traditions is an important consideration for site managers, visitors, policy makers, planners and tourism operators. Visitors should be encouraged to behave as welcomed guests, respecting the values and lifestyles of the host community, rejecting possible theft or illicit trade in cultural property and conducting themselves in a responsible manner which would generate a renewed welcome, should they return.

Planning for tourism activities should provide appropriate facilities for the comfort, safety and well-being of the visitor, that enhance the enjoyment of the visit but do not adversely impact on the significant features or ecological characteristics.

Principle 4

Host communities and indigenous peoples should be involved in planning for conservation and tourism.

The rights and interests of the host community, at regional and local levels, property owners and relevant indigenous peoples who may exercise traditional rights or responsibilities over their own land and its significant sites, should be respected. They should be involved in establishing goals, strategies, policies and protocols for the identification, conservation, management, presentation and interpretation of their heritage resources, cultural practices and contemporary cultural expressions, in the tourism context.

While the heritage of any specific place or region may have a universal dimension, the needs and wishes of some communities or indigenous peoples to restrict or manage physical, spiritual or intellectual access to certain cultural practices, knowledge, beliefs, activities, artefacts or sites should be respected.

Principle 5

Tourism and conservation activities should benefit the host community.

Policy makers should promote measures for the equitable distribution of the benefits of tourism to be shared across countries or regions, improving the levels of socio-economic development and contributing where necessary to poverty alleviation.

Conservation management and tourism activities should provide equitable economic, social and cultural benefits to the men and women of the host or local community, at all levels, through education, training and the creation of full-time employment opportunities.

A significant proportion of the revenue specifically derived from tourism programmes to heritage places should be allotted to the protection, conservation and presentation of those places, including their natural and cultural contexts. Where possible, visitors should be advised of this revenue allocation.

Tourism programmes should encourage the training and employment of guides and site interpreters from the host community to enhance the skills of local people in the presentation and interpretation of their cultural values.

Heritage interpretation and education programmes among the people of the host community should encourage the involvement of local site interpreters. The programmes should promote a knowledge and respect for their heritage, encouraging the local people to take a direct interest in its care and conservation. Conservation management and tourism programmes should include education and training opportunities for policy makers, planners, researchers, designers, architects, interpreters, conservators and tourism operators. Participants should be encouraged to understand and help resolve the at times conflicting issues, opportunities and problems encountered by their colleagues.

Principle 6

Tourism promotion programmes should protect and enhance Natural and Cultural Heritage characteristics.

Tourism promotion programmes should create realistic expectations and responsibly inform potential visitors of the specific heritage characteristics of a place or host community, thereby encouraging them to behave appropriately.

Places and collections of heritage significance should be promoted and managed in ways which protect their authenticity and enhance the visitor experience by minimising fluctuations in arrivals and avoiding excessive numbers of visitors at any one time.

Tourism promotion programmes should provide a wider distribution of benefits and relieve the pressures on more popular places by encouraging visitors to experience the wider cultural and natural heritage characteristics of the region or locality.

The promotion, distribution and sale of local crafts and other products should provide a reasonable social and economic return to the host community, while ensuring that their cultural integrity is not degraded.

5

TOURISM AN EVERGREEN TRADE

Agritourism is a style of vacation in which hospitality is offered on farms. This may include the opportunity to assist with farming tasks during the visit. Agritourism is often practiced in wine growing regions, as in Italy, France and Spain. In America, Agritourism is wide-spread and includes any farm open to the public at least part of the year. Tourists can pick fruits and vegetables, ride horses, taste honey, learn about wine, shop in gift shops and farm stands for local and regional produce or hand-crafted gifts, and much more. Agritourism is being developed as a valuable component of a business model to support many agricultural entities when the farm products they produce are no longer economically competitive otherwise. To help promote the single agritourism operations, some farms get together to form festivals, tours or other events.

People are more interested in how their food is produced and want to meet the producers and talk with them about what goes into food production. Children who visit the farms often have not seen a live duck, or goat, and have not picked an apple right off the tree. This form of expanded agri-tourism has given birth to what are often called "entertainment farms." These farms cater to the pick-your-own crowd, offering not only regular farm products, but also food, mazes, open-pen animals, train rides, picnic facilities and pick-your-own produce. Dude ranches offer tourists the chance to work on cattle ranches and sometimes include cattle drives.

ARCHAEOLOGICAL TOURISM

Archaeotourism or Archaeological tourism is an alternative form of cultural tourism, which aims to promote the passion for historical-archaeology and the conservation of historical sites.

Establishment

Investigator Georgeos Diaz-Montexano, who initiated a series of publications in 1995 about ArchaeoTourism, such as "Arqueología y Enigmas de la Historia", "Arqueología Sin Fronteras", "La Esfinge. Revista de Egiptologia" and "ArqueoHistoria", brought awareness to the concept of archaeological tourism. Shortly after writing these publications, he founded the first specialized society on Archaeotourism, ArqueoTour (2000). For these efforts, he is considered by some to be the founder of archaeotourism.

Like Ecological tourism (or Ecotourism), Archaeological tourism is promoted to encourage the development of cultural associations, and companies and cooperatives can be found that dedicate themselves to offer this type of service.

The best definition of archaeotourism can be found in the words of its founders:

The passion by the past is something inherent to the human being. As it says well: "Town that does not know from where town comes that does not know to where it goes".

The Archaeotourism or archaeological tourism is ideal for which they look for a higher knowledge and sublimates, tie to the meditation and the relaxation, in perfect syntony with the surroundings or ecosystem that is, integration with the Mother Nature, but always in old places, next to the ruins of the "enigmatic missing civilizations".

Sites and places magician-monks or asylums. From the most remote prehistoric times. From the era of the dinosaurios to the Medieval Age. In order to develop his activities it has a nourished group of authentic experts in each one of the matters.

Therefore, archaeologists, paleontologists, anthropologists, historians and specialists in trips will unite their knowledge under a same objective: to offer to the traveller a wonderful and unforgettable experience, an intensive course and of introduction to each one of these manifestations of the human knowledge. This way the visitor will not be a simple traveller, will be in addition an apprentice in sciences to the past.

Some times will feel a paleontologist discovering tracks of dinosaurious and others will feel like Indiana Jones in the Damn Temple, mainly when penetrating in the mysterious caverns and artificial caves that long ago served from temples our ancestors. Enigmatic places loaded of an atmosphere of magic and mystery that, sometimes, surpass to all fiction created by the cinema...

Archaeological tourism can include all products associated with public archaeological promotion, including visits to archaeological sites, museums, interpretation centers, reinactment of historical occurrences, the rediscovery of native products, festivals, or theater.

Although archaeological tourism is quite recent, many international institutions and governments have already begun to contemplate viable alternative activity for the sustainable economic-social development. Several countries have for years had programs resembling the main points of Archaeological tourism for economic income, including Egypt, Mexico and Peru.

BOOKSTORE TOURISM

Bookstore tourism is a type of cultural tourism that promotes independent bookstores as a group travel destination. It started as a grassroots effort to support locally owned and operated bookshops, many of which have struggled to compete with large bookstore chains and online retailers.

The project was initiated in 2003 by Larry Portzline, a writer and college instructor in Harrisburg, Pennsylvania who led "bookstore road trips" to other cities and recognized its potential as a group travel niche and marketing tool. He promoted the concept with a how-to book and a web site, and groups around the U.S. soon began offering similar excursions, usually via a chartered bus, and often incorporating book signings, author home tours, and historical sites. In 2005-06, the Southern California Booksellers Association and Northern California Independent Booksellers Association embraced bookstore tourism, offering trips to independent bookstores in Los Angeles, San Diego and San Francisco.

The Bookstore Tourism movement encourages schools, libraries, reading groups, and organizations of all sizes to create day-trips and literary outings to cities and towns with a concentration of independent bookstores. It also encourages local booksellers to attract bibliophiles to their communities by employing bookstore tourism as an economic development tool.

Others benefiting include local retailers, restaurants, bus companies, and travel professionals.

The effort also provides organizations with an outreach opportunity to support reading and literacy.

Portzline has traveled across the country to promote the concept. In Fall 2006 he launched the National Council on Bookstore Tourism (NCBT), a nonprofit organization and trade association that will partner with booksellers, libraries, educators, literary festivals, the travel industry and economic development agencies at the national, state and local levels. In 2006 he created a promotional video featuring group "bookstore road trips" in New York City's Greenwich Village and in Los Angeles area "beach towns" and posted it on the NCBT website.

CULTURAL TOURISM

'Cultural tourism' (or culture tourism) is the subset of tourism concerned with a country or region's culture, especially its arts. It generally focuses on traditional communities who has diverse customs, unique form of art and distinct social practices, which basically distinguishes it from other types/forms of culture. Cultural tourism includes tourism in urban areas, particularly historic or large cities and their cultural facilities such as museums and theatres.

It can also include tourism in rural areas showcasing the traditions of indigenous cultural communities (i.e. festivals, rituals), and their values and lifestyle. It is generally agreed that cultural tourists spend substantially more than standard tourists do. This form of tourism is also becoming generally more popular throughout Europe.

Destination

By definition, the term destination refers broadly to any given area where tourism is a relatively important activity, like for instance having an economy significantly influenced by tourism revenues. However, it is complicated by the fact that a single, recognizable destination may include several cities, towns or municipalities, provinces, or other government entities-in island archipelago it may be the entire country.

Types

Due to globalization, technology and the onset of cultural tourism and ecotourism, the number of living cultural areas is continually declining. For an indigenous culture that has stayed largely separated from the surrounding majority, tourism can present both advantages and problems. On the positive side are the unique cultural practices and arts that attract the curiosity of tourists and provide opportunities for tourism and economic development. On the negative side is the issue of how to control tourism so that those same cultural amenities are not destroyed and the people do not feel violated.

A Few Examples

Chiloé is Chile's largest island, located at the midway point between the capital, Santiago, and the country's extreme south at Tierra del Fuego. Chiloé is the site of the Chiloé Model Forest, member of the same network as the Calakmul and Eastern Ontario Model Forests. Having evolved for centuries isolated from mainland Chile, the "Chilotes" developed a strong, self-reliant culture, rich in folklore, mythology and tradition. This very identity is what constitutes the island's major attraction for domestic tourists in Chile and increasingly, for international tourists.

As in the Calakmul case above, tourism to Chiloé is very strongly based on the island's cultural heritage, predominantly consisting of crafts markets, appreciation of cultural landscapes, museum exhibitions, seafood cuisine and architectural heritage (Chiloé's old churches). However, the average tourist to the island will have little opportunity to see Chilotes involved in their living cultural activities, such as the elaborate preparation of the islands famous "curanto" meal, rich in shellfish, meat and potatoes, the management practices of their farm and forest lands, boat building and more.

In order to overcome the cultural and organizational barriers that keep suppliers of living cultural heritage and tour operators apart, the Chiloé diocese of Ancud established a private foundation called "Fundación con Todos" (One for All Foundation). Among other activities, the Foundation has played a key role in helping a number of Chilote households organize themselves into an "agrotourism" network. The Foundation helped Chilote households make the preparation required to accommodate tourists (including training in sanitation and maintenance of facilities, the provision of basic infrastructure) and complemented this effort with a professional marketing campaign. These works were undertaken with the financial support of other agencies.

Again, in cooperation with the EOMF and the Chiloé Model Forest, a cultural and natural heritage tour was organized to Argentina and Chile, including a three-day visit to Chiloé, permitting some of the Chilote households to host a group of cultural heritage tourists for the first time. The visits were very successful and should be the first of more to come, helping establish the credibility of Chiloé's agrotourism network among other tour operators.

Orrissa Tribes

Nestling on the eastern coast of India, Orissa is one of the most exquisite regions dominated by exotic sandy beaches, plenteous wild life, and holy temples famous for their architectural splendor and primitive lifestyle. The charm of the city is still well-nigh chaste and unrevealed by the visitors, up to its full extent. The other lure of the city lies in its tribal population dotted with more than 62 tribal communities. The tribal communities of Orissa constitute about 23% of its total population. Orissa is inhabited by tribes like Saora or Sabar that had a respectable mentioning in the epic of Mahabharata.

Mostly the Orissa tribes are high land habitats with opulent ethnic trait, cultures and customs dominated by varying languages. The culture conscious tribes are able to preserve their social customs and dignified values. The most primitive tribes are Bondas, Gadabas, Koyas, Kondhas and Sauras.

The culture of tribal Orissa is affluent with their own folk songs and dances, their tattoos. Tribal culture of Orissa is well depicted in its modern city in form of poems, art and craft or music.

The tribes have adapted the Hindu traditions and culture from centuries, which is mixed with their own culture giving a distinct zest to the entire racial. Songs and dances are the essence of the tribal culture of Orissa. The traditions and the ceremonies for wedding, birth and death all are represented by singing songs, rural dances along with feasts.

The Tribal Folk Orissan tribes are strong, assiduous and simple hospitable tribes, normally like to be reserved and maintain distance from the people of other communities, as they are too shy. The major occupation of these tribes is agriculture and fishing and hunting.

Men usually wear loin attire and women rap long stretch of cloth around them. Women are adorned with ornaments like bangles, armlets, bracelets, necklaces, rings, hairpins etc usually made of silvers, aluminum, and brass. The practice of tattooing is prevalent among women folk. Girls above 5 years are found with tattoo mark on their faces and hands.

Festival Celebration Numbers of deities are worshiped by the tribes for their happy life. Many festivals are also celebrated with much of enthusiasm and excitement. The ceremony rituals are observed through out the year in order to appease their deities and ascendant.

The most significant festival of the year are the chaita parab and push parab-this day all able men of the village go on a hunting expedition. The tribes with their cultural dance, song and music all distinguish custom of their artistic life, which demarcate them from the other non tribal groups.

Orissa acquire every thing Orissa is a state, embellished with hilly terrain of the Eastern Ghats, where primitive tribes dwell and a beautiful stretch of the Indo-Aryans coast where modern life persists. A blend of 2 discrete civilization with contrast cultures, beautiful landscapes, beaches, rich wildlife, offers the best of India to its visitors.

As the issue of globalization takes place to this modern time, the challenge of preserving the few remaining cultural community around the world is becoming hard. In a tribal based community, reaching economic advancement with minimal negative impacts is an essential objective to any destination planner.

Since they are using the culture of the region as the main attraction, sustainable destination development of the area is vital for them to prevent the negative impacts (i.e. destroying the authentic identity of the tribal community) due to tourism.

Management Issues

Certainly, the principle of "one size fits all" doesn't apply to destination planning. The needs, expectations, and anticipated benefits from tourism vary greatly from one destination to another. This is clearly exemplified as local communities living in regions with tourism potential (destinations) develop a vision for what kind of tourism they want to facilitate, depending on issues and concerns they want to be settled or satisfied.

Destination Planning Resources

It is important that the destination planner takes into account the diverse definition of culture as the term is subjective. Satisfying tourists' interests such as landscapes, seascapes, art, nature, traditions, ways of life and other products associated to them-which may be categorized cultural in the broadest sense of the word, is a prime consideration as it marks the initial phase of the development of a cultural destination.

The quality of service and destination, which doesn't solely depend on the cultural heritage but more importantly to the cultural environment, can further be developed by setting controls and policies which shall govern the community and its stakeholders. It is therefore safe to say that the planner should be on the ball with the varying meaning of culture itself as this fuels the formulation of development policies that shall entail efficient planning and monitored growth (e.g. strict policy on the protection and preservation of the community).

Local Community, Tourists, the Destination and Sustainable Tourism

While satisfying tourists' interests and demands may be a top priority, it is also imperative to ruminate the subsystems of the destination's (residents). Development pressures should be anticipated and set to their minimum level so as to conserve the area's resources and prevent a saturation of the destination as to not abuse the product and the residents correspondingly. The plan should incorporate the locals to its gain by training and employing them and in the process encourage them to participate to the travel business. Keep in mind that the plan should make travellers not only aware about the destination but also concern on how to help it sustain its character while broadening their travelling experience.

Planning Tools

The core of a planner's job is to design an appropriate planning process and facilitate community decision. Ample information which is a crucial requirement is contributed through various technical researches and analyzes. Here are some of the helpful tools commonly used by planners to aid them:

1. Key Informant Interviews
2. Libraries, Internet, and Survey Research
3. Census and Statistical Analysis
4. Spatial Analysis with Geographical Information System (GIS) and Global Positioning System (GPS) technologies

Key Institutions

Participating structures are primarily led by the government's local authorities and the official tourism board or council, with the involvement of various NGOs, community and indigenous representatives, development organizations, and the academe.

Cultural and Ecotourism in the Mountainous Regions of Central Asia and in the Himalayas

Tourism is coming to the previously isolated but spectacular mountainous regions of Central Asia, the Hindu Kush and the Himalayas. Closed for so many years to visitors from abroad, it now attracts a growing number of foreign tourists by its unique culture and splendid natural beauty. However, while this influx of tourists is bringing economic opportunities and employment to local populations, helping to promote these little-known regions of the world, it has also brought challenges along with it: to ensure that it is well-managed and that its benefits are shared by all.

As a response to this concern, the Norwegian Government, as well as the UNESCO, organized an interdisciplinary project called the Development of Cultural and Eco-tourism in the Mountainous Regions of Central Asia and the Himalayas project. It aims to establish links and promote cooperation between local communities, national and international NGOs, and tour agencies in order to heighten the role of the local community and involve them fully in the employment opportunities and income-generating activities that tourism can bring. Project activities include training local tour guides, producing high-quality craft items and promoting home-stays and bed-and-breakfast type accommodation. As of now, the project is drawing on the expertise of international NGOs and tourism professionals in the seven participating countries, making a practical and positive contribution to alleviating poverty by helping local communities to draw the maximum benefit from their region's tourism potential, while protecting the environmental and cultural heritage of the region concerned.

GRIEF TOURISM

Dark tourism or Grief tourism is tourism involving travel to sites associated with death and suffering. Thanatourism, derived from the Ancient Greek word thanatos for the personification of death, is associated with dark tourism but refers more specifically to violent death; it is used in fewer contexts than the terms dark tourism and grief tourism.

This includes sites of pilgrimage such the site of St Peter's death in Rome; castles and battlefields such as Culloden near Inverness, Scotland; sites of disaster, either natural or man made such as Ground Zero in New York; prisons now open to the public such as Beaumaris Prison in Anglesey, Wales; and purpose built centers such as the London Dungeon.

One of the most notorious destinations for dark tourism is the Nazi extermination camp at Auschwitz in Poland.

DISASTER TOURISM

Disaster tourism is the act of traveling to a disaster area as a matter of curiosity. The behavior can be a nuisance if it hinders rescue, relief, and recovery operations.

Disaster tourism took hold in the Greater New Orleans Area in the aftermath of Hurricane Katrina. There are now guided bus tours to neighborhoods that were severely damaged by storm-related flooding. Some local residents have criticized these tours as unethical, because the tour companies are profiting from the misery of their communities and families. The Army Corp of

Engineers has noted that traffic from tour buses and other tourist vehicles have interfered with the movement of trucks and other cleanup equipment on single-lane residential roads.

Furthermore, during the first six months after the storm, most of these neighborhoods lacked electricity, phone access, street signs, or access to emergency medical or police assistance. Simply traveling to these neighborhoods was hazardous. For these reasons, organized disaster tours are now banned from two of the most severely damaged areas in the city, the Lower 9th and St. Bernard Parish near the Industrial Canal.

On the other hand, such communities as Gentilly and Lakeview, along the 17th Street Canal, have welcomed organized tour groups as a means to publicize the scale of the destruction and attract more aid to the city. Much of the recovery effort in the New Orleans relies on out-of-state volunteers and donations.

Numerous non-profit organization, including Habitat for Humanity International and Catholic Charities, have converged on the city to gut and rebuild homes. There is also a movement by local residents to bring congressmen and other national leaders to the city and view the damage in person, since

recovery efforts have been hampered by the failure of many homeowners and businesses to receive claims from their insurance providers.

DRUG TOURISM

Drug tourism is travel for the purpose of obtaining or using drugs for personal use that are unavailable or illegal in one's home jurisdiction. This would include crossing a national border to obtain drugs over the counter that are not sold in one's own country, or traveling to another country in order to obtain or use narcotics that are illegal in one's own country, or even traveling from one U.S. state to another in order to buy alcohol or tobacco more easily (although this last situation is often considered too trivial to qualify as drug tourism).

Drug tourism has many legal implications, and persons engaging in it sometimes risk prosecution for drug smuggling or other drug-related charges in their home jurisdictions or in the jurisdictions they are visiting, especially if they bring their purchases home rather than using them abroad. The act of traveling for the purpose of buying or using drugs is itself a criminal offense in some jurisdictions.

Amsterdam is a popular destinations for drug tourists, due to the Dutch government's acceptance of marijuana use and possession. Another Dutch city which is visited frequently by drug tourists is Maastricht because of its position close to the borders of Germany and Belgium. Other popular destinations include Southeast Asia and South America. Drug tourism thrives because legislation controlling the sale, possession, and use of drugs varies dramatically from one jurisdiction to another.

ECOTOURISM

Ecotourism, also known as ecological tourism, is a form of tourism which appeals to the ecologically and socially conscious. Generally speaking, ecotourism focuses on local culture, wilderness adventures, volunteering, personal growth, and learning new ways to live on the planet; typically involving travel to destinations where flora, fauna, and cultural heritage are the primary attractions.

Responsible ecotourism includes programs that minimize the negative aspects of conventional tourism on the environment, and enhance the cultural integrity of local people. Therefore, in addition to evaluating environmental and cultural factors, an integral part of ecotourism is in the promotion of recycling, energy efficiency, water conservation, and creation of economic opportunities for the local communities.

Many global environmental organizations and aid agencies believe that ecotourism has great potential for sustainable development.

Ideally, ecotourism should satisfy several criteria, such as:

- o conservation of biological diversity and cultural diversity, through ecosystem protection
- o promotion of sustainable use of biodiversity, by providing jobs to local populations
- o sharing of socio-economic benefits with local communities and indigenous people by having their informed consent and participation in the management of ecotourism enterprises.

- o increase of environmental & cultural knowledge
- o minimization of tourism's own environmental impact
- o affordability and lack of waste in the form of luxury
- o local culture, flora and fauna being the main attractions

For many countries, ecotourism is not simply a marginal activity to finance protection of the environment but as a major industry of the national economy. For example, in places such as Costa Rica, Ecuador, Nepal, Kenya, Madagascar, and Antarctica, ecotourism represents a significant portion of the gross domestic product and economic activity.

The concept of ecotourism is widely misunderstood, and in practice is often used as a marketing tool to promote tourism that is related to nature. Critics claim that ecotourism as practiced and abused often consists of placing a hotel in a splendid landscape, to the detriment of the ecosystem. According to them, ecotourism must above all sensitize people with the beauty and the fragility of nature. They condemn some operators as "greenwashing" their operations; using the label of "ecotourism" and "green-friendly", while behaving in environmentally irresponsible ways. Although academics disagree about who can be classified as an ecotourist and there is precious little statistical data, some estimate that more than five million ecotourists-the majority of the ecotourist population-come from the United States, with others from Western Europe, Canada, and Australia.

Currently there are various moves to create national and international ecotourism accrediation programs, although the process is also controversial. Ecotourism certificates have been put in place at Costa Rica, although some critics have dismissed these programs as greenwashing.

Ecotourism, responsible tourism, and sustainable development have become prevalent concepts since the late 1980s, and ecotourism has experienced arguably the fastest growth of all sub-sectors in the tourism industry. The popularity represents a change in tourist perceptions, increased environmental awareness, and a desire to explore natural environments. Such changes have become a statement affirming one's social identity, educational sophistication, and disposable income as it has about preserving the Amazon rainforest or the Caribbean reef for posterity.

With its great potential for environmental protection, the United Nations celebrated the "International Year of Ecotourism" in 2002.

To approach an understanding of the problem, a clear definition must delineate what is, and is not, ecotourism. Ideally, ecotourism satisfies several general criteria, including the conservation of biological diversity and cultural, diversity through ecosystem protection, promotion of sustainable use of biodiversity, share of socio-economic benefits with local communities through informed consent and participation, increase in environmental and cultural knowledge, affordability and reduced waste, and minimization of its own environmental impact. In such ways, it contributes to the long term benefits to both the environment and local communities.

However, in the continuum of tourism activities that stretch from conventional tourism to ecotourism proper, there has been a lot of contention to the limit at which biodiversity preservation, local socio-economic benefits, and environmental impact can be considered "ecotourism". For this reason, environmentalists, special interest groups, and governments define ecotourism differently. Environmental organizations have generally insisted that ecotourism is nature-based, sustainably managed, conservation supporting, and environmentally educated. The tourist industry and governments, however, focus more on the product aspect, treating ecotourism as equivalent to any sort of tourism based in nature. As a further complication, many terms are used under the rubric of ecotourism. Nature tourism, low impact tourism, green tourism, bio-tourism, ecologically responsible tourism, and others have been used in literature and marketing, although they are not necessary synonymous with ecotourism.

The problems associated with defining ecotourism have led to confusion among tourists and academics alike. Definitional problems are also subject of considerable public controversy and concern because of greenwashing, a trend towards the commercialization of tourism schemes disguised as sustainable, nature based, and environmentally friendly ecotourism. According to McLaren, these schemes are environmentally destructive, economically exploitative, and culturally insensitive at its worst. They are also morally disconcerting because they mislead tourists and manipulate their concerns for the environment. Despite objections, greenwashing continues to grow unabated. The Nature's Sacred Paradise, a theme park in Quintana Roo, Mexico, is responsible for displacing local Mayan communities and illegally keeping endangered species in captivity to attract visitors. The development and success of such large scale, energy intensive, and ecologically unsustainable schemes are a testament to the tremendous profits associated with being labeled as ecotourism.

The Negative Psycho-social Impact of Ecotourism

Ecotourism is the trend towards the commercialization of tourism throughout the nation. This trend has become one of the fastest growing sectors of the tourism industry growing annual 10-15% worldwide (Kamuaro, 2007). Ecotourism was first introduced in Africa in the 1950's with the legalization of hunting (Kamuaro, 2007). This need for recreational hunting zones lead to the creation of protected areas, national parks, and game reserves. Today these areas have become important revenue-earning venues with the establishment of lodges and tourist campsites.

One definition of ecotourism is "the practice of low-impact, educational, ecologically and culturally sensitive travel that benefits local communities and host countries" (Honey, 1999). Many of the ecotourism projects are not meeting these standards. Even if some of the guidelines are being executed, the local communities are still facing other negative impacts. South Africa is one of the countries that are reaping significant economic benefits from ecotourism, but negative effects including, physical displacement of persons, gross violation of fundamental rights, and environmental hazards far out weigh the medium-term economic benefits (Kamuaro, 2007). A tremendous amount of money is being spent and human resources continue to be used for ecotourism despite the lack of success stories, and even more money is put into public relation campaigns to dilute the effects of the criticism. Ecotourism channels resources away from other projects that could contribute more sustainable and realistic solutions to pressing social and environmental problems. "The money tourism can generate often ties parks and managements to eco-tourism" (Walpole et al. 2001).

But there is a tension in this relationship because eco-tourism often causes conflict and changes in land-use rights, fails to deliver promises of community-level benefits, damages environments, and has plenty of other social impacts. Indeed many argue repeatedly that eco-tourism is neither ecologically nor socially beneficial, yet it persists as a strategy for conservation and development (West, 2006). While several studies are being done on ways to improve the ecotourism structure, these examples provide reason that it should just stop all together.

The ecotourism system exercises tremendous financial and political influence. The evidence above shows that at the very least a strong case exists for restraining such activities. Funding could be used for field studies aimed at finding alternative solutions to tourism and the diverse problems Africa faces in result of urbanization, industrialization, and over exploitation of agriculture (Kamuaro, 2007). At the local level ecotourism has become a source of conflict over control of land, resources, and tourism profits. There are many problems with the idea of ecotourism.

Environmental, the effects on the local people, and conflicts over profit distribution are only a few of the negative effects of ecotourism. In a perfect world more efforts would be made towards educating tourists of the environmental and social effects of their travels. Very few regulations or laws stand in place as boundaries for the investors in ecotourism. These should be implemented to prohibit the promotion of unsustainable ecotourism projects and materials which project false images of destinations, demeaning local and indigenous cultures.

DIRECT ENVIRONMENTAL IMPACTS

Ecotourism operations typically fail to live up to conservation ideals. It is often overlooked that ecotourism is a highly consumer-centered activity, and that environmental conservation is only a means to further economic growth. Although ecotourism is intended for small groups, even a modest increase in population, however temporary, puts extra pressure on the local environment and necessitates the development of additional infrastructure and amenities. The construction of water treatment plants, sanitation facilities, and lodges come with the exploitation of non-renewable energy sources and the utilization of already limited local resources.

The conversion of natural land to such tourist infrastructure is implicated in deforestation and habitat deterioration of butterflies in Mexico and squirrel monkeys in Costa Rica. In other cases, the environment suffers because local communities are unable to meet the infrastructure demands of ecotourism. The lack of adequate sanitation facilities in many East African parks results in the disposal of campsite sewage in rivers, contaminating the wildlife, livestock, and people who draw drinking water from it.

Aside from environmental degradation with tourist infrastructure, population pressures from ecotourism also leaves behind garbage and pollution associated with the Western lifestyle. Although ecotourists claim to be educationally sophisticated and environmentally concerned, they rarely understand the ecological consequences of their visits and how their day-to-day activities append physical impacts on the environment.

As one scientist observes, they "rarely acknowledge how the meals they eat, the toilets they flush, the water they drink, and so on, are all part of broader regional economic and ecological systems they are helping to reconfigure with their very activities." Nor do ecotourists recognize the great consumption of non-renewable energy required to arrive at their destination, which is typically more remote than conventional tourism destinations. For instance, an exotic journey to a place 10,000 kilometers away consumes about 700 liters of fuel per person.

Ecotourism activities are, in of itself, issues in environmental impact because they disturb fauna and flora. Ecotourists believe that because they are only taking pictures and leaving footprints, they keep ecotourism sites pristine, but even harmless sounding activities such as a nature hike can be ecologically destructive.

In the Annapurna Circuit in Nepal, ecotourists have worn down the marked trails and created alternate routes, contributing to soil impaction, erosion, and plant damage. Where the ecotourism activity involves wildlife viewing, it can scare away animals, disrupt their feeding and nesting sites, or acclimate them to the presence of people. In Kenya, disruption of wildlife observers drive cheetahs off their reserves, increasing the risk of inbreeding and further endangering the species.

Environmental Hazards

We already understand that biodiversity and environmentally intact lands form the basis of ecological stability. Unfortunately, industrialization, urbanization, and unsustainable agriculture practices have all had serious effects on the environment. Ecotourism is now also playing a role in this depletion. While the term ecotourism may sound relatively benign, one of its most serious impacts is its consumption of virgin territories (Kamuaro, 2007). These invasions often include deforestation, disruption of ecological life systems and various forms of pollution, all of which contribute to environmental degradation.

The number of motor vehicles crossing the park increases as tour drivers search for rare species. The number of roads has disrupted the grass cover which has serious effects on plant and animal species. These areas also have a higher rate of disturbances and invasive species because of all the traffic moving off the beaten path into new undiscovered areas (Kamuaro, 2007). Ecotourism also has an affect on species through the value placed on them. "Certain species have gone from being little known or valued by local people to being highly valued commodities.

The commodification of plants may erase their social value and lead to overproduction within protected areas. Local people and their images can also be turned into commodities" (West, 2006). Kamuaro brings up a relatively obvious contradiction, any commercial venture into unspoiled, pristine land with or without the "eco" prefix as a contradiction in terms. To generate revenue you have to have a high number of traffic, tourists, which inevitably means a higher pressure on the environment.

Local Peoples

Most forms of ecotourism are owned by foreign investors and corporations that provide few benefits to local communities. An overwhelming majority of profits are put into the pockets of investors instead of reinvestment into the local economy or environmental protection. The limited numbers of local people who are employed in the economy enter at its lowest level, and are unable to live in tourist areas because of meager wages and a two market system. In some cases, the resentment by local people results in environmental degradation. As a highly publicized case, the Maasai nomads in Kenya killed wildlife in national parks to show aversion to unfair compensation terms and displacement from traditional lands. The lack of economic opportunities for local people also constrains them to degrade the environment as a means of sustenance. The presence of affluent ecotourists encourage the development of destructive markets in wildlife souvenirs, such as the sale of coral trinkets on tropical islands and animal products in Asia, contributing to illegal harvesting and poaching from the environment. In Surinam, sea turtle reserves use a large portion of their budget to guard against these activities.

Displacement of People

One of the most powerful examples of communities being moved in order to create a park is the story of the Masai. About 70% of national parks and game reserves in East Africa are on Masai land (Kamuaro, 2007). The first undesirable impact of tourism was that of the extent of land lost from the Masai culture. Local and national governments took advantage of the Masai's ignorance on the situation and robbed them of huge chunks of grazing land, putting to risk their only socioeconomic livelihood. In Kenya the Masai also have not gained any economic benefits. Despite lose of their land, employment favors better educated workers. Further more the investors in this area are not local and have not put profits back into local economy. In some cases game reserves can be created without informing or consulting local people, who come to find out about the situation when an eviction notice is delivered (Kamuaro, 2007).

Another source of resentment is the manipulation of the local people by their government. "Eco-tourism works to create simplistic images of local people and their uses and understandings of their surroundings. Through the lens of these simplified images, officials direct policies and projects towards the local people and the local people are blamed if the projects fail" (West, 2006). Clearly tourism as a trade is not empowering the local people who make it rich and satisfying. Instead ecotourism exploits and depletes, particularly in African Masai tribes. It has to be reoriented to serve useful to local communities and to become sustainable.

Threats to Indigenous Cultures

Ecotourism often claims that it preserves and "enhances" local cultures. However, evidence shows that with the establishment of protected areas local people have illegally lost their homes, and most often with no compensation (Kamuaro,

2007). What about pushing people onto marginal lands with harsh climates, poor soils, lack of water, and infested with livestock and disease is "enhancing"? The establishment of parks does nothing but create harsh survival realities and deprives the people of their traditional use of land and natural resources. Ethnic groups are increasingly being seen as a "backdrop" to the scenery and wildlife. The local people struggle for cultural survival and freedom of cultural expression while being "observed" by tourists. Local indigenous people also have strong resentment towards the change, "Tourism has been allowed to develop with virtually no controls. Too many lodges have been built, too much firewood is being used and no limits are being placed on tourism vehicles. They regularly drive off-track and harass the wildlife. Their vehicle tracks crisscross the entire Masai Mara. Inevitably the bush is becoming eroded and degraded" (Kamuaro, 2007).

Mismanagement of Ecotourism Sites

While governments are typically entrusted with the administration and enforcement of environmental protection, they often lack the commitment or capability to manage ecotourism sites effectively. The regulations for environmental protection may be vaguely defined, costly to implement, hard to enforce, and uncertain in effectiveness. Government regulatory agencies, as political bodies, are susceptible to making decisions that spend budget on politically beneficial but environmentally unproductive projects.

Because of prestige and conspicuousness, the construction of an attractive visitor's center at an ecotourism site may take precedence over more pressing environmental concerns like acquiring habitat, protecting endemic species, and removing invasive ones. Finally, influential groups can pressure and sway the interests of the government to their favor. The government and its regulators can become vested in the benefits of the ecotourism industry which they are supposed to regulate, causing restrictive environmental regulations and enforcement to become more lenient.

Management of ecotourism sites by private ecotourism companies offers an alternative to the cost of regulation and deficiency of government agencies. It is believed that these companies have a self interest in limited environmental degradation, because tourists will pay more for pristine environments, which translates to higher profit. However, theory indicates that this practice is not economically feasible and will fail to manage the environment.

The model of monopolistic competition states that distinctiveness will entail profits, but profits will promote imitation. A company that protects its ecotourism sites is able to charge a premium for the novel experience and pristine environment. But when other companies view the success of this approach, they also enter the market with similar practices, increasing competition and reducing demand. Eventually, the demand will be reduced until the economic profit is zero. A cost-benefit analysis shows that the company bears the cost of environmental protection without receiving the gains. Without economic incentive, the whole premise of self interest through environmental protection is quashed; instead, ecotourism companies will minimize environment related expenses and maximize tourism demand.

The tragedy of the commons offers another model for economic unsustainability from environmental protection, in ecotourism sites utilized by many companies. Although there is a communal incentive to protect the environment, maximizing the benefits in the long run, a company will conclude that it is in their best interest to utilize the ecotourism site beyond its sustainable level. By increasing the number of ecotourists, for instance, a company gains all the economic benefit while paying only a part of the environmental cost. In the same way, a company recognizes that there is no incentive to actively protect the environment; they bear all the costs, while the benefits are shared by all other companies. The result, again, is mismanagement.

Taken together, the mobility of foreign investment and lack of economic incentive for environmental protection means that ecotourism companies are disposed to establishing themselves in new sites once their existing one is sufficiently degraded.

Regulation and Accreditation

Because the regulation of ecotourism is poorly implemented or nonexistent, ecologically destructive greenwashed operations like underwater hotels, helicopter tours, and wildlife theme parks are categorized as ecotourism along with canoeing, camping, photography, and wildlife observation. The failure to acknowledge responsible, low impact ecotourism puts these companies at a competitive disadvantage.

Many environmentalists have argued for a global standard of accreditation, differentiating ecotourism companies based on their level of environmental commitment. A national or international regulatory board would enforce accreditation procedures, with representation from various groups including governments, hotels, tour operators, travel agents, guides, airlines, local authorities, conservation organizations, and non-governmental organizations. The decisions of the board would be sanctioned by governments, so that non-compliant companies would be legally required to disassociate themselves from the use of the ecotourism brand.

Crinion suggests a Green Stars System based on criteria including a management plan, benefit for the local community, small group interaction, education value, and staff training. Ecotourists who consider their choices would be confident of a genuine ecotourism experience when they see the higher star rating.

In addition, environmental impact assessments could be used as a form of accreditation. Feasibility is evaluated from a scientific basis, and recommendations could be made to optimally plan infrastructure, set tourist capacity, and manage the ecology. This form of accreditation is more sensitive to site specific conditions.

An environmental protection strategy must address the issue of ecotourists removed from the cause-and-effect of their actions on the environment. More initiatives should be carried out to improve their awareness, sensitize them to environmental issues, and care about the places they visit.

Tour guides are an obvious and direct medium to communicate awareness. With the confidence of ecotourists and intimate knowledge of the environment, they can actively discuss conservation issues. A tour guide training program in Costa Rica's Tortuguero National Park has helped mitigate negative environmental impacts by providing information and regulating tourists on the parks' beaches used by nesting endangered sea turtles.

The underdevelopment theory of tourism describes a new form of imperialism by multinational corporations that control ecotourism resources. These corporations finance and profit from the development of large scale ecotourism that causes excessive environmental degradation, loss of traditional culture and way of life, and exploitation of local labor. In Zimbabwe and Nepal's Annapurna region, where underdevelopment is taking place, more than 90 percent of ecotourism revenues are expatriated to the parent countries, and less than 5 percent go into local communities.

The lack of sustainability highlights the need for small scale, slow growth, and locally based ecotourism. Local peoples have a vested interest in the well being of their community, and are therefore more accountable to environmental protection than multinational corporations. The lack of control, westernization, adverse impacts to the environment, loss of culture and traditions outweigh the benefits of establishing large scale ecotourism.

The increased contributions of communities to locally managed ecotourism create viable economic opportunities, including high level management positions, and reduce environmental issues associated with poverty and unemployment. Because the ecotourism experience is marketed to a different lifestyle from large scale ecotourism, the development of facilities and infrastructure does not need to conform to corporate Western tourism standards, and can be much simpler and less expensive. There is a greater multiplier effect on the economy, because local products, materials, and labor are used. Profits accrue locally, and import leakages are reduced. However, even this form of tourism may require foreign investment for promotion or start up. When such investments are required, it is cruical for communities for find a company or non-governmental organization that reflects the philosophy of ecotourism; sensitive to their concerns and willing to cooperate at the expense of profit.

The basic assumption of the multiplier effect is that the economy starts off with unused resources, for example, that many workers are cyclically unemployed and much of industrial capacity is sitting idle or incompletely utilized. By increasing demand in the economy it is then possible to boost production. If the economy was already at full employment, with only structural, frictional, or other supply-side types of unemployment, any attempt to boost demand would only lead to inflation. For various laissez-faire schools of economics which embrace Say's

Law and deny the possibility of Keynesian inefficiency and under-employment of resources, therefore, the multiplier concept is irrelevant or wrong-headed.

As an example, consider the government increasing its expenditure on roads by $1 million, without a corresponding increase in taxation. This sum would go to the road builders, who would hire more workers and distribute the money as wages and profits. The households receiving these incomes will save part of the money and spend the rest on consumer goods. These expenditures in turn will generate more jobs, wages, and profits, and so on with the income and spending circulating around the economy.

The multiplier effect arises because of the induced increases in consumer spending which occur due to the increased incomes--and because of the feedback into increasing business revenues, jobs, and income again. This process does not lead to an economic explosion not only because of the supply-side barriers at potential output (full employment) but because at each "round", the increase in consumer spending is less than the increase in consumer incomes. That is, the marginal propensity to consume (mpc) is less than one, so that each round some extra income goes into saving, leaking out of the cumulative process. Each increase in spending is thus smaller than that of the previous round, preventing an explosion.

SHOCK TOURISM

Extreme tourism or shock tourism is a type of niche tourism involving travel to dangerous places (mountains, jungles, deserts, caves, etc.) or participation in dangerous events. Extreme tourism overlaps with extreme sport. The two share the main attraction, "adrenaline rush" caused by an element of risk, and differing mostly in the degree of engagement and professionalism.

Extreme tourism is a growing business in the countries of the former Soviet Union (Russia, Ukraine, Armenia, etc.) and in South American countries like Peru, Chile and Argentina. The mountainous and rugged terrain of Northern Pakistan has also developed into a popular extreme tourism location.

While traditional tourism requires significant investments in hotels, roads, etc., extreme tourism requires much less to jumpstart a business. In addition to traditional travel-based tourism destinations, various exotic attractions are suggested, such as flyovers in MiGs at 2.5 Mach, ice diving in the White Sea, or travelling across the Chernobyl zone.

FEMALE SEX TOURISM

Female sex tourism is travel by women, partially or fully for the purpose of having sex.

Female sex tourism differs from male sex tourism in that women do not use bars, sex shows and formal tours to meet foreign men. There are "de facto" tours, however, such as airplanes bound to the Gambia in West Africa full of British and Scandinavian women seeking affairs with beach boys.

Often such trips are referred to by women as "romance tourism."

Women usually give clothes, meals, cash and gifts to their male prostitutes. In some destinations, there are "going rates" for male companionship, ranging from $50 to $200. In few destinations, especially in Southern Europe, Turkey, Bali and the French Caribbean, men do not expect to be compensated.

While men tend to go to Asia for sex tourism, women tend to head to the Caribbean, Southern Europe, and Africa. The patterns have been explored by Michel Houellebecq in Platform and in the non-fiction work Romance on the Road, and are important in that they support the idea that sex tourism by both men and women reflects serious problems in the tourists' home countries, including a dating war, or profound conflict between the sexes. Thailand, the Dominican Republic and Cuba are exceptional in that both male and female sex tourists find these places all-purpose sexual emporia.

The primary destinations for female sex tourism are Southern Europe (mainly Italy, Greece, Turkey, Croatia and Spain), the Caribbean (led by Jamaica, Barbados and the Dominican Republic), Ghana and Kenya in Africa, Bali in Indonesia and Phuketin Thailand. Lesser destinations include Nepal, Morocco, Fiji, Ecuador and Costa Rica.

Lesbian sex tourism is nascent but evident in Lesbos (Mytilini) in Greece; Bangkok and Pattaya in Thailand, and on Bali in

Indonesia. Tourist women are called Shirley Valentines (if British), longtails (in Bermuda), yellow cabs (Japan) and, in Jamaica, milk bottles if newly arrived or Stellas if black. Female sex tourism in Barbados has been dubbed "Canadian secretary syndrome."

The men who chase tourist women are kamakia ("fishing harpoons," Greece),galebovi ("seagulls,"Croatia), sharks (Costa Rica), rent-a-dreads, rent-a-rastas, rent-a-gents and the Foreign Service (Caribbean), Kuta Cowboys or pemburu-bule ("whitey hunters," Bali), Marlboro men (Jordan), bomsas or bumsters (the Gambia), sanky pankies (Dominican Republic), "gringa hunter" in Ecuador and "brichero" in Peru.

Background

Barring some isolated cases of women traveling for sex among North American Indian tribes and within Turkey, female travel sex (involving American and English women) began in Rome in the late 1840s, at the same time as feminism's first wave, which encouraged independence and travel.

Affairs and intrigues, particularly between American heiresses and down-on their luck European aristocrats, continued steadily until World War I and inspired Henry James's Daisy Miller, Joaquin Miller's The One Fair Woman, and much of the early output of E.M. Forster.

Female sex travel declined from the time of the Depression until the 1960s, with the exception of India, Nepal and Thailand, where intrepid women from England, France, Czechoslovakia, the United States and elsewhere continued to attract the attention of maharajas and other Asian royals, despite the uproar of World War II.

Coincident with the explosion of leisure travel in the 1960s and feminism's second wave, sex tourism by women re-ignited, first via French Canadian women traveling to Barbados and Swedish and Northern European women to Spain, Greece, Yugoslavia and the Gambia. Female sex travel became ubiquitous throughout the Caribbean, from the tiniest islands through the big destinations of Jamaica, the Dominican Republic and Barbados.

In the 1990s, women from Japan and Taiwan began to appear on the beaches of Bali and Phuket in Thailand.

Today, many other destinations are popular, including Morocco, Nepal, Thailand, Ecuador, Costa Rica, Mexico--everywhere with beaches (or in Nepal's case, mountains) and a surplus of underemployed men.

Female sex tourism's first and second waves coincided not only with feminism but with Victorian-era man shortages that began in England and later cropped in continental Europe and the United States.

Other societal reasons for women seeking intimate companionship abroad include the dating war, as typified by extreme competition between the sexes in schools, the workplace, while dating, in marriages, and even in contentious divorces. The dating war appears to especially drive sex tourism by Australian and Japanese women, and to a lesser extent, German and Scandinavian female tourists.

Another factor in women engaging in holiday romance is identity loss. Many women behave while traveling in a way at odds to how they behave at home, where fear of the "slut" label curbs the kind of hedonistic behavior seen on holiday. Traveling and expatriate women often try on a new, more experimental identity when away from family and friends.

Additional reasons include:

- sexual connoisseurship--an interest in experiencing a variety of men
- a search for healing after a divorce or breakup (see Michelle Thomas, in Major academic publications, below)
- prolonged involuntary celibacy
- the commodification of sex, whereby affection is now something that can be purchased by women, as well as men, as well as the globalization of sex and affection markets
- interest in fulfilling sexual fantasies

Depictions

Non-fiction books include Anne Cumming's The Love Habit and The Love Quest, Fiona Pitt-Kethley's The Pan Principle and Journeys to the Underworld, Cleo Odzer's Patpong Sisters and Lucretia Stewart's The Weather Prophet.

Female sex tourists have been notoriously difficult to find and interview on the record (see de Albuquerque, 1998, in "Major academic publications" subheading, below). Thus some observers have turned to film and fiction to examine the motivations of women who travel for sex, love and affection. Movies include Heading South (Vers le Sud), with Charlotte Rampling which depicts three Western tourists in Haiti in the 1970s, taking their pleasure with local men. Earlier film depictions include How Stella Got Her Groove Back and Shirley Valentine. Stella led to a quantifiable increase in trips by women to Jamaica, according to Michele Faul's Associated Press article, 12/6/1998, " 'Stella' the Movie Attracting Single Women to Jamaica."

Important works of fiction include, in addition to Michel Houellebecq's Platform, Erica Jong's Fear of Flying.

SEX TOURISM

Sex tourism is travel to engage in sexual intercourse or sexual activity with prostitutes, and is typically undertaken internationally by tourists from wealthier countries whose payment for services may then be rendered either in cash or in kind.

The World Tourism Organization, a specialized agency of the United Nations, defines sex tourism as "trips organized from within the tourism sector, or from outside this sector but using its structures and networks, with the primary purpose of effecting a commercial sexual relationship by the tourist with residents at the destination". The U.N. opposes sex tourism citing health, social and cultural consequences for both tourist home countries and destination countries, especially in situations exploiting gender, age, social and economic inequalities in sex tourism destinations.

Attractions for sex tourists can include reduced costs for services in the destination country, along with either legal prostitution or indifferent law enforcement and access to child prostitution.

National destinations for sex tourists include Thailand, Brazil, Dominican Republic, Costa Rica, and Cuba.

An individual city or region can have a particular reputation as a sex tourist destination. Many of these coincide with major red-light districts, and include Amsterdam in the Netherlands; Zona Norte in Tijuana, Mexico; Bangkok, Pattaya and Phuket in Thailand; Vladivostok in Russian Far East, destination for Japanese sex tourists, and Angeles City, the site of a former United States military base in the province of Pampanga, Philippines.

In the United States, prostitution is largely illegal, with the exception of rural areas of the state of Nevada; these have become a sex tourist destination for some Americans. To a lesser extent, several other large cities in the U.S. are also domestic sex tourist destinations despite legal sanctions on prostitution.

Conversely, prostitution is a legal activity in a growing list of other nations worldwide including in many of these destinations.

Female Sex Tourism Destinations

The primary destinations for female sex tourism are Southern Europe (mainly Italy, former Yugoslavia, Turkey, Greece and Spain), the Caribbean (led by Jamaica, Barbados and the Dominican Republic), parts of Africa, Pattaya or Phuket in Thailand. Lesser destinations include Nepal, Morocco, Fiji, Ecuador and Costa Rica. Female sex tourism differs from male sex tourism, in that women do not usually go to specific bars. Women usually give clothes, meals, cash and gifts to their prostitutes, but not all (especially in Southern Europe) expect compensation.

Tourism Involving Sex with Minors

Child Wise defines child sex tourism as "the commercial sexual exploitation of children by foreigners", usually referring to:

- o travel to other countries to engage in sexual acts with children, or
- o foreigners engaging in sexual activity with children while overseas

While most sex tourists only engage in this activity with other adults, some actively look for child prostitutes, while others are not very selective either way regarding age. The WTO makes a distinction between "sex tourism" and "child sex tourism." A tourist who has sex with a child prostitute offends the spirit of the international Convention on the Rights of the Child and the Optional protocol on the sale of children, child prostitution and child pornography, and, in addition to breaking the law in the host country, might well also be doing so in the country the tourist is a national of. A growing number of countries are enacting laws with extra-territorial reach in order to meet their obligations under the covenants above, and consequently punishing citizens who engage in sex with minors whilst overseas. But being difficult to police and enforce these crimes continue nonetheless.

The term "child" is often used as defined by the international conventions above and refers to any person below the age of consent. Many countries have signed the Worst Forms of Child Labour Convention, 1999 and implemented domestic law making having sex with child prostitutes a criminal offence for their nationals or inhabitants including when practised abroad regardless of whether it is forbidden by the laws of the destination country. Singapore has been criticized for having no such law, in spite of being adjacent to the sex tourism destination of Batam in Indonesia, which has many underage sex workers, many of whom have been forced into prostitution.

In 2004 Canada started to prosecute individuals under the sex tourism law. The first individual charged in Canada under this law was Donald Bakker. Australia has long done so: with a conviction in 1996 after enactment of legislation in 1994. Its Government has, for example, caused an international political incident in pressing for the extradition of suspended Solomon Islands Attorney-General Julian Moti, an Australian citizen, to face possible charges over alleged offences dating back to 1997.

According to the Cambodia minister for Woman's Affairs, it is not tourists who are the prime culprits of pedophilia in her country, but the locals.

Legal Issues in the United States

Federal law (see PROTECT Act of 2003) prohibits United States citizens or permanent residents to engage in international travel with the purpose or effect of having commercial sex with a person under the age of 18, or any sex with a person under the age of 16; facilitating such travel is also illegal. Arrests by

Immigration and Customs Enforcement are becoming common, however prosecutions under this law are still very rare.

As of 2005, there has been one effort to prosecute a sex tour operator: Big Apple Oriental Tours of New York was prosecuted for "promotion of prostitution" by the New York State Attorney General after lobbying by feminist human rights groups, however the case has been thrown out twice.

HR 972, the Trafficking Victims Protection Reauthorization Act of 2005 reauthorizes the 2000 law, but it also gives U.S. law enforcement better tools to study human trafficking within the United States and to prosecute those who purchase sex acts. The measure authorizes $50 million for grants to state and local law enforcement to investigate and prosecute persons who engage in the purchase of commercial sex acts.

Scandals

In 2005 it was reported that Philippe Servaty, a newspaper columnist for Le Soir, traveled to Morocco where he persuaded women to engage in sexual activity by promising to marry and bring them to Belgium. He then posted photos online to boast of his conquests, but when his explicit materials were circulated back to Morocco many of the women were arrested, had their lives ruined, committed suicide or disappeared.

University of Leicester sociologists studied this subject as part of a research project for the Economic and Social Research Council and End Child Prostitution and Trafficking campaign. The study included interviews with over 250 Caribbean sex tourists. Among their findings:

- Preconceptions about race and gender influenced their opinions.
- Economically underdeveloped tourist-receiving countries are promoted as being culturally different so that (in the Western tourist's understanding) prostitution and traditional male domination of women have less stigma than similar practices might have in their home countries.

Canadian film makers have been active at reporting on sex tourism. Documentary titles include:

- Falang: Behind Bangkok's Smile by Jordon Clark (2005) (this title at the Internet Movie Database), set in Thailand

- o the CBC series, the Lens episode "Selling Sex in Heaven" (2005) (this title at the Internet Movie Database), set in the Philippines.
- o Channel 4 Cutting Edge episode "The Child Sex Trade" (2003), set in Romania, Italy

Depictions in Fiction and Popular Culture

- o The 2005 film Heading South describes the experiences of a group of middle-aged women in the late 1970s, who travel to Haiti for the purposes of sexual tourism.
- o In the animated TV series South Park the character Chef joins the Super Adventure Club which travels the world having sex with children.
- o Sex tourism is a major theme of Platform, a novel by Michel Houellebecq.
- o In the 2005 film Hostel, directed by Eli Roth, depicts sex tourism in Slovakia
- o The film Macho Dancer deals with male sex workers in Manila. It includes characters who are female prostitutes.

Trafficking

Trafficking of human beings is the recruitment, transportation, transfer, harbouring or receipt of people for the purpose of exploitation. Trafficking involves a process of using illicit means such as threat, use of force, or other forms of coercion, of abduction, of fraud, of deception, of the abuse of power or of a position of vulnerability.

Exploitation includes forcing people into prostitution or other forms of sexual exploitation, forced labour or services, slavery or practices similar to slavery, servitude or the removal of organs. For children exploitation may include also, illicit international adoption, trafficking for early marriage, recruitment as child soldiers, for begging or for sports (such as child camel jockeys or football players), or for recruitment for religious cults.

Human trafficking differs from people smuggling. In the latter, people voluntarily request smuggler's service for fees and there may be no deception involved in the (illegal) agreement. On arrival at their destination, the smuggled person is usually free.

On the other hand, the trafficking victim is enslaved, or the terms of their debt bondage are fraudulent or highly exploitative. The trafficker takes away the basic human rights of the victim. Victims are sometimes tricked and lured by false promises or physically forced. Some traffickers use coercive and manipulative tactics including deception, intimidation, feigned love, isolation, threat and use of physical force, debt bondage, other abuse, or even force-feeding with drugs to control their victims.

In the case of children, such practices are considered child trafficking even if none of the illicit means previously described are used.

Trafficked people usually come from the poorer regions of the world, where opportunities are limited, and are often from the most vulnerable in society, such as runaways, refugees, or other displaced persons, (though they may come from any social background, class or race. People who are seeking entry to other countries may be picked up by traffickers, and-typically-misled into thinking that they will be free after being smuggled across the border. In some cases, they are captured through slave raiding, although this is increasingly rare.

Trafficking of children often involves exploitation of the parents' extreme poverty. The latter may sell children to traffickers in order to pay off debts or gain income or they may be deceived concerning the prospects of training and a better life for their children. In West Africa, trafficked children have often lost one or both parents to the African AIDS crisis.

Women, who form over 80% of trafficking victims, are particularly at risk to become involved in sex trafficking. Potential kidnappers exploit lack of opportunities, promise good jobs or opportunities for study, and then force the victims to become prostitutes, participate in pornography or escort services. Through agents and brokers who arrange the travel and job placements, women are escorted to their destinations and delivered to the employers. Upon reaching their destinations, some women learn that they have been deceived about the nature of the work they will do; most have been lied to about the financial arrangements and conditions of their employment; and all find themselves in coercive and abusive situations from which escape is both difficult and dangerous.

The main motive of a woman (in some cases an underage girl) to accept an offer from a trafficker is better financial opportunities for herself or her family. In many cases traffickers initially offer 'legitimate' work or the promise of an opportunity to study. The main types of work offered are in the catering and hotel industry, in bars and clubs, modeling contracts, or au pair work. Offers of marriage are sometimes used by traffickers as well as threats, intimidation and kidnapping. In the majority of cases, the women end up in prostitution. Also some (migrating) prostitutes become victims of human trafficking. Some women know they will be working as prostitutes, but they have a too-rosy picture of the circumstances and the conditions of the work in the country of destination.

Men are also at risk of being trafficked for unskilled work predominantly involving hard labor. Other forms of trafficking include bonded and sweatshop labor, forced marriage, and domestic servitude. Children are also trafficked for both labor exploitation and sexual exploitation. On a related issue, children are forced to be child soldiers.

Many women are forced into the sex trade after answering false advertisements, and others are simply kidnapped. Thousands of children from Asia, Africa, and South America are sold into the global sex trade every year. Often they are kidnapped or orphaned, and sometimes they are actually sold by their own families.

United States State Department data "estimated 600,000 to 820,000 men, women, and children [are] trafficked across international borders each year, approximately 80 percent are women and girls and up to 50 percent are minors. The data also illustrate that the majority of transnational victims are trafficked into commercial sexual exploitation." Due to the illegal nature of trafficking and differences in methodology, the exact extent is unknown.

An estimated 14,000 people are trafficked into the United States each year, although again because trafficking is illegal, accurate statistics are difficult. According to the Massachusetts based Trafficking Victims Outreach and Services Networkin Massachusetts alone, there were 55 documented cases of human trafficking in 2005 and the first half of 2006 in Massachusetts.

In 2004, the Royal Canadian Mounted Police (RCMP) estimated that 600-800 persons are trafficked into Canada annually and that additional 1,500-2,200 persons are trafficked through Canada into the United States.

In the United Kingdom, 71 women were known to have been trafficked into prostitution in 1998 and the Home Office recognized that the scale is likely greater as the problem is hidden and research estimates that the actual figure could be up to 1,420 women trafficked into the UK during the same period. Trafficking in people is increasing in Africa, South Asia and into North America.

Russia is a major source of women trafficked globally for the purpose of sexual exploitation. Annually, thousands of Russian women end up as prostitutes in China, Japan or South Korea. Russia is also a significant destination and transit country for persons trafficked for sexual and labor exploitation from regional and neighboring countries into Russia, and on to the Gulf states, Europe, Asia, and North America. The ILO estimates that 20 percent of the five million illegal immigrants in Russia are victims of forced labor, which is a form of trafficking. There were reports of trafficking of children and of child sex tourism in Russia. The Government of Russia has made some effort to combat trafficking but has also been criticized for not complying with the minimum standards for the elimination of trafficking.

The majority of child trafficking cases are in Asia, although it is a global problem. In Thailand, non-governmental organisations (NGO) have estimated that up to a third of prostitutes are children under 18, many trafficked from outside Thailand. In Ukraine, a survey conducted by the NGO "La Strada-Ukraine" in 2001-2003, based on a sample of 106 women being trafficked out of Ukraine found that 3% were under 18, and the US State Department reported in 2004 that incidents of minors being trafficked was increasing.

In Asia, Japan is the major destination country for trafficked women, especially from the Philippines and Thailand. The US State Department has rated Japan as either a 'Tier 2' or a 'Tier 2 Watchlist' country every year since 2001 in its annual Trafficking in Persons reports. Both these ratings implied that Japan was (to a greater or lesser extent) not fully compliant with minimum standards for the elimination of human trafficking trade.

In Ukraine, a survey conducted by the NGO "La Strada-Ukraine" in 2001-2003, based on a sample of 106 women being trafficked out of Ukraine found that 3% were under 18, and the US State Department reported in 2004 that incidents of minors being trafficked was increasing.

In the United Kingdom, Vietnamese human trafficking have been discovered in the past few years. Many Vietnamese people are trafficked to work in illegal Vietnamese cannabis factories throughout the country, as the recent police Operation Keymer showed. Another recent police Operation Pentameter discovered illegal Vietnamese are also smuggled in to work in Vietnamese nail salons. Recently the UK authority planned to deport over 500 children back to Vietnam who had been smuggled into the country.

Reporters have witnessed a rapid increase in prostitution in Cambodia, Bosnia, and Kosovo after UN and, in the case of the latter two, NATO peacekeeping forces moved in. Peacekeeping forces have been linked to trafficking and forced prostitution. Proponents of peacekeeping argue that the actions of a few should not incriminate the many participants in the mission, yet NATO and the UN have come under criticism for not taking the issue of forced prostitution linked to peacekeeping missions seriously enough. In the western world, Canada in particular has a major problem with modern-day sexual slavery. In a 2006 report the Future Group, a Canadian humanitarian organization dedicated to ending human trafficking, ranked eight industrialized nations and gave Canada an F for its "abysmal" record treating victims. The report, titled "Falling Short of the Mark: An International Study on the Treatment of Human Trafficking Victims", concluded that Canada "is an international embarrassment" when it comes to combatting this form of slavery.

The report's principal author Benjamin Perrin wrote, "Canada has ignored calls for reform and continues to re-traumatize trafficking victims, with few exceptions, by subjecting them to routine deportation and fails to provide even basic support services."

In the report, the only other country to flunk was the United Kingdom, which received a D, while the United States received a B+ and Australia, Norway, Sweden, Germany and Italy all received grades of B or B-. The report criticizes former Liberal Party of Canada cabinet ministers Irwin Cotler, Joe Volpe and Pierre Pettigrew for "passing the buck" on the issue.

Commenting on the report, the then Minister of Citizenship and Immigration, Monte Solberg told Sun Media Corporation, "It's very damning, and if there are obvious legislative or regulatory fixes that need to be done, those have to become priorities, given especially that we're talking about very vulnerable people."

Some causes of trafficking include:

- o poverty
- o perceived higher standards of life elsewhere
- o lack of employement opportunities
- o organised crime and presence of organised criminal gangs
- o regional imbalances
- o economic disparities
- o social discrimination
- o corruption in governement
- o political instability
- o armed conflict
- o uprooting of communities because of mega projects without proper Resttlement and Rehabilitation packages.
- o Profitability
- o Growing deprivation and marginalization of the poor
- o Insufficient penalties against traffickers
- o According to the UN a major factor that has allowed the growth of sexual trafficking is "Governments and human rights organizations alike have simply judged the woman guilty of prostitution and minimized the trafficker's role."
- o Driven by demand; demand is high for prostitutes and other forms of labor in host countries; therefore there is a very profitable market available to those who wish to become handlers.

Trafficking in people has been facilitated by porous borders and advanced communication technologies, it has become increasingly transnational in scope and highly lucrative. Unlike drugs or arms, people can be "sold" many times. The opening up of Asian markets, porous borders, the end of the Soviet Union and the collapse of the former Yugoslavia have contributed to this globalization.

Government Action

A human trafficking awareness poster from the Canadian Department of Justice.

Actions taken to combat human trafficking vary from government to government. Some have introduced legislation specifically aimed at making human trafficking illegal. Governments can also develop systems of co-operation between different nation's law enforcement agencies and with non-government organisations (NGOs).

Other actions governments could take is raise awareness. This can take on three forms. Firstly in raising awareness amongst potential victims, in particular in countries where human traffickers are active. Secondly, raising awareness amongst police, social welfare workers and immigration officers. And in countries where prostitution is legal or semi-legal, raising awareness amongst the clients of prostitution, to look out for signs of a human trafficking victim.

Laws against trafficking in the United States are prosecuted at the federal level. The overwhelming majority of states do not have laws against human trafficking. For example, in Maryland it is a felony to have sex with a minor, but only a misdemeanor for making it available to those who wish to have sex with a minor. Raising awareness can take on different forms. One method is through the use of awareness films or through posters.

In June 2006, the government of Bangladesh issued a restraining order preventing Sigma Huda, U.N. special reporter on trafficking in persons, from leaving the country to deliver a key report on trafficking before the Human Rights Council in Geneva on June 11, 2007. U.N.

High Commissioner for Human Rights Louise Arbour has asked Bangladesh to clarify corruption charges against a U.N. human rights investigator, which will prevent her from addressing the main U.N. rights body. The Coalition Against Trafficking in

Women issued a statement calling this "an outrage and a violation of her right to freedom of movement and freedom of speech."

International Law

In 2000 the United Nations adopted the Convention against Transnational Organized Crime, also called the Palermo Convention and two Palermo protocols thereto:

- o Protocol to Prevent, Suppress and Punish Trafficking in Persons, especially Women and Children; and
- o Protocol against the Smuggling of Migrants by Land, Sea and Air.

All of these instruments contain elements of the current international law on trafficking in human beings.

Council of Europe

The Council of Europe Convention on Action against Trafficking in Human Beings was adopted by the Council of Europe on 16 May 2005. The aim of the convention is to prevent and combat the trafficking in human beings. Of the 46 members of the Council of Europe, so far 31 have signed the convention and 1 has ratified it.(29 June 2006).

United States Federal Law

The United States federal government has taken a firm stance against human trafficking both within its borders and beyond. Domestically, human trafficking is prosecuted through the Civil Rights Division, Criminal Section of the United States Department of Justice. Older statutes used to protect 13th Amendment rights within United States borders are Title 18 U.S.C., Sections 1581 and 1584. Section 1584 makes it a crime to force a person to work against his will. This compulsion can be effected by use of force, threat of force, threat of legal coercion or by "a climate of fear", that is, an environment wherein individuals believe they may be harmed by leaving or refusing to work. Section 1581 similarly makes it illegal to force a person to work through "debt servitude".

New laws were passed under the Victims of Trafficking and Violence Protection Act of 2000. The new laws responded to a changing face of trafficking in the United States. It allowed for greater statutory maximum sentences for traffickers, provided resources for protection of and assistance for victims of trafficking and created avenues for inter-agency cooperation in the field of human trafficking. It also allows many trafficking victims to remain in the United States and apply for permanent residency. This law also attempted to encourage efforts to prevent human trafficking internationally, by creating annual country reports on trafficking, as well as by tying financial non-humanitarian assistance to foreign countries to real efforts in addressing human trafficking.

International NPOs, such as Human Rights Watch and Amnesty International, have called on the United States to improve its measures aimed at reducing trafficking. They recommend that the United States more fully implement the "United Nations Protocol to Prevent, Suppress and Punish Trafficking in Persons, Especially Women and Children" and the "United Nations Convention against Transnational Organized Crime" and for immigration officers to improve their awareness of trafficking and support the victims of trafficking.

United States State Law on Trafficking Several states have also written laws to address human trafficking in their borders. Florida has written trafficking statutes criminalizing forced labor, sex trafficking, and document servitude. Florida also provides for mandatory law enforcement trainings and victim services.

On May 8, 2006, Connecticut passed an act addressing human trafficking that criminalized coerced work, and made trafficking a violation of the Connecticut RICO Act.

Human Trafficking in Popular Culture

Lilya 4-ever, a film based loosely on the real life of Dangoule Rasalaite, portrays a young woman from the former Soviet Union who is deceived into being trafficked for exploitation in Sweden. Human trafficking has also been portrayed in the Canadian/UK TV drama Sex Traffic.

Based on true events, Svetlana's Journey by Michael Cory Davis depicts the trials of a 13-year-old who loses her family and is sold to human traffickers by her adoptive family. Drugged, raped, and forced to endure continuous abuse by her 'clients' and traffickers, she finally commits suicide.

The 2007 film Trade deals with human trafficking out of Mexico and a brother's attempt to rescue his kidnapped and trafficked young sister. It is based on Peter Landesman's article about sex slaves, which was featured as the cover story in the January 24, 2004 issue of New York Times Magazine.

The film The Transporter deals with the hero, Frank Martin, played by Jason Statham, trying to stop a container full of men and women being illegally transported. Human Trafficking (2005) (TV) by Christian Duguay stars Mira Sorvino, Donald Sutherland, and Richard Carlyle. A sixteen-year-old girl from the Ukraine, a single mother from Russia, an orphaned seventeen-year-old girl from Romania, and a twelve-year-old American tourist become the victims of international sex slave traffickers. Sorvino and Sutherland are the Immigration and Customs Enforcement (ICE) agents who struggle to save them.

FREE INDEPENDENT TRAVELER/TOURIST (FIT)

With world travel market having undergone significant changes over the last few years a new type of tourist has emerged known as the Free Independent Traveler or Tourist (FIT). The definition is broad but tends to refer to people over 35, often, though not necessarily, of above average income who like to travel in small groups, usually couples. They eschew mass tourism and the holiday package concept promoted by Travel operators, in favour of a more individualistic approach to travel.

There are two implications to the idea of the Free Independent Traveler. One is important in the context of a marketing niche with a distinct economic behaviour whilst the other concentrates more on the philosophy of travel. This distinction can be summarised in how they are described. For the economic importance of tourism and for marketing purposes they are Free Independent Travelers (Upper case as they are an identifiable group within the market) whilst the people themselves are perhaps more attracted to the possibilities and lack of limitations in the concept of being a free, independent traveler.

Free Independent Travelers as an Alternative Movement

They tend to be environmentally aware, enjoy experiencing new ways of life and are enthusiastic, off the beaten track explorers practising for travel what the Slow Food Movement does for eating. They enjoy good food, architecture, and the heritage of local cultures. They tend to reject the traditional Package holiday model and even the Dynamic packaging system of doing things. People may garner information from a wide variety of sources or tips. The Guardian Newspaper's ivebeenthere site or Lonely Planet's forum are all examples and represent the fundamental difference between the FIT and other types of travel that this is about sharing and passing on of ideas and knowledge in accordance with the much talked about Web 2.0.

The FIT vacation is a custom built cocktail then with suggestions from friends, forums, speciality providers or others creating the idea around which the vacation is built. The FITs themselves are responsible for adding components in place of the traditional package operators. The rise of low cost airlines in the US and Europe has also increased the supply of alternative and lower cost short haul destinations fueling demand for these newly available markets. Southwest Airlines in the US, Ryanair and easyJet in Europe and later Spanish, German and nationally orientated airlines grew up adding destinations and creating an internationally networked portfolio of air-routes delivering people to destinations that were not previously available at a commercial, international level.

The internet is fundamental to the rise of the FIT, offering them the suggestions, for example, of a good meal out in Rome from a fellow FIT, across the globe, who ate there last week.

GARDEN TOURISM

Garden tourism is a type of niche tourism involving visits or travel to botanical gardens and places which are significant in the history of gardening. Garden tourists often travel individually in countries with which they are familiar but often prefer to join organized garden tours in countries where they might experience difficulties with language, travel or finding accommodation in the vicinity of the garden.

The list of famous gardens which attract garden tourists from afar includes: Sissinghurst Castle Carden and Stourhead in England, Versailles and Giverny in France, Keukenhof in Holland, Villa d'Este and Villa Lante in Italy, Alhambra in Spain, Longwood Gardens and Filoli in the USA, Taj Mahal in India,

Ryoan-ji in Japan. In the year 2000 the Alhambra and the Taj Mahal both received over 2 million visitors. This poses problems for the landscape manager.

Michel de Montaigne was one of the earliest garden tourists to record his impressions of gardens (c1580). John Evelyn also recorded his visits to gardens in France and Italy, as did Fynes Moryson. At the start of the twenty-first century Britain had the largest number of gardens open to the public for tourist visits: over 3,500 gardens are listed in Gardens of England and Wales Open for Charity (the 'Yellow Book').

GUEST RANCH

"Dude ranch" redirects here. For the blink-182 album, see Dude Ranch (album).

The guest ranch, also known as a dude ranch, is a type of ranch oriented towards visitors or tourism. It is a phenomenon of the romanticization of the American West after the official closing of the United States frontier in the late 19th century. The Western adventures of hardy aristocrats like Theodore Roosevelt were made available to paying guests from cities or the East, called "tenderfeet," "greenhorns," or "dudes" in the West. After World War I, the transcontinental railroad network brought these paying visitors to the local depot, where a wagon would be waiting for them. Some guest ranch visitors expected a somewhat edited version of the "cowboy life," while others were more tolerant of the odors and timetable of a working ranch. Guest ranches have also become a feature of the Australian Outback.

In the United States, guest ranches are a long-established tradition and continue to be a popular vacation destination. Depending on the climate, some guest ranches are open only in the summer or winter, others offer "year-round" service in all four seasons. College students are often recruited to work at guest ranches during the summer months. Common jobs offered to college students include: housekeeping, wrangler, dining staff, and office staff or babysitters.

Some guest ranches cater to hunters. Some feature native wildlife such as whitetail deer, mule deer, bison or elk. Others feature exotic species imported from other nations such as Africa and India. Both types of ranches are highly controversial. While many traditional ranches allow hunters and outfitters on their land to hunt native game, the act of confining game to guarantee a kill is considered unsporting by some people.

The introduction of non-native species on ranches is even more controversial because of concerns that these "exotics" may escape and contaminate the gene pool of native species or spread previously unknown disease. The advocates of hunting ranches argue in turn that they help protect native herds from over-hunting and the stocking of exotic species actually increases their numbers and may help save them from extinction.

HERITAGE TOURISM

Cultural heritage tourism (or just heritage tourism) is a branch of tourism oriented towards the cultural heritage of the location where tourism is occurring. Culture has always been a major object of travel, as the development of the Grand Tour from the 16th century onwards attests. In the 20th century, some people have claimed, culture ceased to be the objective of tourism: tourism is now culture. Cultural attractions play an important role in tourism at all levels, from the global highlights of world culture to attractions that underpin local identities. (Richards, 1996)

According to the Weiler and Hall, culture, heritage and the arts have long contributed to appeal of tourist destination. However, in recent years 'culture' has been rediscovered as an important marketing tool to attract those travellers with special interests in heritage and arts. According to the Hollinshead, cultural heritage tourism defines as cultural heritage tourism is the fastest growing segment of the tourism industry because there is a trend toward an increase specialization among tourist. This trend is evident in the rise in the volume of tourists who seek adventure, culture, history, archaeology and interaction with local people.

Cultural heritage tourism is important for various reasons; it has a positive economic and social impact, it establishes and reinforces identity, it helps preserve the cultural heritage, with culture as an instrument it facilitates harmony and understanding among people, it supports culture and helps renew tourism (Richards, 1996).

Cultural heritage tourism has a number of objectives that must be met within the context of sustainable development such as; the conservation of cultural resources, accurate interpretation of resources, authentic visitors experience, and the stimulation of the earned revenues of cultural resources. We can see therefore, that cultural heritage tourism is not only concerned with identification, management and protection of the heritage values but it must also be involved in understanding the impact of tourism on communities and regions, achieving economic and social benefits, providing financial resources for protection, as well as marketing and promotion. (J. M. Fladmark, 1994)

Heritage tourism involves visiting historical or industrial sites that may include old canals, railways, battlegrounds, etc. The overall purpose is to gain an appreciation of the past. It also refers to the marketing of a location to members of a diaspora who have distant family roots there.

Decolonization and immigration form the major background of much contemporary heritage tourism. Falling travel costs have also made heritage tourism possible for more people.

Another possible form involves religious travel or pilgrimages. Many Catholics from around the world come to the Vatican and other sites such as Lourdes or Fátima. Large numbers of Jews have both visited Israel and emigrated there. Many have also gone to Holocaust sites and memorials. Islam commands its followers to take the hajj to Mecca, thus differentiating it somewhat from tourism in the usual sense, though the trip can also be a culturally important event for the pilgrim.

Heritage Tourism can also be attributed to historical events that have been dramatised to make them more entertaining. For example a historical tour of a town or city using a theme such as ghosts or vikings.

LITERARY TOURISM

Literary Tourism is a type of cultural tourism that deals with places and events from fictional texts as well as the lives of their authors. This could include following the route a fictional character charts in a novel, visiting particular settings from a story or tracking down the haunts of a novelist.

Literary tourists are specifically interested in how places have influenced writing and at the same time how writing has created place. In order to become a literary tourist you only need a novel and an inquisitive mind-set, however there are literary guides, literary maps and literary tours to help you on your way.

In addition to visiting author and book sites, literary tourists often engage in bookstore tourism, browsing local bookshops for titles specifically related to the sites as well as other regional books and authors.

MUSIC TOURISM

Music tourism is the act of visiting a city or town in order to see a gig or festival. With the presence of the tourist, money is spent and the local economy benefits. This sort of tourism is particularly important to small villages such as Glastonbury, as well as large cities like Glasgow.

NAKED HIKING

Naked walking, naked hiking, or Freehiking is a sub-set of the modern form of social nudity. For some people, naked hiking may appear to be some form of energetic sport; however, for most it is simply a pleasant recreational pastime, with no social agenda.

Naturism has traditionally been an activity engaged in a private space or landed club environment. Modern naturism is moving towards a public space, as well including a more active component.

Although naturists have always been interested in health and fitness, indeed this was a prerequisite to many early gatherings, and most clubs have volleyball nets and table tennis tables, there has always been a slight reluctance to walk, run or cycle naked. One reason for this has been the secluded nature of the early clubs, private from prying eyes and textiles, and the limited area in which the early pioneers had to work with.

Modern naturism in nude-tolerant societies is moving out of the private enclosure and towards the arena of public nudity, where it is deemed ok to be not only naked in public, but where it is also ok to be active (from a stroll to action sports) in the nude. The point about being active is that many people appear to find static nudity acceptable, for example in the media (porn magazines or page 3 girls in newspapers), and theatre (non-moving Greek-statue-like nudity), but moving nudity, in contrast, seems to generate heated feeling.

Attention and Opinion

Naked outdoor activity is a subject expounded clearly in the publications of the Nacktiv site. People simply go about their normal day to day business, or recreational activities, naked. The more naked bodies people see in a public setting the more likely they are to question the advertising and media industries' onesided linking of sex with nudity. Public active nudists go out of their way to be discreet, and are to be seen walking in remote mountain areas, through quiet forests and woods, across distant fields and scrubland, and not in densely populated areas, often not meeting anyone else at all.

In the United Kingdom, Steve Gough, known as The Naked Rambler, received much media coverage for walking naked from Land's End to John o' Groats in 2003-2004 and again in 2005-2006. He was arrested and imprisoned several times during both his walks. In both 2005 and 2006 the European Alps were crossed naked during a one week hiking (tour), there was little media coverage and no-one was arrested or troubled.

Special Considerations

Although extremists might insist that naked hiking should be all-naked, and nothing but naked, as in all things one should remain practical and sensible about such activities.

Sensible footwear might mean bare feet on the beach, but wearing mountain boots in the mountains. Sunstroke or sunburn is a danger by any activity, naked or not, but naked hiking in the high mountains exposes the body to an increased level of sunshine not found at sea level, so sunscreen and a sun hat are essential items. Bugs, such as mosquitoes and midges, can be particularly troublesome, especially in sensitive areas, so anti-bug formulas are often needed by participants in this activity. Walking through a bunch of stinging nettles, or a field full of high thistles, can be an interesting experience (even with shorts on). Naturally, extra care must be taken.

NEO TOURISM

Neo Tourism is a term coined by the Korea tourism organization that comprehensively describes the newly changing trend of the tourism.

Definition of Neo Tourism

Following the changes in the economic, social and cultural paradigm of the last century, the form of tourism is changing as well. "Neo Tourism" is a term that comprehensively describes the new aspects of such changes and diversification of the tourism. The "Neo Tourism" incorporates concepts such as 'Sustainable tourism' which puts emphasis on the environmental sustainability and 'Special Interest Tourism (SIT)' which reflects postmodern social phenomenon.

The Origin of Neo Tourism

Initially the term "Neo Tourism" was generated to explain a form of tourism which has not existed before, to say, "New Tourism". However, with continuous advents of various types of tourism, it has become necessary to categorize those concepts in further details and eventually the "Neo Tourism" has taken more concrete meaning as such including the essential key words in the category. Those essential key words are as follows.

- o Postmodernism
- o Sustainability
- o Digitalization

Application of Neo Tourism

The term of "Neo Tourism" can explain the following types of tourism.

- o Tourism that satisfies individual interests and purposes appearing with post-modern social change
- o Tourism that avoids the environmental destruction and ensure experiencing the untouched nature
- o Tourism that manages various matters such as gathering information and making reservation through Internet.

The term "Neo Tourism" can be used from the suppliers' point of view as well as the customers' in the following concepts.

- o Creating a new type of tourism product by connecting tourism industry with other industries. (ex. Medical tourism, Edu Tourism)
- o Developing environmentally and socially sustainable tourist attractions
- o Utilizing IT technology such as internet and ubiquitous systems to promote and sale the tourism products

POP-CULTURE TOURISM

Pop-culture tourism is the act of traveling to locations featured in literature, film, music, or any other form of popular entertainment.

Popular destinations have included:

- o Los Angeles, California film studios.
- o the Iowa cornfields featured in Field of Dreams
- o New Zealand after The Lord of the Rings was filmed there
- o The Louvre in which the book and movie The Da Vinci Code takes place
- o Tom's Restaurant which is known to many as Monk's from Seinfeld
- o Prince Edward Island, in which the Canadian novel Anne of Green Gables takes place, is a popular attraction for tourists, notably from Japan.
- o South Korea because of the recent Hallyu phenomenon in East Asia.
- o Japan for japanophiles or lovers of Japanese pop-culture.
- o North Bend, Washington and in particular Twede's Cafe where much of the television show Twin Peaks was shot.
- o Roslyn, Washington, which stood in for Cicely Alaska in the television show Northern Exposure.
- o Tunisia, location of the filming of the Star Wars movies.

Pop-culture tourism is in some respects akin to pilgrimage, with its modern equivalents of places of pilgrimage, such as Elvis Presley's Graceland and the grave of Jim Morrison in Père Lachaise Cemetery. Another pop-culture tourism destination is Vulcan, Alberta Canada. In the early 1990s this small rural community began to explore ways it could capitalize on the coincidence of the Town's name being the same as popular Star Trek Character, Mr. Spock's home planet: Vulcan, to develop its local tourism industry.

PILGRIMAGE

In religion and spirituality, a pilgrimage is a long journey or search of great moral significance. Sometimes, it is a journey to a sacred place or shrine of importance to a person's beliefs and faith. Members of every major religion participate in pilgrimages. A person who makes such a journey is called a pilgrim.

Buddhism offers four sites of pilgrimage: the Buddha's birthplace at Kapilavastu, the site where he attained Enlightenment Bodh Gaya, where he first preached at Benares, and where he achieved Parinirvana at Kusinagara.

In the kingdoms of Israel and Judah the visitation of certain ancient cult-centers was repressed in the 7th century BC, when the worship was restricted to Jahweh at the temple in Jerusalem. In Syria, the shrine of Astarte at the headwater spring of the river Adonis survived until it was destroyed by order of Emperor Constantine in the 4th century AD.

In mainland Greece, a stream of individuals made their way to Delphi or the oracle of Zeus at Dodona, and once every four years, at the period of the Olympic games, the temple of Zeus at Olympia formed the goal of swarms of pilgrims from every part of the Hellenic world. When Alexander the Great reached Egypt, he put his whole vast enterprise on hold, while he made his way with a small band deep into the Libyan desert, to consult the oracle of Ammun. During the imperium of his Ptolemaic heirs, the shrine of Isis at Philae received many votive inscriptions from Greeks on behalf of their kindred far away at home.

Although a pilgrimage is normally viewed in the context of religion, the personality cults cultivated by communist leaders ironically gave birth to pilgrimages of their own. Prior to the demise of the USSR in 1991, a visit to Lenin's Mausoleum in Red Square, Moscow can be said to have had all the characteristics exhibiting a pilgrimage-for Communists. This type of pilgrimage to a personality cult is still evident today on people who pay visits of homage to Mao Tse Tung, Kim Il Sung, and Ho Chi Minh.

Effects on Trade

Pilgrims contributed an important element to long-distance trade before the modern era, and brought prosperity to successful pilgrimage sites, an economic phenomenon unequalled until the tourist trade of the 20th century. Encouraging pilgrims was a motivation for assembling (and sometimes fabricating) relics and for writing hagiographies of local saints, filled with inspiring accounts of miracle cures. Lourdes and other modern pilgrimage sites keep this spirit alive.

Modern Pilgrimage

Pilgrimages are still made throughout the world: modern-day pilgrimages include the Way of St. James, the Hajj, and the pilgrimage to Mount Kailash. In modern usage, the terms pilgrim and pilgrimage can also have a somewhat devalued meaning as they are often applied in a secular context. For example, fans of Elvis Presley may choose to visit his home, Graceland, in Memphis, Tennessee. Similarly one may refer to a cultural center such as Venice as a "tourists' Mecca".

Bahá'í Faith

A Bahá'í pilgrimage currently consists of visiting the holy places in Haifa, Akká, and Bahjí in Northwest Israel. Bahá'ís do not have access to other places designated as sites for pilgrimage.

Bahá'u'lláh decreed pilgrimage in His Motherbook (Kitáb-i-Aqdas) to two places: the House of Bahá'u'lláh in Baghdad, Iraq, and the House of the Báb in Shiraz, Iran.

In two separate Tablets, known as Suriy-i-Hajj, He prescribed specific rites for each of these pilgrimages (lifting the injunction regarding the shaving of one's head for pilgrimage in the Kitáb-i-Aqdas). It is obligatory to make the pilgrimage, "if one can afford it and is able to do so, and if no obstacle stands in one's way". Bahá'ís are free to choose between the two Houses, as either has been deemed sufficient. And although women are not bound to perform pilgrimage, they are certainly not prohibited to do so.

Later, `Abdu'l-Bahá designated the Shrine of Bahá'u'lláh at Bahji (the Qiblih) as a site of visitation. No rites have been prescribed for this.

Buddhism

Gautama Buddha spoke of the four sites most worthy of pilgrimage for his followers to visit:

- o Lumbini: birth place (in Nepal)
- o Bodh Gaya: place of Enlightenment
- o Sarnath: (formally Isipathana) where he delivered his first teaching
- o Kusinara: (now Kusinagar, India) where he attained mahaparinirvana (passed away).

Other pilgrimage places in India and Nepal connected to the life of Gautama Buddha are: Savatthi, Pataliputta, Nalanda, Gaya, Vesali, Sankasia, Kapilavastu, Kosambi, Rajagaha, Varanasi.

Other famous places for buddhist pilgrimage in various countries include:

- o India: Sanchi, Ellora, Ajanta.
- o Thailand: Sukhothai, Ayutthaya, Wat Phra Kaew, Wat Doi Suthep.
- o Tibet: Lhasa (traditional home of the Dalai Lama), Mount Kailash, Lake Nam-tso.
- o Cambodia: Angkor Wat, Silver Pagoda.
- o Sri Lanka: Polonnaruwa, Temple of the Tooth (Kandy), Anuradhapura.
- o Laos: Luang Prabang.
- o Myanmar: Bagan, Sagaing Hill.
- o Nepal: Bodhnath, Swayambhunath.
- o Indonesia: Borobudur.
- o China: Yung-kang, Lung-men caves.
- o Japan: Kyoto, Nara.

Communism

- o USSR: Moscow, Mausoleum of Lenin in Red Square.
- o China: Peking, Mausoleum of Mao Tse Tung in Tiananmen Square.
- o Germany: Trier, Birthplace of Karl Marx in Trier

Christianity

Pilgrimages were first made to sites connected with the birth, life, crucifixion and resurrection of Jesus. Surviving descriptions of Christian pilgrimages to the Holy Land date from the 4th century, when pilgrimage was encouraged by church fathers like Saint Jerome. Pilgrimages also began to be made to Rome and other sites associated with the Apostles, Saints and Christian martyrs, as well as to places where there have been apparitions of the Virgin Mary. The crusades to the holy land are also considered to be mass armed pilgrimages.

The second largest single pilgrimage in the history of Christendom was to the Funeral of Pope John Paul II after his death on April 2, 2005. An estimated four million people travelled to Vatican City, in addition to the almost three million people already living in Rome, to see the body of Pope John Paul II lie in state. World Youth Day is a major Catholic Pilgrimage, specifically for people aged 16-35. It is held internationally every 2-3 years. In 2005, young Catholics visited Cologne, Germany. In 1995, the largest gathering of all time was to World Youth Day in Manila, Philippines, where four million people from all over the world attended.

The major Christian pilgrimages are to:

- Jerusalem. Site of the crucifixion and resurrection of Jesus.
- Rome on roads such as the Via Francigena. Site of the deaths of Saint Peter, Saint Paul and other early martyrs. Location of sacred relics of various saints, relics of the Passion, important churches and headquarters of the Catholic Church.
- Constantinople (today Istanbul, Turkey). Former capital of the Byzantine Empire and the see of one of the five ancient Patriarchates and spiritual see of the Eastern Orthodox Church. Hagia Sophia, former cathedral and burial place of many Ecumenical Patriarchs.
- Lourdes, France. Apparition of the Virgin Mary. The second most visited Christian pilgrimage site after Rome.
- Santiago de Compostela in Spain on the Way of St James (Spanish: El Camino de Santiago). This famous medieval

pilgrimage to the shrine of Saint James is still popular today.

Other important Christian pilgrimage sites include:

- o Assisi, Italy, St. Francis of Assisi and St Clare, relics
- o Ávila, Spain, St Theresa of Avila, relics
- o Bethlehem, in Israel, Birthplace of Jesus and King David.
- o Canterbury Cathedral associated with Saint Thomas Becket.
- o Cap-de-la-Madeleine, Quebec, Canada in honour of Our Lady of the Cape.
- o Cathedral of Chartres, France.
- o Miercurea Ciuc, Transylvania, Romania. Whit Sunday gathering of (mostly ethnic Hungarian) Catholics.
- o Croagh Patrick, Ireland. Saint Patrick.
- o Conques, France
- o Cologne, Germany. Relics of the Three Magi.
- o Czestochowa, Poland.Black Madonna of Czestochowa is housed pernamently in theJasna Góra Monastery
- o Glastonbury, England. St Joseph of Arimathea.
- o Goa, India. St. Francis Xavier
- o Hill of Crosses, Lithuania
- o House of the Virgin Mary, Turkey. Pope John-Paul II declared the Shrine of Virgin Mary as a pilgrimage place for Christians.
- o Issoudun, France. Notre-Dame du Sacré-Coeur
- o Kapel in 't Zand, Limburg
- o Kevelaer, Germany
- o Knock, Ireland
- o Lichen, Sanctuary of Our Lady of Lichen
- o Lisieux, France. Saint Therese of Lisieux, burial place.
- o Lourdes, France. Apparition of the Virgin Mary. Place of healing.
- o Mariazell, Austria. Marian Shrine to Austria and Hungary

- Medugorje, Bosnia-Herzegovina. Apparitions of the Virgin Mary at the present.
- Mount Athos, Greece. Orthodox monastic centre.
- Mount Nebo, Jordan. Traditional site of the death of Moses.
- Mount Sinai, Egypt, holy mountain to the ancient Hebrews, traditional site has been commemorated since time of Constantine
- Nazareth, Israel, hometown of Jesus
- Fatima, Portugal. Apparition of the Virgin Mary.
- Padua, Italy, St Anthony, relics
- Paris (Sacred-Heart Basilica Basilica of the Sacré Cœur; and Saint Catherine Labouré)
- Rosslyn Chapel, Scotland
- Sacri Monti, Italy. The Sacred Mountains of Piedmont and Lombardy.
- San Giovanni Rotondo, Italy, St Pio from Pietrelcina
- Guadalupe, Spain
- Sea of Galilee, Israel, site of Jesus' early ministry.
- Shrine of Our Lady of Guadalupe, Mexico City. Apparition of the Virgin Mary.
- St. Andrews, Scotland, it is said that Saint Andrew was given, by God, directions to the location of St Andrews
- St. Patrick's Purgatory, Donegal, Ireland
- St. Thomas Mount, India. Place where St. Thomas was martyed.
- Taizé Community, France, modern monastery that actively encourages pilgrimages to it
- Nidaros Cathedral, Norway
- Turin, Italy. Holy Shroud.
- Vailankanni, India. 16th-century Mary apparition site.
- Vierzehnheiligen, Germany.
- Walsingham, England. Virgin Mary apparition site.
- Wittenberg, Germany. Church of Martin Luther and centre of the Protestant Reformation.

Hinduism

Hindus are required to undertake pilgrimages during their lifetime. Most Hindus who can afford to go on such journeys travel to numerous sites including those below:

- Badrinath
- Kedarnath
- Gangotri
- Yamunotri
- Rishikesh
- Haridwar
- Benares
- Mandher Devi temple in Mandhradevi
- Vrindavan
- Mayapur
- Udupi
- Kateel
- Talapady
- Tirupati
- Palani
- Kukke Subramanya

The first four sites in the list above together comprise the Chardham, or four holy pilgrimage destinations. It is believed that travelling to these places leads to moksha, the release from samsara (cycle of rebirths). Vrindavan is most important place of pilgrimage for every Vaishnava, especially for the followers of Gaudiya Vaishnavism who regard Krishna as the original Personality of Godhead (God). Here one can attain love of God (prema).

Islam

Pilgrimage to Mecca-the Hajj-is one of the Five Pillars of Islam. It should be attempted at least once in the lifetime of all able-bodied Muslims who can afford to do so. It is the most important of all Muslim Pilgrimages.

Many Muslims also undergo ziyarat, which is a pilgrimage to sites associated with the prophet Muhammad, his companions, or other venerated figures in Islamic history, such as Shi'a imams or Sufi saints. Sites of pilgrimage include mosques, graves, battlefields, mountains, and caves. Local Pilgrimage traditions-those undertaken as ziarah visits to local graves, are also found throughout Muslim countries.

In some countries, the grave sites of heroes have very strong ziyarah traditions as visiting the graves at auspicious times is a display of national and community identity. Some traditions within Islam have negative attitudes towards grave visiting.

The third religiously sanctioned pilgrimage for Muslims is to the Al Quds mount in Jerusalem which hosts Al-Aqsa Mosque and the Dome of the Rock.

Judaism

Within Judaism, the Temple in Jerusalem was the center of the Jewish religion, until its destruction in 70 AD, and all who were able were under obligation to visit and offer sacrifices known as the korbanot, particularly during the Jewish holidays in Jerusalem.

Following the destruction of the Second Temple and the onset of the diaspora, the centrality of pilgrimage to Jerusalem in Judaism was discontinued. In its place came prayers and rituals hoping for a return to Zion and the accompanying restoration of regular pilgrimages (see Jerusalem, Jews and Judaism).

Until recent centuries, pilgrimage has been a fairly difficult and arduous adventure. But now, Jews from many countries make periodic pilgrimages to the holy sites of their religion.

The western retaining wall of the original temple, known as the Wailing Wall, or Western Wall remains in the Old City of Jerusalem and this has been the most sacred site for Zionist Jews. Pilgrimage to this area was off-limits from 1948 to 1967, when East Jerusalem was controlled by Jordan. Some Reform and Conservative Jews who no longer consider themselves exiles, still enjoy visiting Israel even if it is not an official "pilgrimage."

SACRED TRAVEL

Sacred travel, or metaphysical tourism, is a growing niche of the travel market. It attracts New Age believers, primarily middle-aged women, and involves tours and travel to "spiritual hotspots" on the Earth.

Destinations are often ancient sites where there is a mystery concerning their origin or purpose, such as Machu Picchu in Peru, The Pyramids of Egypt, or Stonehenge in England. Some Christian sites such as the locations of the Black Madonnas and the Rosslyn Chapel in Scotland are also popular.

These travelers see the journey as more than just tourism and take the trips in order to heal themselves and the world. Part of this may involve rituals involving, (supposedly), leaving their bodies, possession by spirits (channelling), and recovery of past life memories.

SAFARI

A safari is an overland journey. It usually refers to a trip by tourists to Africa, traditionally for a big-game hunt and in more modern times to watch and photograph big game and other wildlife as a safari holiday.

There is a certain theme or style associated with the word, which includes khaki clothing, pith helmets, and animal skins-like leopard's skin.

Etymology

Entering the English language in the late 19th century, the word safari means 'journey' in Swahili language. Originally from the Arabic (safara) meaning travel The verb for "to travel" in Swahili is "safiri", the noun for the journey is "safari". These words are used for any type of journey e.g. by bus from Nairobi to Mombasa.

Touristic Usage

Most people in the West still believe that a true safari can only be in East Africa, that is Kenya and Tanzania, and not in Africa as a whole. That is to say that if you were in South Africa doing some big game watching, you wouldn't be "on safari" even though the word is broadly used, because the word "safari" comes from the Swahili-speaking people who can be found along the Swahili Coast. Today the word is used generally to mean anything from big game viewing, photography, or even game hunting.

VIRTUAL TOURISM

Virtual tourism refers to pre-planning alternative touristic activity before your departure, by integrating multiple digital resources to explore regions of the world without having to physically travel. It helps focus attention onto people, places and exploring changes over time.

By using the internet, travel literature (travel guides and travelogues), Journals, Papers and television visual learning courseware graphically shows information necessary to make an informed decision about which places to visit and historic or scenic byways to explore.

It is an economical activity that employs people from several different specific areas, such as journalists and photographers, geographers, editors, cameras, writers, etc... and it is one activity related to promoting nature-based or people-powered outdoor recreation involving adventure-based tourism.

VOLUNTEER VACATION

Volunteer vacations are an opportunity for people to make a positive difference in the lives of others or to help improve or contribute to society, culture, or the environment while on vacation.

It is also a chance for people of nearly any age to immerse themselves in foreign or challenging circumstances, experience a different culture first-hand, and learn more about the world they live in.

According to the Travel Industry Association of America, more than 55 million Americans have participated in a volunteer vacation, and about 100 million more are considering taking one. Volunteer vacations attract people from all walks of life and all age groups-students on break or who take a year off between high school and college, singles, couples, families with young children, and older adults.

Despite obvious differences among these people, they typically share a desire to "do something good" while also experiencing new places and challenges in locales they might not otherwise visit.

People choose to take a volunteer vacation for a variety of reasons, and often more than one applies. First and foremost is a desire to help-be it children, the elderly, the handicapped, animals, or the natural environment.

Some people have a specific cause in mind; say, protecting endangered gorillas or preserving the coral reefs off the coast of Australia, and they target organizations that offer such opportunities.

Other people have a more general idea of what they want to do; for example, help alleviate hunger or teach children to read.

Along with an altruistic reason for volunteering there are often others, such as a desire to see exotic or unusual places, an opportunity to experience new challenges, a chance to practice a foreign language, having an experience that will enhance their resume and/or job opportunities, and the fact that such trips usually provide a substantial tax deduction.

When choosing a volunteer vacation opportunity, prospective travelers should consider several questions.

- Where to go? Volunteer vacation opportunities are available in every corner of the world, from the United States to Australia, China, Iceland, and the Amazon.
- How much does it cost? The program fees participants pay to take part in volunteer vacations typically (but not always) include room and board, project fees, travel medical insurance, and travel within the country in which the volunteer activity occurs. The fees usually do not include transportation to the country. Potential volunteers should check with the sponsoring organization to determine which costs are included in the program fee, and to learn how much of the fee is tax deductible.
- How challenging is it? Some volunteer vacations require a certain level of physical strength and stamina, especially those that involve working outdoors. Potential volunteers should always clearly understand the physical expectations and requirements and be sure they are medically capable of meeting them.
- What are the accommodations? Lodging options vary widely and may involve pitching a tent, living in unheated huts, staying with native families, sharing a dormitory-

type residence, or checking into a comfortable hotel. Questions about food, water, linens, availability of power (including computer and cell phone access), medical care, and local transportation should be addressed during the evaluation process.

- o How long? Most volunteer vacations last from one to four weeks; some can extend on for months. The vast variety of volunteer vacation opportunities usually means people can find more than one vacation that fits their needs.
- o Any special skills needed? People who have special skills-teachers, nurses, veterinarians, biologists, accountants, lawyers, photographers, farmers-are always welcome and in fact urgently needed in some locations. Most volunteer opportunities, however, only ask that people have a desire to help and a willingness to learn and follow directions.
- o Is language a barrier? Since so many volunteer vacations are in remote, foreign locations, knowledge of another language in addition to English can be helpful and in some cases, strongly recommended. However, most potential volunteers do not need to know a second language.
- o What about free time? The amount of time volunteers have to spend sightseeing or doing other activities away from their volunteer tasks varies with each assignment, as do the types of activities that are available. This information is usually provided by the sponsoring organization, and it can be helpful to talk or correspond with other people who have volunteered in the location previously.
- o Who can participate? Volunteer vacations are available for singles, couples, students, families, and older adults. The age limitation is typically 16 to 18 years of age; a parent or guardian usually must accompany any person younger than 16. Volunteer vacations geared for families with younger children have their own special regulations.

HOW TO FIND A VOLUNTEER VACATION

Both for-profit and nonprofit organizations and companies offer volunteer vacations. Some organizations sponsor opportunities that focus on a specific issue, such as saving sea turtles or building homes for the needy, while others offer a broad spectrum of projects that center on areas such as education, poverty, public health, endangered species, and habitat preservation. While some organizations have projects in only a few countries, others offer options in dozens of locations on nearly every continent.

People interested in learning more about volunteer vacations in general or selecting one in particular can begin by exploring volunteer vacation directories or targeting organizations that offer specific opportunities.

Volunteer Vacation Directories

People who are uncertain about the type of volunteer vacation they want to take may find it best to start by checking a directory of opportunities by category. Charity Guide is a nonprofit that provides information on volunteer vacations in several different categories: environmental protection, children's issues, animal welfare, and health and safety.

Travel with a Challenge provides a directory that caters to mature volunteers (age 45 years and older). Transitions Abroad is a portal for volunteer vacations involving social issues around the globe.

Organizations that Sponsor Volunteer Vacations

Potential volunteers can also scour the opportunities offered by organizations that sponsor volunteer vacations. Airline Ambassadors International distributes medical and other aid to children, families, and underprivileged communities around the world.

Global Service Corp. focuses its efforts in two countries, Tanzania and Thailand, and offers projects that last from two weeks up to six months. People interested in environmental and animal issues can choose from more than 130 projects in 47 countries offered by the nonprofit group Earthwatch. Cross

Cultural Solutions has projects lasting from one to twelve weeks located in eleven countries.

One-week opportunities are the mainstay of Globe Aware, which sponsors projects in nine countries. Community development, conservation, and teaching are just a few of the types of projects offered by i-to-i in more than two dozen countries. One unique type of organization is Peace Villages Foundation, a Non-Profit Franchise run and paid for entirely by volunteers.

People who don't find what they're looking for with a sponsoring organization or who have a pet cause or favorite charity can contact the particular group or charity on their own and ask about volunteer vacation opportunities.

WINE TOURISM

Wine tourism refers to tourism whose purpose is or includes the tasting, consumption, or purchase of wine, often at or near the source. Wine tourism can consist of visits to wineries, vineyards, and restaurants known to offer unique vintages, as well as organized wine tours, wine festivals, or other special events.

Many wine regions around the world have found it financially beneficial to promote such tourism; accordingly, growers associations and others in the hospitality industry in wine regions have spent significant amounts of money over the years to promote such tourism.

The National Wine Centre of Australia is a tourism venue that showcases the entire Australian wine industry. It is an education hub for tourists, the general public and full time students.

The National Wine Centre is a teaching centre for wine-related academic programs of The University of Adelaide, Australia. The University of Adelaide, "the wine university", is one of the top two educators in the world for wine studies along with the University of California-Davis.

Flinders University in Australia offers a degree program in food and wine tourism.

SUSTAINABLE TOURISM

There are many different definitions of sustainable tourism, or responsible tourism, that have been developed over the last decade. Most tend to assume that all tourists are responsible for respecting and conserving a location's economic, environmental, and socio-cultural balances.

Global economists forecast continuing international tourism growth, ranging between three and six percent annually, depending on the location.

As one of the world's largest and fastest growing industries, this continuous growth will place great stress on remaining biodiverse habitats, often used to support mass tourism.

Sustainable tourists are aware of these dangers and seek to protect their favorite destinations, and to protect tourism as an industry. Sustainable tourists face many responsibilities to reduce tourism's impact on communities, including:

- informing themselves of the culture, politics, and economy of the communities being visited.
- anticipating and respecting local cultures' expectations and assumptions.
- contributing to intercultural understanding and tolerance.
- supporting the integrity of local cultures by favoring businesses which conserve cultural heritage
- supporting local economies by purchasing local goods and participating with small, local businesses.
- conserving resources by seeking out businesses that are environmentally conscious, and by using the least possible amount of non-renewable resources.

The Multilateral Investment Fund MIF Focus on destinations where there is already a critical mass of tourism businesses, MIF projects aim to boost the competitiveness of locally owned small and medium enterprises, helping them to organize themselves and work toward the shared goals of increasing income, employment and economic development.

See the Sustainable Tourism Action Plan and project proposal Guidelines.

Ecotourism

Ecotourism, according to Heather Robinson (2006), is a subset of sustainable tourism, differing by its focus on ecology.

Ecotourism is sustainable tourism that "contributes actively to the conservation of natural and cultural heritage; includes local and indigenous communities in its planning, development and operation, contributing to their well-being; interprets the natural and cultural heritage of the destination to visitors; and lends itself better to independent travellers, as well as to organized tours for small size groups.

In simple words ecotourism means while practicing any kind of tourism one should not harm nature.

For today's fast changing world only the practice of ecotourism can save nature from ever growing human population. Ecotourism is the best way to practice any kind of tourism whether it is wildlife tourism, adventure tourism, or heritage tourism.

It is the duty of all mankind to preserve nature and different species, only then can they survive for a long time; mankind should respect nature and its rules.

Man should preserve nature for the upcoming generation, so they also feel the pleasure of being in nature as people of this and earlier generations felt.

Green Conventions, Meetings and Events

Large conventions, meetings and other major organized events drive the travel, tourism and hospitality industry.

Cities and convention centers compete to attract such commerce, commerce which has heavy impacts on resource use and the environment.

Major sporting events, such as the Olympic Games, present special problems regarding environmental burdens and degradation. But burdens imposed by the regular convention industry can be vastly more significant.

Green conventions and events are a new but growing sector and marketing point within the convention and hospitality industry.

More environmentally aware organizations, corporations and government agencies are now seeking more sustainable event practices, greener hotels, restaurants and convention venues, and more energy efficient or climate neutral travel and ground transportation.

Additionally, some convention centers have begun to take direct action in reducing the impact of the conventions they host.

One example is the Moscone Center in San Francisco, California, which has a very aggressive recycling program, a large solar power system, and other programs aimed at reducing impact and increasing efficiency.

With the advent of the internet, some traditional conventions are being replaced with virtual conventions, where the attendees remain in their home physical location and "attend" the convention by use of a web-based interface programmed for the task.

This sort of "virtual" meeting eliminates all of the impacts associated with travel, accommodation, food wastage, and other necessary impacts of traditional, physical conventions.

6

Tourism: The World Largest Industry

The World Travel and Tourism Council (WTTC) estimate that in 1999 travel and tourism were directly and indirectly responsible for generating across the global economy:

11% of GDP;

200 million jobs;

8% of total employment; and

5.5 million new jobs per year until 2010.

Worldwide, the number of international tourist trips rose by 8.7% per year on average between 1980 and 1997. Fastest growth was in the East Asia/Pacific region (which includes China, Hong Kong, Singapore and Thailand) and in the Americas. The latest 1999 preliminary figures from the World Tourism Organisation suggest the UK has fallen below China to sixth place and that the East Asia and the Pacific region as a whole continued to have strong growth rates and to have recovered from a slight downturn following the financial crisis. Arrivals in the region increased by 10.7% last year. Malaysia was particularly successful, with a growth rate of 43%.

The profile of employment within the tourism industry (high proportions of female, young and part-time workers) meant that, after the retail sector, the hospitality sector is the sector with most workers affected by the national minimum wage (NMW) which came in to force on 1 April 1999.

The Low Pay Commission undertook some research in to the immediate affects of introducing the minimum wage. A survey of members of the British Hospitality Association found that the impact seemed to be limited to the hotel and catering sectors with nearly three-quarters reporting no effect on their business. The survey found that only 12% of businesses in London and the South East were affected, compared to between 27% and 38% of firms in other regions. The Commission said that introduction of the minimum wage was positively accepted in the sector. It quoted evidence from Tourism South and West Wales who said that a number of employers had expressed the view that "the introduction of the NMW has ensured that we can lay the low wage ghost which has haunted the careers in tourism and hospitality for so long".

The British Hospitality Association's main compliant about the NMW is the lack of regional variation.

VAT on Hotels

There is a general feeling in the tourism industry that one of the reasons that the UK is losing its market share of world tourism (see section VII) is because hotel prices are not competitive. The UK has one of the highest rates of VAT on accommodation in the EU; only Denmark levies a higher rate.

A study conducted on behalf of the BTA by Deloitte & Touche, The Economic Effects of Changing VAT Rates on the British Tourism and Leisure Industry, found the evidence of that international tourism receipts and expenditure are strongly influenced by the price of the UK's tourism services.

The report highlighted the experiences of the Irish Republic whose government halved the VAT on visitor accommodation and restaurant meals in the mid 1980s. Following this reduction visitor numbers increased sharply, generating an increase in foreign exchange earnings of more than 50%. There was also a switch in behaviour of Irish residents who became more likely to holiday in Ireland. The report said that reducing the rate of VAT applying to visitor accommodation from 17.5% to 8%, would cost the Exchequer £400 million a year through the direct loss of VAT receipts.

However against this are the gains from additional income and corporation tax receipts and savings in social security payments which would rise from £400 million a year to more than £700 million after ten years. It would also result in the creation of about 50,000 new jobs.

The British Hospitality Association (BHA) has lobbied hard on this matter, Martin Couchman, Deputy Chief Executive, BHA said:

The imposition of VAT at such a high rate has an impact on the industry's prices, and this is holding this country back in the highly competitive international tourism market. We could be even more successful-and attract more visitors-if the level of VAT was reduced. The Government however has made it clear that they are not considering reducing the rate of VAT on accommodation: Mr. Hoyle: To ask the Chancellor of the Exchequer (1) what assessment he has made of the advantages and disadvantages of reducing VAT on hotel room charges; (2) what plans he has to use the taxation system to promote the UK tourism industry.

Dawn Primarolo: The Government currently have no such plans. UK tourism is enjoying record success and the tourism industry is about to benefit from the long term strategy "Tomorrow's Tourism: a growth industry for the new millennium" recently announced by my right hon. Friend the Secretary of State for Culture, Media and Sport.

This issue was debated at length in the Lords on 12 November 1998, when Lord Gordon of Strathblane argued for a cut in VAT on hotel accommodation to 12.5% or 8%. Speaking for the Government Lord McIntosh of Haringey said: [...] The noble Lord, Lord Rowallan, seems to believe that if one cuts the rate of

VAT on hotel accommodation by 10 per cent. one is somehow cutting prices by the same percentage. Nothing could be further from the truth. Only 34 per cent. Of tourism spend in this country is on hotel accommodation. If VAT were cut to 8 per cent, that would be a reduction of 3 per cent. in total tourism spend. If it were reduced to the average of 12.5 per cent., to which my noble friend Lord Gordon of Strathblane referred, that would produce a cut of less than 2 per cent. in total spend. That is the absolute maximum because 12 per cent. of expenditure on hotels is by UK business visitors who can recoup the tax anyway.

Some £427 million is spent by overseas conference visitors to this country, many of whom can recover VAT. Also, 18 per cent. of hotel expenditure involves establishments that are below the VAT threshold. The effect on prices of cuts in VAT of the kind proposed would be only 1 per cent. or 2 per cent., to be generous. Noble Lords are right to say that tourism expenditure is price sensitive but the claim that matters can be improved by the sort of cut in VAT proposed is not proven. In fact, it is highly improbable. [...]

Licensing Laws

The Government has recently published a white paper containing their proposed changes to the licensing laws, Time for Reform: Proposals for the Modernisation of out Licensing Laws.

The proposals include:

A single integrated scheme for licensing premises which sell alcohol, provide public entertainment or provide refreshment at night.

A new system of personal licences which allow holders to sell or to serve alcohol for consumption on or off any premises possessing a premises licence. (Places providing public entertainment or refreshment at night which does not involve alcohol, would require a premises licence only.)

To minimise public disorder resulting form fixed closing time, flexible opening hours with the potential for up to 24 hour opening 7 days a week, subject to consideration of the impact on local residents.

The Government hopes that the changes will end the confusion of overseas visitors. The Tourism Minister, Janet Anderson said "Many visitors come form countries were liquor licensing laws are quite different. They find our regulations archaic and confusing. They are taken aback when time is called at 11pm in a public house, or told in a restaurant that they cannot order a bottle of wine because it is midnight"

The British Hospitality Association reacted favourably to the proposals:

The British Hospitality Association welcomes the White Paper on licensing reform as a major step towards freeing the hotel and restaurant industry from archaic restrictions and regulations concerning the service of drink.

"The White Paper is most welcome," says Phil Phillips, the BHA's technical services manager. "It contains many of the amendments to the licensing legislation that we were seeking. For once, government has listened to the industry's reasoned arguments and introduced sensible proposals which treat members of the public as adults. "It will have the added benefit of helping tourism because it provides flexibility. It will enable businesses to tailor opening hours to meet local trade demands and allows visitors to Britain to have a drink whenever they want it-something which has been denied them in the past and which has always been an irritant to them."

TOMORROW'S TOURISM ACTION POINTS

Tourism Summit

Progress on the 15 Action Points set out in Tomorrow's Tourism

1. A blueprint for the sustainable development of tourism to safeguard our countryside, heritage and culture for future generations Leading role given to ETC, which has set up Task Force and will publish a strategy paper in Autumn 2000. Rural and Urban White Papers to be published later this year.
2. Initiatives to widen access to tourism for the 40% of people who do not take a long holiday ETC has conducted research into holiday non-participation. Research results and outputs from working group sessions will help shape ETC policy. In March ETC will publish "Accessible Britain 2000", a practical travel guide for people with disabilities.
3. More money for a more focused and aggressive overseas promotion programme to bring in more overseas visitors The Government has granted the BTA an extra £5 million over the period 1999-2000 to 2001-2002. The BTA now has a target to increase from £27 to £30 its return on investment of each £1 of grant-in-aid.
4. New internet systems to deliver more world-wide tourist bookings for Britain and to provide information on attractions and travel options The BTA is on course to

launch 36 new websites-one for each country where it is active or has an information service-by early 2000. 19 are already live. Some RTBs now have IT strategies and most regional websites now link to national product databases. Pilot project launched to integrate transport and accommodation data

5. New computerised booking and information systems to make it easier for people to book accommodation and travel The ETC is promoting Impact Through IT-guidelines for tourism organisations on the use of destination management systems. ETC is also working to secure compatibility of data between different systems. BTA's VisitBritain website now offers on line booking or e-mail enquiry facilities for some hotels and some local pilot schemes are underway
6. A major careers festival and image campaign to raise the profile and promote the image of careers in the hospitality industry Held successfully in June 1999. Reached over 100,000 potential employees. Second festival planned for October 2000
7. A hospitality industry programme to sign up 500 employers to work towards Investors in People standard to help raise the quality of training in the industry 800 have already signed up and 1000 more are going to be signed up. The Hospitality Training Foundation are leading this campaign
8. New strategic national body for England to provide leadership to the English tourism industry The English Tourism Council (ETC) was launched on 12 July with a new Framework for Action. Under the new Chairman, it has reconstituted the Tourism Forum; set up Task Forces to deal with key issues like: transport, sustainable tourism, resort regeneration and future trends; and made progress on other issues including these Action Points
9. A new grading scheme for all hotels and guest houses to give holiday makers and business travellers consistent quality they can rely on The ETC, together with the AA and the RAC, launched the new quality standards to consumers on 13 September. Participation in the new scheme has continued to grow (self-catering 10%, serviced 13%, from 98/99).

10. New targets for hotel development in London and a further £4.5 million for marketing to\ exploit its potential as a premier location for business travellers and holiday makers and as a gateway to Britain The Government has announced a further £4.5 million for the overseas promotion of London over the period 1999-2000 to 2001-02. Hotel targets are on schedule
11. More integrated promotion of our wonderful cultural, heritage and countryside attractions to enable visitors to enjoy the full range of what Britain has to offer More integration taking place in regional & local destination marketing, and new BTA promotions will help meet this objective. RTBs supporting work on regional & local cultural strategies. BTA co-ordinates UK Cultural and Tourism Group to share experiences and good practice in cultural tourism
12. The development of innovative niche markets, such as film tourism and sports tourism, to unlock the full potential of Britain's unique cultural and natural heritage ETC has completed research on potential niche markets, and will be working on market development strategies for the best markets identified. BTA Movie map was launched in July 1999. "Green Britain" map launched in September 1999. BTA launched the sports tourism strategy in January 2000.
13. Encouraging the regeneration of traditional resorts to allow leisure and business visitors to enjoy high-quality amenities and services The Government has reflected the needs of resort areas in the new maps proposed for the Objective 2 Structural Fund and Assisted Areas. The ETC is undertaking research, including on best practice. Its Resorts Task Force will consider ways in which resorts can develop sensible, effective regeneration plans and is due to report by the end of 2000.
14. More central government support for the regions to give each part of the country better resources to develop their own identity and strengths Creation of ETC has freed more money to go to RTBs. ETC decisions on RTB bids were announced on 9 February 2000 with allocations

made on the merit of individual regional proposals and how they best fit with the national strategy; and lead RTBs identified in key areas.

15. A high profile annual Tourism Summit bringing together industry and government to monitor progress, plan future action and keep all sides working in partnership towards the same objectives Held on 1 March 2000.

TOURISM INDUSTRY OF NEWZEALAND

A key characteristic of New Zealand's tourism industry is its importance to our economy. Tourism has a substantial role in job-creation and export earnings. It is a demand-driven, service-oriented industry experiencing rapid growth and innovation. The industry now faces the challenge of balancing economic, social and environmental dimensions to achieve sustainable growth.

Economic Driver

Tourism plays a key role in the growth of our economy through employment, foreign exchange earnings, investment and regional development. Tourism directly and indirectly contributes almost 10% of New Zealand's GDP.

Tourism is one of New Zealand's largest export industries, with international visitor expenditure in 2002 of $6.1 billion. The most recently available data for Domestic tourism is for the 2001 calendar year, which reports Domestic tourism generated $6.9 billion. See more information on visitor expenditure in the International Visitor Survey and Domestic Travel Study.

Tourism is a vehicle for regional and community development. Many tourists look for unique, unspoilt or 'off the beaten track' locations, so are drawn to small towns and provincial regions that often most need economic development. Tourist interest in the Maori culture also fosters development of Maori communities and businesses.

The New Zealand tourism industry is made up of 10 major public-listed companies and between 13,500 and 18,000 small to medium enterprises.

Tourism supports nearly one job in ten in New Zealand, with around 90,000 full-time equivalent jobs provided directly through tourism and an estimated 60,000 indirectly. See the Tourism

Satellite Account for more information about tourism's contribution to the economy.

Tourism is defined by customer demand. When a tourist takes a taxi, for example, that taxi service becomes part of the tourism industry. In this respect, tourism cuts across a broad range of industries, including:

- o transport,
- o accommodation,
- o retail,
- o catering and
- o financial services.

Many other sectors benefit through provision of goods and services that support tourism businesses, for example:

- o construction,
- o printing and publishing,
- o manufacturing and
- o insurance.

As a result, tourism policy issues involve a broad spectrum of areas and interests. Read more about the different policy issues in the Policy section.

Whilst international tourist arrivals have been growing rapidly over the last two decades, New Zealand remains a niche destination. Our geographic location makes us a long-haul destination-it takes over 8 hours to get here from most countries.

We have a different appeal than high volume tourist destinations like France, Spain, USA and the UK. Research indicates that New Zealand appeals to people seeking adventure, connection with nature, relaxation and revitalisation. Read more about New Zealand's appeal.

Draws on "Public Goods"

Tourism often draws on public facilities and goods such as oceans & rivers, beaches, parks and reserves. By drawing on these resources, tourism impacts on host communities. Careful planning and resource management is required to preserve the quality of these public goods for both tourists and host communities.

Read about resource management and sustainable development in the New Zealand Tourism Strategy 2010.

Sold Overseas and Consumed Onshore

International tourism is a unique type of export-products & services are sold to customers overseas but consumed in New Zealand. This presents the challenge of ensuring that the total tourism experience is consistent with visitor expectations when they purchase their trips to NZ. Read more about consumer needs and motivations and perceptions of New Zealand.

Intangible and Perishable Experiences

Tourism largely involves intangible experiences that customers cannot keep, except in photos, videos and memories. Tourism products and services tend to be perishable in nature-for example-excess hotel rooms, airline seats or bungy jumps on one day cannot be accumulated for use at a later date.

Support Networks

There are many tourism associations to support different aspects of the tourism sector. The lead industry body is the Tourism Industry Association New Zealand-a membership based organisation representing the interests of over 3,500 businesses from throughout the tourism industry. Their purpose is to provide leadership, guidance and appropriate services for the benefit of its members in order to contribute to a viable and sustainable tourism industry.

Sector-specific organisations include the Inbound Tour Operators Council (ITOC), Holiday Accommodation Parks Association of New Zealand (HAPNZ) and the Adventure Tourism Council.

The worldwide tourism industry currently accounts for 760 million people and accounts for roughly a tenth of global employment and capital formation. In most countries, especially low income countries, tourism is seen as a viable option for economic growth, but current unsustainable tourism practices can impact the health and well-being of the environment and community as well as tourism itself. In many low-income countries tourism is significant to the economy or is growing, and long-haul travel is growing at the fastest rate doubled from 1997-2001)

In most industries, CSR standards and practices have been developed by the private sector to respond to external pressure. In tourism, however, the use of codes of conduct and certification is not widespread and is not based as yet upon agreed international standards. It is difficult to make generalisations about CSR without first examining the context in which sustainable tourism operates, its demand and also assessing the numerous certification schemes, codes of conduct and best practices within the industry.

The purpose of this report is to inform FIAS advisory work on CSR and certification with regards to the feasibility and desirability for low income countries to use certification and accreditation as tools for sustainable development. This study is in response to the World Bank's research on CSR codes of conduct and social and environmental guidelines. The World Bank's CSR Practice Investment Climate Department commissioned research to determine whether adopting national certification schemes built on private sector standards and whether these initiatives can be used to enhance both the country and visitor experiences. It is assumed that enhancement would result in better promotion and marketing, which would lead to increased market opportunities through better linkages into the supply chain.

This report is based on both extensive secondary research and a large number of key informant interviews. First, a review of existing research on codes of conduct and certification schemes was undertaken, followed by a review of research on the demand for sustainable tourism. Supplementary interviews with key stakeholders, experts, scheme directors, tour operators and travel providers were then carried out to assess demand for sustainable tourism, the success of certification schemes and consumers' willingness to pay. Companies approached to be interviewed included the largest tour operators, specialty operators in both Europe and North America, certification programs and industry experts (see Appendix A for the full list of organisations interviewed).

It should be recognised that this report is not exhaustive in its nature as not all codes of conduct or certification schemes were analysed. In addition, some potential interviewees could not be contacted, and therefore some opinions may have been omitted. Once codes and certification schemes were identified, they were assessed with regard to broad CSR categories, such as their human rights, labour rights, environmental standards and social and community impact.

The tourism sector's codes of conduct and certification schemes were analysed to gauge their effectiveness and market potential. Interviews with certification players as well as large and eco/ adventure tourism operators and travel providers were also undertaken to evaluate the benefits of certification schemes and to determine demand for sustainable tourism. In the interest of obtaining as much information as possible from interviewees, assurances were given that no direct quotes would be used to identify them or their company. Therefore, all statements are those of the authors' and should not be attributed to any particular interviewee. Sustainable development has been defined as development that meets the needs of present and host regions while protecting and enhancing opportunities for the future.

Sustainable tourism, in addition to the criteria of sustainable development requires a holistic, integrated perspective that takes into account all the industries and resources upon which tourism relies. The set of criteria or principles that define the conditions for its achievement comprises:

Protect and conserve sustainable resources

Be a multi-stakeholder approach

Be environmentally responsible

Maintain the well-being and involvement of the local population or host

Provide meaningful and fairly remunerated employment for the host population

Have economic benefit

Have a long-term view

Have a triple-bottom line approach (environmental, social and economic)

Be equitable

Government must play a leadership role (e.g., impose a 'greater good' approach)

Obtain optimum guest satisfaction and educate tourists about environmental and social concerns

The definition of corporate social responsibility (CSR) has many similar elements to sustainable tourism in that both focus on how stakeholders should be identified and engaged and that initiatives should be measured to determine their impact on others.

Whereas CSR relates to a company's obligation to be accountable to all of its stakeholders in all its operations and activities with the aim of achieving sustainable development not only in the economical dimension but also in the social and environmental dimensions, sustainable tourism was first seen mainly from an environmental perspective and has only recently incorporated social and community aspects.

Today, it is commonly recognised that sustainable tourism is more than just environmental conservation of a natural area, but that is must also address the quality of life of those visiting it and those being visited.

Sustainable tourism development is about making all tourism more compatible with the needs and resources of a destination area. Tourism needs to take into account a holistic and comprehensive approach that balances tourism development with other activities yet tourism is made up of many sectors and is very fragmented, therefore effects and monitoring processes through one company or mechanism has been difficult.

The supply chain of product to end user is not often controlled by solely one party or individual and different elements are often operated by multiple stakeholders. This therefore has led to difficulties in controlling elements of corporate social responsibility.

At Kotu Beach in The Gambia, staff at the Bungalow Beach and Kombo Beach hotels have helped to make a big difference to the earnings of local people and create a more relaxed environment for their guests. Until recently guests at the hotels were constantly approached on the beach by various local vendors offering them goods such as fruit and fruit juices.

The hotel guests so disliked being harassed they were discouraged from using the beach and both the hotels and tour operators viewed it as a major issue. In an innovative project completed in 2002, the juice pressers, fruit sellers and the craft sellers in the local market worked with the local hoteliers to understand and find ways to overcome the problem.

It used a multi-stakeholder approach to bring together the informal guides, fruit sellers, juice pressers and craft sellers with the tour operators and hoteliers to discuss how things could be improved. The juice pressers and fruit sellers were keen to reduce the level of hassle on the beach. Each adopted codes of conduct which they now enforce as a group. The hotels also assist the women's' marketing efforts by putting up 'What's On' boards in the hotels to advertise the stall. The women have higher earnings and the hotel guests can use the beach again without being disturbed. Incomes at the craft market increased three-fold between the two seasons-the tourists spend more when they are not pestered in the market and some new products and better merchandising have also helped.

A number of rural communities in Asia have been engaged to make cushions and tapestries for the guestrooms of Banyan Tree resorts. These initiatives complement ongoing efforts by Banyan Tree Gallery to showcase cottage crafts and the work of indigenous artisans at its lifestyle galleries, as well as the Museum Shops, a collection of outlets in Singapore museums from which visitors can purchase a piece of ancient Asian art recreated as contemporary ornaments, accessories and stationery. This arrangement has the two-fold benefit of keeping traditional arts and crafts alive while providing Asian communities with a means of earning a living.

Labour Standards as Part of Sustainable Tourism

Environmental aspects have been the priority of official certification programmes and voluntary initiatives since the early 1980's and only recently have social or community issues been added. Human rights and labour issues have been more focused upon in developing countries rather than in Europe and North America, partially because social legislation has been more comprehensive in Western countries. Additionally, more advanced concepts such as "the triple bottom line" (environmental, social and economic) are just now being incorporated into definitions and initiatives.

There are a number of labour issues which affect the tourism industry. These include women's rights, fair wages, long working hours, qualification and skills requirements for employees, inability to join trade unions, importing of labour and displacement of traditional employment to benefit from tourism dollars. Tourism workers often do not earn a living wage and are dependent on tips and service charges. Many workers have temporary contracts or none at all, work long hours and are employed in low skilled areas such as waitressing and/or house cleaning.

According to the ILO, tourism workers and managers are often "imported" by the large international hotel and leisure chains (six of the seven leading multinationals of the sector are North American), which pick up the major part of the profits. By contrast, local populations benefit only from low or semi-skilled, poorly paid jobs (cooks, maintenance workers, chambermaids, barmen, gardeners, bus drivers, etc.).

According to a report recently submitted to a tripartite meeting of the ILO, this sector is known for low pay (for example, in the European Union, it is less than 20 per cent of the average salary), difficult working conditions (irregular schedules, Sunday/holiday work, unpaid overtime), and many clandestine jobs. Women make up 70 percent of the labour force in tourism and there are numerous cases of youth or child workers (half the workers in the sector are up to 25 years old).

Although few tourism codes of conduct, industry policies or schemes so far have specifically addressed labour or human rights concerns, child labour and prostitution have been widely addressed in the Caribbean, Thailand and parts of Africa through initiatives such as ECPAT (End Child Prostitution, Child Pornography and Trafficking of Children for Sexual Purposes). Awareness of exploitative labour has also increased due to campaigns such as the recent initiative by Tourism Concern: Sand, sea and sweatshops.

Since 2002, major hotel groups, airlines and tour operators have signed up to the code which involves

- establishing an ethical policy regarding commercial exploitation of children
- training staff
- providing information to officials about abuse at various destinations
- and providing information to travellers (in-flight videos and flyers)

Some programs which have developed out of ECPAT include The Youth Career Development Program which has expanded to be the Youth Career Initiative (YCI). YCI contributes towards the eradication of the commercial sexual exploitation of children by giving girls aged 17 to 20 employment training for the hotel and travel industry. The program targets youths from poor communities and the program uses hotel expertise in human resources development to provide disadvantaged youths with the skills to work in the hotel and travel industry. The program started in Thailand in 1995 and has grown from 9 graduates and one hotel in 1995 to 550 graduates and 23 hotels in 2003. The program is now being extended to the Philippines, Romania and South Africa. Governments, NGO's and the industry are only now starting to address these issues, and although environmental elements and biodiversity issues are a crucial underpinning to achieving wider sustainable tourism development goals, it is now being recognised that labour and community equality/participation issues do affect the success of the tourism product and experience.

THE DEMAND

Within the tourism industry it is generally agreed that there are increasing overall societal and environmental concerns, and that this will increase the demand for more sustainable destinations and travel preferences. These, in turn, will increase the pressure for destination management policies and tour operator responsibility. The destination developments of the 1960/70s, which were the result of overbuilding, are expected to face severe decline as consumers look for more attractive destinations that feature a clean environment and well preserved natural and cultural attractions. Another trend affecting sustainable tourism is health and wellness.

Active or adventure holidays, wellness and spa products and sun destinations are likely to increase in popularity. Authenticity or 'experiential tourism' is another trend. Artificial type destinations (e.g., theme parks), which do not meet higher consumer quality standards, will decrease as the consumer searches for the greater authenticity. Furthermore, there has also been an increase in tourists seeking meaning from their vacation experiences with a resultant noticeable increase in the number of organisations that offer volunteer based travel or educational travel, notably from non-traditional NGO's such as Volunteer Services Overseas (VSO), etc.

The market share of sustainable tourism is difficult to assess as many consumers do not just purchase one type of holiday. During the same year, they may choose a typical package sun and sand holiday as well as one that specifically caters to nature and adventure. Sustainable tourists are approximately 50% free and independent travellers (FIT) and 50% package tour travellers (those travelling with a tour operator)

The majority of tourists seeking nature or adventure type holidays typically travel with niche or small scale operators as mass operators tend to accommodate sun, sea and sand packages. The number of operators offering more nature or adventure tours has increased in Europe over the past few years, whereas in North America, specialty travel operators have existed for over a decade.

Overall, the percentage of consumers who consciously look for sustainable travel packages or ecotourism has been estimated to be as high as 5% of the overall market for travel, although up to 30% feel that it would be 'nice to have' but without an accompanying willingness to pay (World Tourism Organisation-WTO). With increased awareness of general societal issues regarding sustainability, this number is expected to increase somewhat.

Sustainable tourism demand is difficult to assess as most figures are anecdotal evidence of market share. A number of surveys have been completed over recent years which have assessed demand for more sustainable forms of travel. A report by the WTO in 1997 presented information to indicate that ecotourism (not sustainable tourism) accounts for 20% of the world tourism market. The International Ecotourism Society Report, whose statistics were cited worldwide in other reports, indicated that ecotourism contributed US$154 billion in receipts for 2000 and was growing at a rate of 20% per year compared with 7% for tourism overall. This number has not been substantiated in any recent reports.

According to National Geographic, there are 55 million 'geo-travellers' in the United States who are environmentally and socially responsible and have ceaseless expectations for unique and culturally authentic travel experiences that protect and preserve the ecological and cultural environment. 38% of these travellers would be willing to pay a premium to patronise travel companies that use sustainable environmental practices (although it should be noted that only 1% of US travellers take holidays overseas). In Europe, 95 % of Swiss tourists consider respect for local culture to be highly important when choosing a holiday and approximately 87% of respondents in a responsibletravel.com survey suggested they were also interested in locally produced food, local culture and using local guides when on holiday.

The Association of British Travel Agents (ABTA) survey said that it was very important that their holiday did not damage the environment (45%) and that it benefited the people of the destination they were travelling to (for example, through jobs and business opportunities (30%). None of the tour operators interviewed have found that their clientele was willing to pay a premium for these criteria to any substantial degree.

Although consumers may indicate that they expect environmental and social issues to be taken into consideration on their holidays, they do not take it upon themselves to ensure these criteria are being met. Responsibility for ensuring more sustainable tourism falls in the hands of the operator. In the UK, over 80% say tour operators should have responsibility for preserving the local environment and culture and ensuring that local people benefit from tourism.

The same percentage of people are more likely to book a holiday with a company with a 'responsible' travel policy-a 28% increase since 2001. A report in 2000 declared that 55% of consumers believed that travel agents have a responsibility to provide the information, while 48% think tour operators should provide it. Social or environmental considerations, although they may be expected to be addressed in the brochure or on the website of an operator or travel provider, are not demanded when booking travel packages. From interviews with large and specialty operators it was found that no specific consumer requests for specific environmental or social criteria were requested or enquired about when booking their holidays. The only customer issues or questions were regarding stray animals or if there was an animal protection group to look after stray dogs or donkeys clients had encountered.

Additionally, environmental and social criteria do not affect most tour operators' choice when selecting their package components as their primary focus is on price and second on quality. In a study done in 2003, almost 70% of tour operator clients expressed no concern or interest in eco-social issues when selecting their products and only 8% expressed a specific interest when selecting their tour Overall, less than 10% of the market booking ecotours in the US is requesting information from their operators on eco-social standards.

Examining eco-tourism, a WTO report in 2002 prepared for the International Year of Ecotourism (IYE) found that ecotourism was closer to 5% of the market compared to 20% as reported in 2000 and although awareness had increased, there was little evidence that ecotourism had been growing, let alone rapidly. Furthermore, although a 2003 survey of successful ecolodge owners and regional ecotourism experts worldwide found that the U.S. market was cited to be the largest and most significant ecotourism market in the world the GeoTourism study found that less than 10% of the 55 million that were classified as geotourists preferred to travel outside of the United States therefore hardly contributing to tourism revenues in low income countries.

Consumer Motivations

Consumer surveys indicate that there is a willingness to pay for more sustainable types of tourism. In the STI survey (2004) 75.4% of self-declared environmentally oriented consumers declared they were willing to pay $1-20 extra per ticket to mitigate the green house gas effects of their travel. Seventy-seven declared they would switch online travel sites to one that made contributions on their behalf to offset the portion of their emissions.

The National Geographic geotourism survey suggested that 61% of those interested in environmentally and socially sensitive travel would pay 5-10% more to use such companies. The Mori (2002) study suggests that package holiday makers would pay more if money went towards preservation of the local environment and reversing some negative environmental effects of tourism (47%), workers in the destination are guaranteed good wages and working conditions (49%), hotels serve food produced locally (36%) or money went to support a local charity (22%).

These consumers said they would be willing to pay up to 10% more for a holiday (1-2% more = 36% of holiday makers, 5% more-39%, 10% more = 18%). In practice, however, there was no evidence that this research led to actual purchase behaviour. From interviews conducted, there was no indication that consumers were willing to pay more for sustainable tourism products even though they may indicate it in research. As one industry leader noted, "In several surveys done in the last years, a considerable number of people always affirm they would be ready to pay for it.

But unfortunately the reality shows that the customer's decisions are often dominated by other criteria, and mostly by price. There is obviously a contradiction between intention and behaviour. It is what we call a cognitive dissonance. However, in many destinations, it is common practice that tourists on an excursion in wildlife reserves pay an extra fee for nature protection activities and this is well accepted". For example, TUI offered a program for ski holiday tourists to purchase a tree to reduce carbon emissions (£10 purchased a tree and a map of where it was planted). Only 1 in 20 bookings subscribed to the program even though it was listed on a full page of the holiday brochure. Specialty operators also did not have much participation, either.

Explore, the UK's largest adventure operator, offered clients to offset their emissions through Climate Care. There has only been a 3% participation rate. By contrast, niche operators see environmental and social issues as part of their core business and often have programs to support such initiatives. These operators are more likely to search for accommodations or areas which are seen as 'green', however, due to a lack of critical mass and awareness by operators, there are few examples of companies using certified accommodations. Sustainability issues are also not perceived to be a key factor in the tourist decision-making process.

A report in 2000 notes that surveys have been unable to conclude that environmental, social or sustainability criteria are a key concern in holiday decision-making by tourists-even so-called ecotourists are not often motivated to travel because of interest in being 'responsible' or 'environmentally concerned. It is clear that marketers need to connect consumer motivations with actual purchasing. As one expert noted, "consumers are willing to make a greener choice if the product comes from a company [or destination] they already know and trust, it doesn't require (m)any behavioural changes to use, and it's at least as good as what they're already buying in terms of aesthetics, style, taste, etc.".

The majority of travel globally is still mass tourism which consists mainly of sun, sea and sand tourism package holidays provided by large operators (TUI, First Choice, Mytravel). Price, accommodation quality and personal security rank as the most important considerations of booking holidays. Consumers are susceptible to health and safety issues, however, with cleanliness and quality being major factors in their destination choice. From existing research and interviews with tour operators and other experts, it can be concluded that consumers would change their destination choice as a result of bad press about health (e.g. dirty beaches) or safety issues, but not for lack of environmental or social responsibility on the part of suppliers. If evidence suggests that consumers are looking for more sustainable product in tourism yet are driven mainly by price or health issues, there is a need to rethink a strategy to shift product and packaging so that product offered to the consumer integrates wider issues of sustainability.

CERTIFICATION SCHEMES

Certification can be described as the process of assuring consumers and industry that the company being assessed has met a set of minimum standards. Within the tourism industry, certification started in the early 1990's. Since 1992, a number of schemes have been developed.

The purpose of certification has been to achieve voluntary standards of performance which meet or exceed baseline standards or legislation. The process starts with a body that sets credible certification standards (through standards which are industry relevant, measurable and obtainable). The certification body must be without conflict of interest and the indicators should be recognised by an accreditation body. The applicant or business then is assessed according to the indicators and, if successful, receives recognition, usually through the form of a logo, to inform the consumer that they have met minimum criteria. The aim of certification is to foster responsible environmental, social and cultural behaviour and provide a quality product to consumers. To be considered reliable, certification programs need to have a 3 rd party audit and effective assessment as well as clearly defined accreditation criteria. According to Toth (2002), elements of a credible certification system include:

- Adequate, appropriate standards developed/accepted by all affected interests-interpretation of standards;
- Trained, qualified assessors-standard defining training and qualifications;
- Professional/ethical operations at all levels with no biases or conflicts of interest;
- Qualified, financially stable certifying body-if there are multiple certifiers, an accreditation mechanism is needed;
- Even-handed certification and accreditation;
- Transparency;
- Defined procedures;
- Appeals mechanism;
- Recognition by relevant agencies and/or customers-compliance with accepted criteria (e.g. ISO/IEC Guides) facilitates recognition; and
- Acceptance in the marketplace or by regulators-marketing and promotion.

It should be noted that the above definition defines elements of a credible certification system, not necessarily one that incorporates all elements of sustainable tourism. As many schemes do not address social or labour issues in detail, these issues have not been addressed to date.

SCHEMES DEVELOPMENT

There are many certification schemes regarding tourism that relate to sustainability. The best known NGO or country initiatives include Voluntary Initiatives for Sustainable Tourism VISIT (Europe-wide), the Costa Rican standard Certification for Sustainable Tourism (CST), Green Deal Guatemala), and Scotland's Green Tourism Business Scheme (GTBS). The best known industry certification programmes are Green Globe and

Blue Flag. Green Globe offers product as well as destination certification, while Blue Flag certifies beaches. There are two industry based standards which do not solely address tourism: ISO 14001 which addresses environmental impacts and ISO 9001 which addresses quality assurance (both mainly used by larger hotels rather than small operators or accommodations). The majority of funding and attention towards certification has addressed tourism-only schemes. These are the 'eco' schemes that focus mainly upon SME's. A number of eco certification projects are in the pilot or development phase such as Mexico, The Caribbean, Sub-Saharan Africa and Peru and countries such as Kenya and Botswana are considering them.

The majority of European ecolabels have related to environmental criteria, however, developing countries such as the Americas and South Africa have included social and cultural aspects as major components. Development of certification and eco-labels has been irregular and although there are benefits of putting forth such programs to set baseline standards, programs are not world-wide, nor is there a critical mass of certified products. There are few programs in low income countries as 2/3 of the approximately 7,000 certified tourism products are in Europe. Approximately 40% of programs started before 1996 with an additional 40% between 1996-2000 and a number of new initiatives developed since 2000 (European Centre for Ecological and Agricultural Tourism (ECEAT), eastern European programs and Central and South America).

Programs and practices vary region to region. Most schemes are national in scope, such as the CST, Guatemalan Green Deal and South Africa's Fair Trade Tourism label. The model for certification in Latin America is the CST and this is now being expanded to become the Network of the Americas to include Guatemala, Brazil, Ecuador and other newly proposed schemes. Most countries in this region have implemented (or plan to such as Mexico & Peru) a national program using the CST as a model 'although the costs of starting and operating a certification program have meant there has been little progress'.

Although publicised as a model for tourism certification, the CST program has few certified products and the Network of the Americas does not have many in total (e.g., only 21 products have been certified in Guatemala).

In Europe, the VISIT program has created an inclusive system to raise standards and cooperation among current European programs, and markets approximately 4,000 certified products through ethical trade fairs (green travel market) and to tour operators. The most successful certification program, Blue Flag, has extended its program outside Europe to the Caribbean, North America and Africa although this program only applies to the certification of beaches.

Green Globe is an industry standard which currently operates out of Australia but has certified properties worldwide. Destination certification has been gaining momentum in recent years due to issues of sustainable destination management and Green Globe's program offers a comprehensive approach for multiple players. Measurability and implementation of this scheme, however, has been questioned. Green Globe is one scheme that does offer certification of more than just ecotourism or small scale products as they offer services for tour operators, hotels, destinations, etc. Some larger scale companies have obtained certification (all-inclusive resorts such as Sandals, Casuarina Beach, Almond Beach and some Hilton and Marriott properties). In 2002, a project called the Sustainable Tourism Stewardship Council (STSC) was set up with the aim of harmonising and providing mutual recognition of schemes, and to set up an international accreditation agency-but little progress has been made since its inception. Reasons include the lack of an over-riding body to adopt international certification, confusion of existing criteria and competition between existing schemes (who did not want to merge their labels).

The majority of certification schemes accredit accommodations (approximately 63%), whereas only 7% address tour operators, mainly ground operators specifically dealing with ecotourism. Approximately 40% of the criteria or indicators in standards relate to management issues and the remaining 60% relate to specific actions such as environmental benchmarking (34%), economic indicators (8%) or socio-cultural criteria (12%). The majority of programs to date (with the exception of Green Globe, Blue Flag and ISO) have targeted small operations or ecolodges rather than larger scale tourism accommodations.

Standards can be divided into product standards (reflecting the appropriate characteristics a product is expected to have) or process standards (reflecting the appropriate characteristics from products to final distribution).

Larger tourism operators, mainly hotels, have few connections with smaller certification schemes and opt instead for international standards such as ISO 9001 which provides a quality assurance accreditation or ISO 14001 which provides environmental accreditation. These schemes are not widely adopted, however, due to a lack of awareness and marketing and many larger chains having their own internal monitoring or benchmarking systems.

Benefits and Issues

The benefits of certification are seen to be wide-spread although the majority of programs uphold marketing and training as their primary benefits. With the designation of a logo, certification is thought to give companies a competitive advantage and increased linkages into the distribution chain and to consumers through marketing (inclusions on web sites, travel fairs, brochure recognition), all of which would be assumed to give businesses competitiveness. Additional benefits perceived from certification include:

- The ability to distinguish sustainable tourism from 'greenwashing'
- The encouragement of voluntary improvements
- Showcasing best practices
- The use of the standard as a blueprint for future development
- Training of management procedures
- Cost savings
- Peer recognition
- Achievement beyond legislation compliance

Determinants of success of schemes have been linked to marketing which to date, has been largely unsatisfactory with the exception of some ECEAT schemes due to the small number of certified products and therefore reduced appeal to large operators to use them in their product choice. Also, the sheer number of schemes and labels makes it difficult for tour operators to incorporate them as they would have to educate the consumer about the standards behind each one and differences among them.

This is beyond what tour operators deem practical for hard copy brochures. Larger certified operators (through organisations such as Green Globe or ISO) have seen cost savings and overall improved management structures. Some benefits to the community are improved environmental conditions of facilities or infrastructure improvements such as new access roads (although often larger hotel chains build water or sewage plants only for the hotel complex rather than the community or village at large). As most certification schemes do not include labour or social/ community issues, the local community has not greatly benefited. In addition, companies have not generally seen marketing benefits, and therefore have participated in schemes largely for cost savings or reporting purposes.

Ecolabels in Eastern Europe were developed to promote organic farms and rural accommodation and promote them to the increasing number of tourists visiting these regions. The Czech Republic's scheme has seen 135 accommodations certified which have been promoted through publications of the Countryside Holiday Guidebook and or the Heritage Trails. As many visitors to Eastern European countries have been VFR (visiting friends and relatives) or independent tourists, farm stays and rural accommodation was a unique and relatively new type of tourism which has since led to the growth of agro-tourism in Europe. The newest initiative is the new "national ecolabel for tourist services" which has been accepted by the Czech Government three weeks ago and will be used as a tool for the new governmental "Tourism Policy" since 2007 (because of the EU programming period 2007-2013).

Failures of certification schemes

Issues around certification are widespread and varied. As Font (2003) suggests, the majority of certification schemes for tour operators address ecotourism operations rather than large mass market operators who supply the majority of the world's tourism and have the main access to the market. Therefore it has not helped respond to industry pressure as most operators have not heard of the numerous schemes or choose their product based on price. Additionally, there is a lack of critical mass as less than 1% of tourism businesses are certified. Thus, tour operators do not have enough products to choose from and often schemes do not ensure quality standards in their accreditation. Issues include:

- Lack of critical mass (too few certified products, certification is not wide-spread)
- Too many certification programs and other industry awards have led to confusion Lack of awareness by industry, consumers and government
- Lack of unified brand (too many programs compete against each other, duplicate efforts, yet vary in their criteria)
- Low consumer demand and a general tiredness with labels of all kinds
- Lack of credibility (local certification schemes with no international recognition)
- Lack of proven marketing benefits (and lack of marketing by certification bodies)
- Lack of incentives for hotels or businesses to join
- Lack of readiness to disclose information (Businesses do not wish to disclose information to obtain certification)
- Cost of adherence (e.g., Green Globe, ISO) and perception that recognition/label can be 'bought'

Types of and Participation in Schemes

The most successful certification program to date has been Blue Flag, an internationally recognised program for measuring the health of beaches. Over 2,700 beaches have been certified. Success can be linked to health and safety as tourists do not want to bathe on polluted beaches. As noted earlier, beach health and cleanliness is a motivating factor in choosing a holiday therefore, having an internationally known system that assures beach health is an economic incentive for a hotel owner near a beach. The Blue Flag program greatly reduces the cost of evaluation by using existing infrastructure to take measurements of the environment.

Overall, certification within the tourism industry has been difficult to achieve because tourism is multifaceted and includes a mix of services and products. Most certification and supplier development is voluntary (between 10-25% of suppliers have met the voluntary sustainability related standards), but there is little consensus that certification is actually viable. There are also few accommodations or organisations that have been certified. In Europe, where the most ecolabel or certification programs exist, less than 0.5% of accommodations have been certified. The four best known certification programs for ecotourism and SMEs (ECOTEL, CST, NEAP and Green Globe) have less than 2000 members in total. In Costa Rica only 5% of hotels have been certified, with only 46% of them advertising their certification.

It has been suggested by the new InterAmerican Bank MIF project for a Sustainable Tourism Certification System that certification for sustainability of tourism will increase competitiveness and market access of small and medium sized enterprises in Latin America. The EU has funded the VISIT scheme and the Green Travel Market to promote certified products and the Cooperative Research Centre for Sustainable Tourism (CRC) in Australia has partnered with Green Globe. However, a thorough review of existing reports on this topic shows that there are no market demand studies available to support this assumption.

Many programs also focus specifically on eco-lodges or other small scale accommodation, such as agro-tourism accommodations. Although this form of tourism can bring positive benefits to the areas in which it operates, its very nature does not make it suitable for mass tourism operators who control the vast majority of travel. There is also a lack of awareness among businesses, although the GTBS in Scotland affirmed that they had good take-up over the first three years, and that their membership is now increasing by about 30% per annum. In Costa Rica, initial participation in the program was also high, however, to date there are few hotels that have achieved a full five star rating. The CST stated that the department was receiving approximately 300 requests for certification per year before the 'oath of legality' (must be notorized by a Public Notary) was put into place. Now they are only receiving 10 requests per year.

There is also a lack of awareness among consumers. In Christchurch, New Zealand, interviews with 295 visitors found that only one-fifth recalled any place with ecolabels, and only 13% had ever heard of any tourism ecolabel. In a survey of 100 tourists in Australia, not one of them chose his or her hotel based on Eco-Australia certification. It is estimated that less than 1% of consumers were aware of the existence or criteria of any tourism certification program (for consistency). Some certification programs assessed did not claim to attract increased business but focused instead on improving management procedures and reduce cost savings. The GTBS said applicants have higher occupancy rates than average for Scotland. This, however, must be accepted with caution as these applicants tend to be well managed companies who would likely achieve these results even without certification. In Guatemala, companies gain more through management techniques to reduce costs and improve efficiency than they do through marketing.

There are also problems with transparency as some businesses in Guatemala do not want to disclose their practices in order to obtain an ecolabel. Certification cannot be seen to counter the problem of 'greenwashing' as schemes are mainly small scale and there is not enough industry pressure to make a difference. There is no world-wide method of monitoring certification and therefore overall compliance and improvement is hard to gauge.

Roles and Costs

Approximately 60% of certification programs are led by private tourism organisations or NGO's; the remainder are government led. The investment for the development of eco-labels differs from the maintenance of the programs. Development of programs is almost evenly split between NGO's, public and private sector (1/3 each, respectively), whereas almost 2/3 of programs are engaged in a multi-stakeholder collaborative approach regarding decision-making and advice giving. The costs of developing certification programs are often put upon governments, however, large governance structures are pricey and programs may need a further layer of organisations to help industry implement the standards.

There is a high cost for SME's to apply for certification unless it is subsidised by government (application procedure and operation of program), and it is often not the priority of the government to run these schemes. Past studies showed that examples from Fiji, Dominican Republic and Venezuela failed in their early attempts to set up programs. NGO's are not able to afford the start-up costs of wide-scale certification projects and are therefore either government subsidised or address specific areas (e.g. Ecuador's Smart Voyager program in the Galapagos, PAN Parks in Europe, Kenya lodge accreditation). Unless subsidised, not all firms will have the same potential access to become certified.

Most programs have addressed these issues through scaled fee structures which are linked to overall company turnover or number of staff. In Costa Rica, the government has successfully subsidised first time applications to the CST. In Australia, costs are kept low but this then impacts the amount of marketing possible. Green Globe, as an industry run program, has higher costs and is linked to the stage of certification. While some certification programs can provide sufficient benefits, cost is an issue for both the company (who may find it costly to implement criteria to become certified) and the program itself as it needs to run its operations and audit the companies applying.

Some companies find ways to repay the fees as they find that meeting some of the criteria make them more eco-efficient and therefore they can justify further certification costs based on the savings realised. For smaller companies, certification programs might need to consider encouraging applications from co-operatives of small firms or under a destination umbrella. Costs are seen by many businesses as high due to the time needed for site visits and filling out forms and questionnaires. Certification can help reduce operating and management costs, although it should be noted that not all adherences to social criteria reduce cost.

Research has shown that substantial energy, waste and water savings can be realised by implementing sustainability criteria into operating processes and procedures. Credible environmental tourism certification programs, with respected standards and rigorous criteria, should be careful in considering broadening their approach to include social issues. 'A tokenist introduction of social issues might instead lead to criticisms for being environmental programs under a sustainability label' and could also raise costs and expertise needed to administer them. It is generally quite difficult to measure social/community impacts through certification.

If certification is to continue to move forward, sustainability criteria need to be assessed alongside health and safety standards as quality assurance is critical to selling a better product. Although eco-certification claims to address environmental and sometimes social criteria, basic health and safety factors are not always considered and some certified ecolodges in Central America have been found to lack basic hygiene and safety. Although ISO 9000 addresses quality assurance, it is not linked to other schemes and has only been adopted by some hotels rather than entire chains or others in the tourism sector.

The main selection criteria for customers to choose their travel packages remain price, safety and quality. Environmental and social criteria will only be considered when these primary criteria are satisfied.

Government roles have mainly involved providing an institutional framework as well as grants or loans. An advantage of government led schemes is that they are usually longer term in focus. Promotion of best practices has also taken place and there is an expectation that governments will take a more active role. Through the assessment of schemes, however, there is no evidence to support that governments are effective at marketing such schemes and often there is a lack of willingness to share information or cooperate with other schemes. There are few motivations for governments to be involved in certification.

There is no market potential as the number of consumers actively supportive is minimal, and most often governments have adopted schemes as part of their wider development strategy (e.g., Costa Rica's Chamber of Commerce (CANATUR) was instrumental in setting up the scheme but has had no part in marketing it). From previous research on the subject and discussions with existing certification programs, it has been suggested that international governmental bodies need to play a more active role.

One is a cooperative arrangement with the WTO, and the other a more integrated relationship. An International Sustainable Tourism Commission (ISTC)-an autonomous body functioning as an executing agency of the WTO-has been proposed. There is no evidence, however, to suggest that there would be an increase in certification if this were to be the case as many countries who already offer programs do not want to give up their brand and there is currently a lack of global criteria used in certification.

NGOs

NGO's have also been responsible for running some certification programs, however the high costs of operations questions the feasibility and long term sustainability of this option. The role of NGO's has been to raise awareness and apply legislative pressure. As certification schemes need large upfront and ongoing investments, subsidies are required, and often NGOs partner with industry associations to implement programs. Politically active NGOs are also exerting pressure, particularly on public companies, to take more of a leadership role with respect to CSR.

There are some industry schemes such as Green Globe, ECOTEL, ISO and CERES. Industry also plays a role in operating schemes such as Guatemala's Alianza Verde (Green Deal). Positive aspects of independent certification are that programs are self-sufficient and would not be relying upon government support. Industry-led schemes are also more willing to share information and partner with other certification schemes to move towards a wider brand and reduce costs for themselves and operators.

Certification incentives could help build industry buy-in. Interviews with tour operators and existing research suggests that tax write-offs, preferential access to areas (e.g., beach property or remote parks) and preferential marketing for supporting schemes would be beneficial, however, the majority of businesses use certification as a means of cost savings, improving management practices and to comply with the requirements for corporate reporting. The main weakness of certification is the overall lack of reporting and monitoring. Certification has been seen to positively affect resource management but does not necessarily deal with labour or social issues and therefore most companies who promote their certification also provide additional forms of reporting.

Certification also has mainly addressed small companies rather than larger operators, accommodation providers and other service providers who make up the majority of the market.

The Spier estate comprises a 155-room hotel, conference facilities, golf course and winery. Their triple bottom line approach to sustainability has the vision to create a sustainable "micro-ecology" which enhances heritage and culture, generates wealth for all stakeholders, helps meet social and economic needs, and provides the infrastructure to encourage new community lifestyles compatible with the vision for the Winelands. Over 150 indicators measure aspects from compliance with employee regulations, energy and water usage, to the impact of the HIV/AIDS prevention and treatment initiatives. Some of the ways that Spier has contributed to CSR initiatives include:

- Procurement of natural gas from local, black owned business
- The establishment of a crafts market on the estate where individuals sell their craftwork
- obtaining the S.A. Fair Trademark (FTSSA)
- reduced wastewater by 20%
- created 19% new employment abiding by laws of equal opportunity
- given 65 hectares of land and water to 16 small farmers from historically disadvantaged backgrounds (as part of a wider land-reform program)

To advance certification schemes a number of options have been put forward by NGO's, industry and government. The WTO guidelines call for higher government intervention to move sustainable tourism forward. National and regional certification schemes declare there is a need for higher government intervention through the establishment of a global set of criteria, promotion and monitoring. They have also noted that a joined-up government approaches to policy development in destinations (participation from both government and industry associations) is needed to help promote certification and that the overall supply chain needs to be focused upon.

Interviewees have been suggesting that overall awareness and one overarching standard is needed if certification is to continue but that financial incentives, verification procedures and mandatory reporting are the most effective means to ensure participation and compliance. Since larger brands and companies dominate the sector, they can have more influence than small scale, bottom-up, locally based initiatives in the adoption of sustainability criteria and reporting. Currently it is the NGOs, politicians and the financial market which are pushing for sustainability measures to be incorporated. Publicly traded companies, in particular, are being forced into compliance since financial analysts want to avoid risks at all costs; these companies are benchmarked against other global players such as Cendant, Marriott, Hilton, Carnival Cruises, etc., and CSR is therefore seen as key for their investor relations. However, the majority of the certification initiatives within the tourism sector to date have focused on the small scale voluntary initiatives that are not facing pressure to conform.

Operators within the supply chain that report their compliance are in many ways better monitored than if they were certified. TUI, in particular is very strong about tracking and demonstrating continual improvement, and assisting their suppliers through expertise in achieving these improvements. Accor, an international hotel chain also monitors through its purchasing organisations in each country.

In 2002, Accor's Purchasing Department Developed a Sustainable Development

Purchasing Charter which aimed to promote and monitor good labour and environmental practices in the 15 countries where it has a purchasing organisation. In 2003 the charter was sent to Accor's 2,000 preferred suppliers (the group's total spend is more than 1 billion Euros) who were asked to complete a questionnaire in order for the company to monitor supplier compliance. In 2003, Accor also set out a new Subcontracting Charter that clearly defines working conditions for outside cleaning personnel in hotels managed directly by Accor, covering areas from work schedules to training programs and the calculation of hours paid.

CODES OF CONDUCT AND ROLES OF REPORTING

Codes of conduct were first developed in the 1970/80's and were predominantly focused on visitor management and environmental management. Their aim was to raise awareness in industry. There are a number of these codes within the tourism industry, put out by international bodies (WTO, UN, TOI, TIES, etc.), however, there is not industry wide awareness nor is there any monitoring of compliance. The tourism industry is fragmented and difficult to monitor due to the complexity of stakeholders in the value-chain. Codes of conduct tend to be voluntary or informal and vary considerably from sector to sector (hotel, cruise, airline, and operator) and in what they cover (labour, environment, social, economic). There are two types of codes of conduct. One is put out by organisations such as the WTO or industry associations and the latter are self-imposed guideline of what the corporation deems ethical business behaviour and it's done to reassure investors and consumers.

This research supports a recent World Bank Group report that there is virtually no effective monitoring or implementation mechanism yet in place for CSR practices, and that even defining sustainable tourism can be difficult as criteria are interpreted differently by different stakeholders. There are, however, a growing number of guidelines and charters on sustainable tourism which have been put forth by both government and industry.

Governments have endorsed the concept of sustainable tourism and signed on to multiple charters, such as the Lanzarote Charter for Sustainable Tourism in 1995 or the EU's 'Working Together for the Future of European Tourism'. However, few charters or country codes actually outline specific measurable targets, as most tourism policies have been driven by economics and divorced from environmental and social costs. There has been raised awareness by destinations in mature stages of development that conservation and social issues could be a challenge as many communities were economically dependant on tourism. There has also been an increase in the adoption of Local Agenda 21 principles for destination management in the past few years. Currently no government body has regulated the need for reporting in the tourism sector.

Hilton has adopted a new Standard for Business Partners and Suppliers which includes standards on child or forced labour, employee representation, health, safety and environmental management, discrimination, disciplinary practices and employee compensation and working hours.

Hotel chains have been addressing their environmental concerns for some years. A number of them set up the International Hotel Environmental Initiative in 1992 which focused on environmental improvements and is now starting to address social and community issues. Most of the larger hotel chains comply with environmental standards and have environmental policies and standards ranging from in-house benchmarking systems (Accor, Hilton Group, etc.) to environmental standards manuals (Rezidor, Starwood, Fairmont, etc.).

Although not widespread in adoption, some hotels are now promoting when they achieve international certification such as ISO 9001 and 14001 (some Taj, TUI, ITC Hotels, Sol Melia, Baja Inn Hotels). Some hotels have subscribed to local certification systems (such as Rezidor hotels in Scotland attaining the Green Tourism Business Scheme or Rezidor and Scandic hotels in Scandinavia receiving the Nordic Swan ecolabel), however they are few in numbers. There are growing examples of hotel companies who have helped sustainability through backward linkages in lower income countries, but to date hotels and large tour companies are not pressured into having to receive a social and/or environmental license to operate as most communities and developing destinations do not have awareness of tourism, let alone the negative issues which may surround it.

Orient-Express inherited a large plot of land as part of the staff accommodation complex in Aguas Calientes, Peru. Orient Express employees who live within the hotel complex and local church workers have started growing their own vegetables which they sell back to the hotel, the Machu Picchu Sanctuary Lodge. In this area of Peru, the hotel had problems finding quality food items, especially vegetables, and now purchases these from their employees.

Reporting

Industry has historically suggested that it will respond to consumer demand for sustainable tourism and that this is where the demand must come from, however, there is evidence that increased CSR is the result of the increased pressure by NGOs, politicians and the financial market to monitor or evaluate codes of conduct or tourism policies which address sustainable or responsible tourism. Reporting comes from constant need for ongoing-communication with suppliers. A notable organisation that is driving progress in this area is the Global Reporting Initiative (GRI), which aims to 'raise the level of sustainability reporting to that of financial reporting'.

The Tour Operators' Initiative, in cooperation with the GRI, developed a Sector Supplement to the GRI 2002 Sustainability Reporting Guidelines providing Tour Operators' performance indicators. Forty-seven indicators were developed to measure tour operators' performance in addressing the environmental, economic and social impacts of their business operations. The tour operators' supplement adds to, but does not replace, the 2002 GRI Sustainability Reporting Guidelines' section on performance indicators. The supplement was not designed to capture sector-specific aspects of the various service industries associated with a package, such as transport, accommodation, and other tourism services.

Many companies produce reports that are aimed at their own employees, in order to help explain and support the roll-out of a company's new sustainability policy.

Some companies also report for reasons of reputation; such companies are keen to capture their leadership work and/or combat negative perceptions that may have arisen about their sector or brand. A social report can also be a useful communication tool to highlight responsible business practice across a company's worldwide operations. Publicly traded companies need to report on CSR initiatives as part of their investor relations and to demonstrate that they are proactive in reducing potential risks. Thus, larger hotel chains, for instance, have moved significantly towards CSR reporting and have been included in the Dow Jones Sustainability Indicator and FTSE4GOOD index (Accor, Hilton and Intercontinental).

Industry association-led initiatives include the Tour Operators Initiative (TOI) and the IHEI. Both these organisations do not have a specific code of conduct but rather coordinate efforts of tour operators or hotels, respectively, to harmonise performance indicators, monitoring, reporting and tools to assist supply chain partners. The three-year programme aims to standardise sustainability checklists with those of certification programs. The project's goal is to merge/assimilate criteria of the FTO with VISIT (VISIT covers mostly environmental criteria, whereas the FTO includes social and labour issues). The aim is to achieve transparency, a cost-effective distribution system, and to link different supply chain initiatives to provide a common toolkit for travel providers.

It must be recognised that without political stability, security and basic infrastructure, tourism will not be fostered by any of the larger international companies, as risks to customers would be deemed too large, and therefore CSR cannot be considered in largely non-democratic countries.

CONCLUSIONS

Certification has resulted from confusion over terms in tourism such as 'sensitive, green, and eco', and the desire to legitimise them has led to multiple schemes being developed worldwide. While certification schemes may be described as ways for SMEs in lower income countries to obtain access to market, interviews with both major and specialist tour operators, travel providers and certification programs do not support this view. Most of the certification schemes have only certified small numbers of attractions or businesses and have not linked into the wider distribution channels due to low awareness and lack of critical mass. In addition, the majority of certification schemes address ecotourism operations rather than large mass market operators who supply the majority of the world's tourism and have the main access to the market.

There also remains considerable variety in standards, criteria and indicators in certification usage. From this study it can be ascertained that although Costa Rica and other countries have widely known and recognised schemes, they are not able to keep up due to lack of staff and finances for operation. Voluntary standards have not been found to increase access to trade unless governments have assisted with mandatory legislation or trade access structures. Industry is cynical about government taking responsibility for the implementation of sustainable tourism practices and also that investment into better social and environmental performance will increase access to market.

There are a lack of internationally accepted principles for certification criteria (although programs such as VISIT and the Network of the Americas are a partial attempt to overcome this) and there is currently a lack of critical mass of products. Certification was also found to be unsuccessful in allowing greater access to new market segments with the exception of some Eastern European countries who noted that organic farms and rural based accommodations gained an increasing number of tourists (providing they were in accessible locations with other amenities/attractions nearby).

The lack of awareness about certification programs and the low incentive for international operators or larger players to take part are largely to blame. Certification schemes at their very best will only allow access to niche market segments, unless they become more widespread and focus on more than just ecotourism and small scale ventures. Operators and certification programmes and research studies have suggested that a global brand is needed if certification is to be pursued more seriously.

One brand would help certification to be internationally recognised and also comply with generally accepted international criteria, and thus have a stronger chance of brand recognition in industry. However, no single approach has so far been put forward successfully due to the varying degrees of infrastructure in countries and the lack of sufficient markets to attract certifiable product. If certification is to be moved forward, there is a need to link certification with quality.

"Case after case has demonstrated that consumer demand develops long after a certification program is well established," according to Amos Bien of The International Ecotourism Society (TIES). The recent report on ecotourism certification suggests that consumer demand takes between 8-15 years (sometimes as long as 20) to develop and that quality, safety and price must be satisfied before the consumer will consider other factors. There is also a need to create demand for sustainable tourism among the travelling public through the linkage with existing quality standards. One example where quality has been linked to certification programs is Green Globe, which has partnered with Australia's AAA to award green stars to products, thereby using an existing quality standard to promote eco friendliness. Their advertising notes research that suggest 62% of travellers say that endorsement will encourage them to consider one accommodation over the other.

Although ISO 9001 is a quality standard it is not linked with other certification standards. In addition, the education of governments about the benefits of long-term planning to ensure sustainability of the destination will also provide them with the skills to understand that long-term planning can ensure a more quality rather than quantity focused approach. Most industry players noted they would be willing to abide by a national level certification scheme as long as it was transparent, did not raise costs of product and achieved a critical mass of certified products.

In order to achieve effective certification schemes or guidelines in low income countries, a multi-stakeholder participatory approach was suggested that included international organisations, such as tour operators or industry associations, to represent individual companies and contribute to the development/adoption of schemes. Recommendations also included that there needs to be an assurance that Government engages with effective systems and builds proper partnerships and that there is a long-term commitment to the process.

Industry is not willing to increase its costs unless it can be translated into increased profits or the cost can be transferred to the consumer. Incentives for gaining participation into schemes by larger operators who could push certification through their supply-chain were suggested, particular tax incentives, preferential access into natural areas and marketing incentives.

It should be noted, however, that there are a number of issues within certification schemes themselves which need to be addressed before governments propose this on a wide scale to industry. For certification to advance it needs to be credible, demand driven, open and transparent, self supporting, accessible and link into a consensus of international standards.

This report advocates that countries with more developed infrastructure are better placed to reduce negative effects of tourism than the development of certification schemes, and that adopting CSR and measures of reporting will have a greater positive effect on industry overall. In many low income countries there are problems of lack of tourism planning, established tourism ministries as well as clear roles and objectives. Therefore focusing on public-private partnership to forward the CSR agenda should have a greater overall positive impact and advance sustainable tourism in the industry. However, if certification is to continue, recommendations include:

Rather than develop new certification schemes in each country, have governments endorse existing and internationally known standards, such as ISO 14001 and 9001 and ILO standards

Continue with efforts to merge certification systems and provide for recognition or convergence of schemes to ensure wider participation and the inclusion of labour and community elements within certification and evaluation initiatives Create a more homogenous market and avoid overregulation in service sectors For elements which are not covered by international agencies (ISO etc.) develop or adopt one internationally recognised brand with baseline criteria to cut down on confusion and multiple criteria Focus on larger tourism companies and international brands operating in developing countries in addition to ecolodges and SMEs to promote wider scale adoption Promote existing industry codes of conduct or guidelines to ensure they are widely disseminated, implemented and monitored/evaluated

Move towards mandatory certification and reporting (for national recognition of sustainable tourism, a critical mass must be achieved) Integrate quality assurance and health & safety standards into schemes or link with other programs (e.g. GTBS links to a quality assurance accreditation scheme)

Focus on capacity building and awareness campaigns primarily to engage business-to-business marketing and government-to-business marketing and awareness.

- Ensure that local certification is implemented through a credible local or regional association to ensure participation and ease of access (but still linked to the overall global brand)
- Award achievement rather than commitment (to ensure confidence)
- Encourage individual business reporting which would improve awareness and obtain confidence in the credibility of certification initiatives
- Recommendations for Achieving Sustainable Tourism and Access to Market for Low Income Countries Supply Chain Initiatives

In order to enhance sustainable tourism development in low income countries, there is a need to focus on elements of the tourism industry which can affect a greater number of products and businesses and contribute environmentally, socially and economically to lower income countries. SMEs as well as larger businesses in developing countries need to align themselves with

European and North American buyers through abiding by CSR and sustainable tourism initiatives that are widely adopted (for example, TUI has made clear that they will not rely upon external auditors for checking accommodations in their programs; therefore businesses reporting on achievements will help link them to buyers who are looking for conformance).

Restrictions or initiatives for more sustainable tourism may not come from low income countries as they are more than ever dependant on the free market economy. Restrictions must come from buyers in Northern Asia, Europe and North America and there need to be incentives for industry to apply supply chain CSR/sustainable tourism standards. Supply chain initiatives can aid in creating more sustainable forms of tourism through:

- Employment: commitments from tourism companies to employ local people at fair wages and provide job training
- Local economic linkages: local procurement of food, supplies and services
- Minimising negative cultural and environmental impacts: through sustainable charters and codes adopted by large industries (such as abiding by international environmental and social regulations which may be ignored or not monitored in local destinations). Also through corporate reporting, education to consumers and businesses on traditional cultures and behaviour will be promoted
- Participation in planning and decision-making processes: through the procurement of local operators and services, community and local views will be fed back through the supply chain
- Linking quality assurance and certification: if buyers adopt criteria for their suppliers, suppliers may use certification programs to obtain the necessary training and knowledge to attain baseline or minimum standards

Recommendations: Encourage SMEs to focus their criteria to match those of international buyers so that they can align themselves with buyers who demand CSR criteria.

Governments should increase pressure on industry associations to ensure supply-chain practices are publicly accessible Provide standards for reporting, including common terminology, disclosure of information, methods of evaluating performance, quality management systems and assessment of evaluation bodies

Provide incentives for both small and larger tourism businesses to adopt supply chain sustainable tourism/CSR criteria. Incentives suggested include:

* Rewarding good practice or suppliers that meet minimum standards set
* Facilitating more business to business marketing-through distribution channels; instead of business to consumer marketing as this is not yet strong enough to influence the consumer
* Promoting best practices that showcase that success needs to include Profit and Returns on Investment in order to build the business case for the industry

Ensure low income countries incorporate tourism into their development policies and provide incentives for larger international companies to adopt certification measures and supply chain guidelines which will benefit SMEs and the local community.

Business reporting on social and environmental issues has potentially helped increase loyalty and a sense of distinctiveness. Some businesses ascertain that promoting their responsible/ sustainable business practices can give them a better market position by distinguishing and differentiating their approach.

Initiatives must be industry led as labour standards and other elements of sustainability are not visible to the consumer but crucial nonetheless to the long-term wellbeing of the destination. CSR reporting means a company is more transparent and accountable to external stakeholders, enabling investors to avoid risk and consumers to support more sustainable businesses, therefore having a multiplier effect. Reporting was deemed essential by the corporate interviewees to ensure that efforts are maintained, and initiatives continued. It also makes it possible for others in the supply chain and at destinations to duplicate successful practices. Currently there is low brand loyalty as consumers make decisions primarily based on price; CSR initiatives could potentially lead to increased brand loyalty and product differentiation. As there is currently little consumer support or awareness, information databases need to be linked so that environmental and social criteria can be provided to the client when they are booking their holiday.

Recommendations: Governments should focus their capacity-building efforts on suppliers, using such methods as legislated compliance (e.g., environmental, reputation and business probity), ensuring that resources are available for training and learning by suppliers and, where needed, fill resource gaps Increase public-private partnerships of training for environmental and social awareness and mitigation strategies Offer incentives and reporting guidelines to the tourism sector distributed through industry associations. Support training and sharing of best practices Encourage industry associations to make adherence to sustainable or responsible tourism policies a condition of membership and to report on progress Encourage CSR reporting from tour operators, airlines, cruises, hotels and destinations themselves so that they can understand the impact they themselves are having. Reporting will also provide measurable criteria by which companies and destinations can be compared.

Providing for a Sustainable Industry

To ensure that a more sustainable form of tourism is pursued, there is a need for stricter legislation coupled with joined-up government. Both industry and certification bodies interviewed noted that a such an approach adopts a concerted effort using all the arms of government-central, regional and local government and public agencies, as well as the private and voluntary sectors to form private/public partnerships. Integration into wider sustainable development plans as well as destination management plans is imperative, and a bottom-up as well as a top-down policy approach is needed.

Pressure on governments to incorporate tourism into their wider development policies may help raise awareness about the need for sustainable tourism and the benefits of long-term planning approaches, however there is a strong need for training of employees and industry players at the local level. Stricter legislation in low income and developing countries is often fraught with issues of corruption, lack of monitoring and lack of governance, as there are often neither tourism master plans that incorporate sustainable tourism practices or measures nor incentives for industry to adopt them on their own initiative. To date, few developing countries have imposed social or environmental criteria to foreign investors, seeing only short term economic gains instead of long-term, holistic, sustainable tourism development.

Recommendations: Ensure transparency through a multi-stakeholder process Include sustainable tourism in all levels of policy formulation from national tourism policy to local destination management plans Recognise the difference between local vs. international stakeholders and the incentives or encouragement they need to adopt more sustainable forms of tourism practices Ensure that tourism is seen as a core or pillar in countries' wider development plans and policies

Ensure that development of tourism in low income countries includes education and training of local communities Provide for sustainability experts to be included in new tourism developments to ensure social and environmental criteria are considered in proposals and funding Ensure stakeholders are identified and consulted throughout the tourism development process and play an active role in decision-making Promote positive investment structures for integrated tourism master planning-focusing on risk mitigation through sustainable development and planning of tourism.

Sustainable tourism can help overcome many of the negative impacts associated with tourism development. Based on the interviews conducted, it is clear that guidelines alone are not strong enough to overcome the short-term profit motive of many operators, governments and destinations. At the same time, national certification programs are too numerous, with too many varying criteria, and not enough accredited product to be effective at this point in time. The analysis indicated that there are emerging trends and recommendations to be gained from this examination, however, it is not suggested that these codes or schemes are standardised within the tourism sector, nor is there a convergence of themes within them with the exception of the International Labour Organisation (ILO) and environmental criteria which often addresses similar issues of waste, water and energy management.

In summary, the conclusions of this report are fourfold. First, there is little overt demand for sustainable tourism therefore more research is needed to determine how product can be shifted to include sustainability. If the consumer and the industry are driven by price then there is a need to re-think the strategy of how to include sustainability within current cost structures. Second, there is low awareness and success of certification programs to date.

There is a need to further develop the concept of an international certification label for the travel and tourism industry that is inclusive (environmental, social, cultural etc.), affordable, monitored, and reported. As there are already a number of recognised and internationally accepted schemes, these should be promoted to extend their reach rather than developing new schemes which add to the confusion of both the industry and the consumer.

Third, in order to achieve more sustainable forms of tourism, it needs to move away from voluntary measures towards reporting where progress can be measured and buyers and suppliers held accountable for their actions.

Fourth, CSR could help with a number of issues facing tourism with regard to promoting sustainable tourism practices, however, industry must see government involvement and support if they are to increase their own involvements in CSR. There is a need for governments to step up to the challenge of ensuring more sustainable forms of tourism will be supported and to reassure investors and players in the tourism sector that government will support and encourage sustainable tourism management and development.

The purpose of this checklist is to attempt to align CSR practices within the tourism industry and public sector development of tourism. It contains a series of criteria that strive for optimal roles for good business practices and development. It should be noted that different criteria will be different for each sector of the industry (for example airlines would not be operating tours or tour operators would not be gaining acquiring land). In addition, due to the nature of the tourism industry, many businesses within this sector may be too small to fulfil all criteria and this tool should be used as a guideline only.

A number of elements of this checklist are critical to ensure the development of a sustainable tourism industry. This does not mean that other elements are not important, however, the elements marked with an * are the minimum standards for which broad enforcement/compliance is desirable and realistic. It should be noted that different countries will have different laws and regulations, and that basic international standards as set out by ILO and other such organizations should be followed in due process.

General Policies and Planning

- Policies to accommodate cultural customs, traditions and practices of staff throughout the organisation*
- Disclosure of loans, monies and taxes from third parties*
- Policy to support voluntary eco-labels and certification where possible
- Public disclosure of health and safety policy for operations, staff, end-user and management in accordance with national and international laws*
- Annual environmental, social and economic report available in public domain*
- Policy and compliance of anti-corruption measures*

Management Systems

- Governance structure*
- Management systems*
- Corporate accountability and risk assurance committee
- Compliance with local laws and regulations*

Employee/HR Principles

- Clear policy and guidelines on labour standards in accordance with local labour law *
- Established working hours and terms of overtime, sick leave*
- Abolishment of child labour, sexual discrimination, forced, bonded or compulsory labour*
- No tolerance of physical, psychological violence or verbal abuse*
- Recognition of right of employee to be represented by trade unions or other associations and recognition for negotiations on behalf of associations*

- Recognition and access for employee feedback and established mechanisms for grievances, redress, appeal
- Respect for human rights (including indigenous and tribal people)*
- Compliance with ILO conventions on child and forced labour*
- Recognise freedom of association; non-discrimination; programmes to combat sexual exploitation of children and to combat and mitigate the social impacts of HIV/AIDS; citizen participation in planning process*
- Provide evidence of recruiting local residents (including destination nationals) for destination posts including management positions (in accordance with local and international law)
- Preference to local employment (within legal constraints)
- Established wages consistent with national standard*
- Honoured reasonable employee benefits-Access to health care, dental, vacation pay, maternity rights, meals or food allowance, transportation allowance, travel, performance bonuses*
- On-the job training for skills and upgrading of skills
- Training for environmental and cultural sensitivity-both within community, corporate culture and to tourists*
- Fair redundancy, compensation and termination terms*

Note: *Many labour standards should reflect compliance with ILO standards Supply chain /procurement procedures*

- Provision of purchasing of local food and equipment from local community
- Creation of networks of environmentally/socially responsible businesses within the destination area
- Use of locally sourced and produced materials, foods, etc. (within legal constraints)
- Describe processes through which suppliers, by type, are consulted during development and implementation of the supply chain management policy,
- Description and disclosure of supply chain policy and targets for social, environmental and economic measures

- Description of suppliers who have sustainability policies and implemented a sustainability management system and/or have a staff person with management responsibility for corporate sustainability.
- Adoption of fair competitive practices for procurement and service contracts*
- Provision of information on quality of products and quality standards
- Fair payment of contracts and service agreements within national legal standards*
- Applied health and safety practices in accordance with national and international laws for suppliers and purchasers*
- Promotion and public encouragement of environmentally and social practices within supply chain
- Published supply chain practices code
- Promotion of labour standards through supply chain

Environmental Reporting/Management Systems

- Established policy and compliance with local and international environmental management, transport and hazardous waste principles*
- Established formal Environmental Management System (EMS) (performance based)
- Disclosure of improved EMS management, operations and organizational structures (attempt to integrate EIA into standard EMS)
- Annual environmental report
- Policy and timely disclosure of environmental reporting to shareholders and public stakeholders including:
- Assessment of significant risk of products, services and/or operations*
- Incorporation of risk assessment and mitigation*
- Conducted and application of environmental impact assessment (EIA) in all new building or construction in accordance to international and local laws*

- Conducted independent EIA to assess and avoid conflict for both environmental implications as well as social/ community implications-obtain clear permission/license to progress from both environmental and social community*

Environmental Management

- Incorporation of published standards for new siting and design for new construction, refurbishment and renovation of property
- Consultation with affected stakeholders regarding risk mitigation
- Disclosure of environmental risks to affected stakeholders within reasonable timeframe*
- Established effective procedures to address environmental damage to resources and risk mitigation plan to overcome hazards or deterioration*
- Environmental impact assessment checklist or guideline to assess adverse social impacts
- Support of conservation efforts
- Standard training of risk management, environmental awareness of products and services*
- Established tour size (tours or excursions group sizes for tours are kept to minimum size (under 16 passengers)
- Established tourist/resident ratio on peak days or season*
- Established standards for impacts for specialized tourism products/services (golf, diving, beaches, hiking, heritage sites, etc.) *
- Use of sustainable forms of tourism for touring or use of low emission gasoline
- Established measures to increase public access, visual and landscape impacts
- Assessment and measures for protection of local Flora y Fauna, wildlife, open spaces and forest, biodiversity, marine/eco/terrestrial habitats, water, air and noise*
- Establishment of Green areas and gardens
- Mitigation of visual and landscape impacts

- Established appropriate scale for design and building of tourist facilities/accommodation
- Use of appropriate building materials (aesthetically sensitive to area and renewable where possible)
- Environmental education to staff, management and consumers of risks and possible reduction of energy, water and waste

Water

- Efficient use of water*
- Reporting on usage of potable water
- Re-use of grey water

Energy

- Use of renewal energy sources*
- Reduced use where possible of energy intensive practices*
- Reporting on fuel usage cost, CO2 emissions Usage of alternate and other energy sources, including solar, wind, geothermal, biomass, small-scale hydro energy, and methane based composting systems
- Waste
- Compliance with national and international regulations of hazardous waste*
- Provision of consumption of annual waste
- Optimal use of Non-corrosive biodegradable chemicals / cleaning products*
- Recycled / eco-friendly products, Post-consumer recycled paper and products
- Established recycling program
- Reduction of non renewable resources where possible *

Pollution

- Assessment and mitigation of noise and air pollution
- Assessment and mitigation of air quality

Guests

- Encouraging responsible use of alcohol

- Evidence of environmentally friendly materials for guest/ client promotional materials
- Education to consumers about local traditions/cultures*
- Education of ecological and biodiversity to guests*
- Assurance that guests do not purchase products made from endangered species*
- Responsible advertising customer satisfaction and feedback
- Encourage customer engagement through
- feedback systems
- awareness and education means surrounding environmental and social issues and protection Community engagement and benefit
- Training programs extended to local community
- Planning gains-infrastructure or public building (e.g. hospitals) that are donated through development
- Appropriate land acquisition *
- Accessibility for public and local community to beaches and attractions and special consideration given regarding local rates and membership*
- Established and accessible community feedback system for feedback and participation in new development*
- Disclosure to employees and community of health and safety risk as well as occupational hazards/diseases/health risks
- Established policy or guidelines for community engagement and non-commercial stakeholders (community groups, NGOs, non-shareholding government authorities, universities etc.)*
- Recognition and protection of the integrity of the community social structure*
- Recognition and respect for local tribal and indigenous groups*

Health and Safety

- Accident and insurance prevention*
- Senior management accountability

- Regular training*
- Systems to respond to and prevent threats
- Clean bathroom, potable water and food storage
- Established house keeping standards
- Clear policies and guidelines established for health and safety measures including accidents and disease*
- Clear policies and guidelines developed for fair and equitable hiring/termination
- Clear policies and guidelines developed to address social issues (e.g. aids/HIV, etc in accordance with national standards) *
- Established effective management system for promoting health and safety*

7

SERVICES OF TRAVEL AGENCIES IN TOURISM

Tourism in India has registered significant growth in the recent years. In 1951, international tourist arrival stood at around 17 thousand only while the same has now gone up to 3.91 million in 2005. The upward trend is expected to remain firm in the coming years. Tourism is also one of the sectors, which employs the largest number of manpower.

There has been a remarkable growth in the recent years, in foreign tourist arrivals to India due to various efforts made, including promoting India through the "incredible India" campaign in overseas markets.

According to the Ministry of Tourism, during January-June 2007, total tourist inflow stood at 23,86887 as against 21,32174 in the same period last year. The total foreign exchange earnings during January-June 2007 stood at US$ 3589.83 million against US$ 3037.04 million for the same period in 2006.

Indian tourism is one of the most diverse products on the global scene. India has 26 world heritage sites. It is divided into 25 bio-geographic zones and has wide ranging eco tourism products. Apart from this, India has a 6,000 km coastline and dozens of beaches.

India's great ethnic diversity translates into a wide variety of cuisine and culture. India also has a large number of villages, plantations and adventure locations.

India is home to a great variety of wildlife and its reserves are well known throughout the world. It also has one of the world's biggest railway systems opening possibilities for those interested in rail tourism. India also has excellent hospitals offering affordable medicare and traditional healthcare systems like Ayurveda. In addition to this India organizes numerous fairs and festivals, which are quite attractive to foreigners.

Tourism sector holds immense potential for Indian economy. Tourism sector has the potential to stimulate other economic sectors through its backward and forward linkages and cross-sectional synergies with sectors like agriculture, horticulture, poultry, handicrafts, transport, construction, etc. Recogonising the importance of this sector, in the recent country budget, the provision for building tourist infrastructure has been increased from US$ 95.6 million in 2006-07 to US$ 117.5 million in 2007-08.

AN ENGINE OF ECONOMIC GROWTH

According to the World Travel and Tourism Council, India' s travel and tourism (T&T) industry is expected to contribute 2.1 percent to Gross Domestic Product in 2006 (INR 713.8 billion or US$16.3 billion).

In the first half of the Annual Plan period of 2005-2006, the Ministry of Tourism has taken several initiatives in the field of infrastructure development and positioning Indian tourism as a major engine for economic growth. These include:

- o Emphasis for developing the existing and new destinations to world-class standards.
- o Improvement of connectivity to important destinations
- o Identification of 10-15 new destinations/ circuits by each state /UT for development to world class standard with all the required infrastructure components.

A VERSATILE SECTOR

- o *Medical Tourism*: The Ministry of Tourism has taken several initiatives, in partnership with the private sector, to promote India as a destination for medical tourism and make it a global health destination. Several promotional measures like road shows and developing publicity material have been undertaken for the same.Some of the main advantages that India has are as under:

  * It has world class doctors and hospitals
  * The cost of treatment is1/5th of costs in the west
  * Eastern healthcare wisdom along with the expertise of western medicine

- *Rural Tourism*: A concept of rural tourism has been developed for showcasing the art, crafts and culture of rural India and for creating gainful employment in villages with tourism potential. Rural tourism holds immense potential for India, where 74 per cent of the population resides in its 7 million villages.Thrust is being provided to rural tourism to spread tourism and its socio-economic benefits to rural regions.
- *Cruise Tourism*: India has a vast and beautiful coastline and hence the potential to develop cruise tourism.
- *Convention Tourism*: International convention Centres of the global standard is considered to be one of the important segments for promoting India as an attractive tourist destination in the global market. Ministry of finance has already identified New Delhi, Mumbai, Bangalore, Goa and Jaipur for opening of world-class convention centres. Several initiatives have been taken up by way of public-private partnership to develop small convention centres of high standard. India is undoubtedly a unique Conference Destination as it offers cultural and heritage sites, the exotic and mystical, excellent facilities of beach and adventure holidays which can be combined as pre and post conference tours.

Investment Opportunities

- Hotel industry
- Service apartments
- Adventure Tourism
- Health Tourism
- Convention centres
- Wildlife Tourism
- Highway Tourism
- Amusement Parks

India	INR (Billion)	% of Tot 2006	Growth*	INR (Billion)	% of Tot 2016	Growth**
Personal Travel and Tourism	935.4	3.8	6.9	2,857.1	4.0	6.7
Business Travel	260.8	-	8.3	822.1	-	7.0
Government Expenditures	41.2	1.0	7.7	119.0	1.0	6.1
Capital Investment	681.5	7.2	8.3	2,314.2	7.5	7.8
Visitor Exports	302.2	3.3	10.9	1,031.3	1.3	7.8
Other Exports	121.5	1.3	14.6	984.6	1.3	17.6
Travel and Tourism Demand	2,342.7	-	8.4	8,128.2	-	8.0
T&T Industry GDP	713.8	2.1	7.2	1,881.9	1.7	5.1
T&T Economy GDP	1,827.6	5.3	7.8	5,542.3	5.0	6.6
T&T Industry Employment	10,679.6	2.4	0.8	10,591.8	2.0	-0.1
T&T Economy Employment	24,349.2	5.4	1.4	27, 015.8	5.1	1.0

Source: World Travel and Tourism Council

*2006 real growth adjusted for inflation (%)

**2007-2016 annualized real growth adjusted for inflation(%)

POLICIES AND SCHEMES OF TOURISM

In order to develop tourism in India in a systematic manner, position it as a major engine of economic growth and to harness its direct and multiplier effects for employment and poverty eradication in an environmentally sustainable manner, the National Tourism Policy was formulated in the year 2002. Broadly, the "Policy" attempts to:-

- o Position tourism as a major engine of economic growth;
- o Harness the direct and multiplier effects of tourism for employment generation, economic development and providing impetus to rural tourism;
- o Focus on domestic tourism as a major driver of tourism growth.
- o Position India as a global brand to take advantage of the burgeoning global travel trade and the vast untapped potential of India as a destination;

- o Acknowledges the critical role of private sector with government working as a pro-active facilitator and catalyst;
- o Create and develop integrated tourism circuits based on India's unique civilization, heritage, and culture in partnership with States, private sector and other agencies; and
- o Ensure that the tourist to India gets physically invigorated, mentally rejuvenated, culturally enriched, spiritually elevated and "feel India from within".

SCHEME FOR PRODUCT DEEVELOPMENT

The focus under this scheme is on improving the existing products and developing new tourism products to world class standards. For infrastructure and product development, the Ministry of Tourism has been providing Central Financial Assistance to the State Governments during the 9th Five Year Plan which resulted in strengthening of the infrastructure and product development in the country.

The scheme has been restructured during the 10th Five Year Plan to meet the present day infrastructure requirements. The past experience had been that a large number of small projects had been funded under the Scheme, spreading the resources very thinly, which at times had not created the desired impact. The focus in the Tenth Plan has been to fund large projects of infrastructure or product development in an integrated manner.

Under the revised scheme, the destinations are carefully selected based on the tourism potential. Master planning of these destinations is undertaken so as to develop them in an integrated holistic manner. The master plan is suppose to tie up all backward and forward linkages, including environmental considerations. Realizing the importance of destination development, the total outlay for this sector has been increased substantially. Important tourist destinations in each State, in consultation with the State Governments, are taken up for development. This include activities ranging from preparation of master plans to implementation of the master plans. The destinations are selected in consultation with the State/UT Governments.

The focus under this scheme is on improving the existing products and developing new tourism products to world class standards. For infrastructure and product development, the Ministry of Tourism has been providing Central Financial Assistance to the State Governments during the 9th Five Year Plan which resulted in strengthening of the infrastructure and product development in the country.

The scheme has been restructured during the 10th Five Year Plan to meet the present day infrastructure requirements. The past experience had been that a large number of small projects had been funded under the Scheme, spreading the resources very thinly, which at times had not created the desired impact. The focus in the Tenth Plan has been to fund large projects of infrastructure or product development in an integrated manner.

Under the revised scheme, the Destinations are carefully selected based on the tourism potential. Master planning of these destinations is undertaken so as to develop them in an integrated holistic manner. The master plan is suppose to tie up all backward and forward linkages, including environmental considerations. Realizing the importance of destination development, the total outlay for this sector has been increased substantially. Important tourist destinations in each State, in consultation with the State Governments, are taken up for development. This include activities ranging from preparation of master plans to implementation of the master plans. The destinations are selected in consultation with the State/UT Governments.

1. *Definition of a Destination:* Destination is a place of tourist interest. For being eligible under this scheme the destination must be among the most visited sites in the State, or a recognized Heritage Monument. A group of attractions located in the same village, town or city would also qualify.
2. *Selection of the Destination:* The destinations will be selected in consultation with State Governments/UT Administrations.
3. *Finalisation of the Project:* The identification of the project, the implementing agency, and the mode of channelisation of funds would be done in consultation with the State Govt./UT Administration. The Ministry of Tourism would bear 100% of the project cost (except refurbishment of monuments which would be funded on 66:33 basis, i.e.

66% CFA) based on the project plan and estimates submitted, excluding the items which are the exclusive responsibility of the State Governments as listed in para 5. The maximum amount that could be sanctioned under this scheme would be Rs. 5.0 crores.

The State Governments would have to bear the responsibility including for the items mentioned in para 5. However for projects in the 'Protected Areas' under ASI or the State Archaeology Deptt. The implementing agency would be CPWD or any other agency to be decided by the Ministry. of Tourism. In such cases funds would be directly released to such implementing agency.

4. *Monitoring Committee:* State level Monitoring Committees would be set up under the Chairmanship of the respective Secretary (Tourism). This Committee would comprise of a nominee of the Ministry of Tourism, Government. of India and a nominee of the executing agency.

5. *Funding Pattern:* All permissible activities will be fully funded by the Ministry of tourism, Government of India. However, the State/UT Governments will be fully responsible for the following components of the project:

   i) Making the land available for development.

   ii) Implementation of rehabilitation package, where shifting of dwelling or commercial units is required. However, the Government of India would provide assistance for construction of Tourist Reception Centres including shopping complexes to house the displaced shops.

   iii) Maintenance and management of the assets created.

   iv) Any other item decided by the High Power Committee.

   v) External infrastructure like Water Supply, Electricity and Roads

6. *Permissible Activities:* The following works may be taken up under the Scheme:

   i) Improvement of the surroundings of the destination. This would include activities like landscaping, development of parks, fencing, compound wall etc.

ii) Illumination of the Tourist destination and the area around/SEL Shows etc.

iii) Providing for improvement in solid waste management and sewerage management.

iv) Construction of Budget Accommodation, Wayside Amenities.

v) Procurement of equipment directly related to tourism, like Water Sports, Adventure Sports, Eco-friendly modes of transport for moving within the Tourism Zone.

vi) Construction of public buildings which are required to be demolished because of implementation of the Master Plan.

vii) Refurbishment of the Monuments. (66:33 basis, i.e. CFA of 66%)

viii) Signages.

ix) Tourist Arrival Centres/Reception Centres/ Interpretation Centres

x) Other work/activities directly related to tourism.

7. *Release of Funds:* The funds would be released to the executing agency as indicated in Para 3 above.

8. *Installments of Release:* On sanction of a work, the first installment of 30% of the approved CFA will be released. The second installment of 50% will be released on receipt of the UC of the first installment. The balance would be released on the completion of the work.

9. *Following Codal Formalities:* The executing agency shall follow all codal formalities while awarding contracts and procurement of equipment and ensure complete transparency in its transactions.

10. *Management of Assets Created:* The infrastructure and assets created will be maintained and managed by the State/UT Governments or their agencies with no financial commitment to Govt. of India except those assets created in protected areas of ASI.

11. *Prescription of the Schedule of Rates:* While executing the works the executing agency shall follow the Schedule of rates prescribed by the CPWD or the State PWD.

12. *Submission of the Utilisation Certificates:* The executing agency shall furnish through the State Government the Utilisation Certificate for release of the second installment. A Completion Certificate has also to be furnished through the State Government before the release of the final installment. In case the works are executed by a Central Agency in a 'Protected Area' the UCs would be obtained from them directly.

ASSISTANCE FOR LARGE REVENUE GENERATING PROJECTS

It is recognized that the development of tourism infrastructure projects requires very large investment that may not be possible out of the budgetary resources of the Government of India alone. In order to remove these shortcomings and to bring in private sector, corporate and institutional resources as well as techno-managerial efficiencies, it is proposed to promote large revenue generating projects for development of tourism infrastructure in public private partnerships and in partnerships with other Government / Semi-Government agencies.

Large revenue generating project, which can be admissible for assistance under this scheme, should be a project, which is also a tourist attraction, or used by tourists and generates revenue through a levy of fee or user charges on the visitors. Projects like Tourist trains, Cruise vessels, Cruise Terminals, Convention Centres, Golf Courses etc. would qualify for assistance. However, this is only an illustrative list.

Hotel & Restaurant component will not be eligible for assistance under the scheme either on a stand-alone basis or as an integral part of some other project. Besides hotel & restaurants, procurement of vehicles and sports facilities like stadiums will also not be eligible for assistance under the scheme.

Integrated Development of Tourist Circuits

Under this Central Financial Assistance scheme the Ministry of Tourism Government of India has been extending assistance to States for development of tourism infrastructure. Experience has shown that in the past funds under the CFA have been used to fund a large number of small isolated projects, spread throughout the length and breadth of the country resulting in the resources being spread very thinly. Therefore, in order to provide quick and substantial impact, during the 10th Five Year Plan, this new scheme of Integrated Development of Tourist Circuits have been taken up. The objective of the scheme is to identify tourist circuits in the country on an annual basis, and develop them to international standards. The aim is to provide all infrastructure facilities required by the tourists within these circuits. The Ministry of Tourism aim at convergence of resources and expertise through coordinated action with States/UTs and private sector.

Under this Central Financial Assistance scheme the Ministry of Tourism Government of India has been extending assistance to States for development of tourism infrastructure. Experience has shown that in the past funds under the CFA have been used to fund a large number of small isolated projects, spread throughout the length and breadth of the country resulting in the resources being spread very thinly. Therefore, in order to provide quick and substantial impact, during the 10th Five Year Plan, this new scheme of Integrated Development of Tourist Circuits have been taken up. The objective of the scheme is to identify tourist circuits in the country on an annual basis, and develop them to international standards. The aim is to provide all infrastructure facilities required by the tourists within these circuits. The Ministry of Tourism aim at convergence of resources and expertise through coordinated action with States/UTs and private sector.

Definition of a Circuit: A tourist Circuit is defined as a route on which at least three major tourist destinations are located such that none of these are in the same town, village or city. At the same time they are not separated by a large distance such that a tourist would not like to cover them in a sequence. It should have well defined entry and exist points. A tourist who enters at the entry point should get motivated to visit all the places identified on the circuit. The objective of having a tourist circuit is to increase the total number of visits to all the destinations on the circuit on one hand and to provide to the tourist the attraction of all the destinations located on the circuit.

Identification of the Circuit: The Circuit to be taken up will be identified by the Ministry of Tourism at the beginning of each year, in consultation with the State Government. While selecting the Circuit, the tourism potential of the places included would be borne in mind. It will be ensured that a circuit is identified for each State/UT in the full Plan period. A circuit could be limited to a State or it could be a regional circuit covering more than a State/UT.

The identification of the project, the implementation agency, and the mode of channelisation of funds would be done in consultation with the State Government/UT Administration. However, for projects in the 'protected areas' under ASI, the implementing agency would be ASI/CPWD or any other agency to be decided by the Ministry of Tourism. The Ministry of Tourism would bear 100% of the project cost (Capital cost only, except for Refurbishment of Monuments where it would be 66:33 i.e. CFA of 66%) based on the project plan and estimates submitted, excluding the items which are the exclusive responsibility of the State Governments as listed in para 3. The maximum amount that could be sanctioned under this scheme would be Rs. 8.00 crores.

Funding Pattern: All activities agreed to by the Ministry of Tourism will be funded on 100% basis i.e. 100% of the capital cost would be borne by the Ministry of Tourism, Government of India, subject to the ceiling of Rs. 8 crores (except, for refurbishment of Monuments where CFA would be 66%). However the State/ UT Governments will be fully responsible for the following components of the project.

i) Making the land available for development.

ii) Implementation of rehabilitation package, where shifting of dwelling or commercial units is required. However the Government of India would provide assistance for construction of Tourist reception centers including shopping complexes to house the displaced shops.

iii) Maintenance and management of the assets created.

iv) Any other item decided by the High Power Committee.

v) External infrastructure, like water supply, Electricity and Roads.

Permissible Activities: The following works may be taken up under the Scheme-

i. Improvement of the surroundings of the destination. This would include activities like landscaping, development of parks, fencing, compound wall etc.

ii. Illumination of the Tourist destination and the area around the SEL Shows etc.

iii. Providing for improvement in solid waste management and sewerage management.

iv. Construction of budget accommodation, wayside amenities.

v. Procurement of equipment directly related to tourism, like water sports, adventure sports, eco-friendly modes of transport for moving within the tourism zone.

vi. Construction of public buildings which are required to be displaced because of implementation of the master plan.

vii. Refurbishment of the monuments.

viii. Signages.

ix. Tourist arrival centers/reception centers/interpretation centers.

x. Other work/activities directly related to tourism.

Release of Financial Assistance: On sanction of a work, the first installment of 30% of the approved CFA will be released, and the second installment of 50% will be released on receipt of utilization certificate of the first installment. The balance would be released on completion of the work.

Codal Formalities: The executing agency shall follow all codal formalities while awarding contracts and procurement of equipments an ensure complete transparency in its transactions.

Management of Assets Created: The infrastructure and assets created will be maintained and managed by the State Government/UT Administration of their agencies with no financial commitment to Government of India, except for those assets which are created in the 'protected areas' of ASI.

Prescription of the Schedule of Rates: While executing the works, the executing agency shall follow the Schedule of rates prescribed by the CPWD or the State PWD.

Submission of the Utilization Certificates: The executing agency shall furnish the utilization certificate through the State Government for release of second instalment, a completion certificate has also to be furnished through the State Government before the release of the final installment. In case the works are executed by a Central Agency in a 'protected area the UC would be obtained from them directly.

Monitoring Committee: A State level monitoring committee would be set up under the Chairmanship of the respective Secretary (Tourism) of the State Government. The Committee would comprise a nominee of the Ministry of Tourism of Government India, and a nominee of the executing agency.

RURAL TOURISM SCHEME

Tourism growth potential can be harnessed as a strategy for Rural Development. The development of a strong platform around the concept of Rural tourism is definitely useful for a country like India, where almost 74% of the population resides in its 7 million villages. Across the world the trends of industrialization and development have had an urban centric approach. Alongside, the stresses of urban lifestyles have led to a "counter-urbanization" syndrome.

This has led to growing interest in the rural areas. At the same time this trend of urbanization has led to falling income levels, lesser job opportunities in the rural areas leading to an urbanization syndrome in the rural areas. Rural Tourism is one of the few activities which can provide a solution to these problems. Besides, there are other factors which are shifting the trend towards rural tourism like increasing levels of awareness, growing interest in heritage and culture and improved accessibility, and environmental consciousness.

In the developed countries, this has resulted in a new style of tourism of visiting village settings to experience and live a relaxed and healthy lifestyle. This concept has taken the shape of a formal kind of Rural Tourism. Under this Scheme, thrust is to promote village tourism as the primary tourism product to spread tourism and its socio-economic benefits to rural and its new geographic regions. Key geographic regions are identified for development and promotion of Rural Tourism.

The implementation is done through a Convergence Committee headed by the District Collector. Activities like improving the environment, hygiene, infrastructure etc. are covered for assistance. Apart from providing financial assistance, the focus is to tap the resources available under different schemes of Department of Rural Development, State Governments and other concerned Departments of the Government of India.

Tourism growth potential can be harnessed as a strategy for Rural Development. The development of a strong platform around the concept of Rural tourism is definitely useful for a country like India, where almost 74% of the population resides in its 7 million villages. Across the world the trends of industrialization and development have had an urban centric approach. Alongside, the stresses of urban lifestyles have led to a "counter-urbanization" syndrome.

This has led to growing interest in the rural areas. At the same time this trend of urbanization has led to falling income levels, lesser job opportunities in the rural areas leading to an urbanization syndrome in the rural areas. Rural Tourism is one of the few activities which can provide a solution to these problems. Besides, there are other factors which are shifting the trend towards rural tourism like increasing levels of awareness, growing interest in heritage and culture and improved accessibility, and environmental consciousness. In the developed countries, this has resulted in a new style of tourism of visiting village settings to experience and live a relaxed and healthy lifestyle.

This concept has taken the shape of a formal kind of Rural Tourism. Under this Scheme, thrust is to promote village tourism as the primary tourism product to spread tourism and its socio-economic benefits to rural and its new geographic regions. Key geographic regions are identified for development and promotion of Rural Tourism. The implementation is done through a Convergence Committee headed by the District Collector. Activities like improving the environment, hygiene, infrastructure etc. are covered for assistance. Apart from providing financial assistance, the focus is to tap the resources available under different schemes of Department of Rural Development, State Governments and other concerned Departments of the Government of India.

Definition of Rural Tourism: Any form of tourism that showcases the rural life, art, culture and heritage at rural locations, thereby benefiting the local community economically and socially as well as enabling interaction between the tourists and the locals for a more enriching tourism experience can be termed as rural tourism. Rural tourism is essentially an activity which takes place in the countryside. It is multi-faceted and may entail farm/agricultural tourism, cultural tourism, nature tourism, adventure tourism, and eco-tourism. As against conventional tourism, rural tourism has certain typical characteristics like; it is experience oriented, the locations are sparsely populated, it is predominantly in natural environment, it meshes with seasonality and local events and is based on preservation of culture, heritage and traditions.

Identification of Villages: Each State/UT Govt. would be requested to furnish one proposal for promotion of Rural tourism. Based on the merits and after a joint inspection by the Deptt. Of Tourism, and the State/UT Govt. if required ten proposals would be identified for implementation in the country.

Preparation of Detailed Plan for Implementation of the Project: After shortlisting the proposals, the State/UT Govts would be requested to draw up a detailed plan of action. The thrust here would be to achieve convergence between the different schemes of the Govt. of India and the State Govts. It should be ensured that atleast 50% of the project should be implemented through achieving convergence of different schemes. Assistance upto Rs. 3 lakhs would be provided to the State Govt. for engaging an expert for preparing the project report.

Assistance under the Scheme: A maximum of Rs. 50 lakhs would be sanctioned under this scheme. The activities listed under the para 5 could be taken up.

Permissible Activities: The following works may be taken up under the Scheme-

i) Improvement of the surroundings of the village. This would include activities like landscaping, development of parks, fencing, compound wall etc.

ii) Improvements to roads within the Panchayat limits. This shall not include any major road which connects the village.

iii) Illumination in the village.

iv) Providing for improvement in solid waste management and sewerage management.

v) Construction of Wayside Amenities.

vi) Procurement of equipments directly related to tourism, like Water Sports, Adventure Sports, Eco-friendly modes of transport for moving within the tourism zone.

vii) Refurbishment of the Monuments. (66:33 basis, i.e. CFA of 66%)

viii) Signages.

ix) Reception Centres.

x) Other work/activities directly related to tourism.

xi) Tourist Accommodation.

Constitution of a Convergence Committee: A Convergence Committee would be set up under the Collector to oversee the implementation of the project.

Execution of the Works: The execution of the work would be entrusted to any Central Govt./State Govt. agency and the funds would be released directly to the implementing agency by the Govt. of India as recommended by the State Govt.

Installments of Release: On sanction of a work the first installment of 30% of the sanctioned amount of CFA will be released. The second installment of 50% would be released on submission of the UC for the first installment. The balance would be released on the completion of the work.

Following Codal Formalities: The executing agency shall follow all codal formalities while awarding contracts and procurement of equipments and ensure complete transparency in its transactions.

Management of Assets Created: The infrastructure and assets created will be maintained and managed by the State/UT Governments or their agencies with no financial commitment to Govt. of India except those assets created in the protected areas of ASI.

Prescription of the Schedule of Rates: While executing the works the executing agency shall follow the Schedule of rates prescribed by the CPWD or the State PWD.

Submission of the Utilisation Certificates: The executing agency shall furnish the Utilisation Certificate through the State Government for release of the second installment. A Completion

Certificate has also to be furnished through the State Govt. before the release of the final installment.

Scheme of Assistance for Large Revenue Generating Projects

It is recognized that the development of tourism infrastructure projects requires very large investment that may not be possible out of the budgetary resources of the Government of India alone. In order to remove these shortcomings and to bring in private sector, corporate and institutional resources as well as techno-managerial efficiencies, it is proposed to promote large revenue generating projects for development of tourism infrastructure in public private partnerships and in partnerships with other Government / Semi-Government agencies.

Scope of the Scheme: Large revenue generating project, which can be admissible for assistance under this scheme, should be a project, which is also a tourist attraction, or used by tourists and generates revenue through a levy of fee or user charges on the visitors. Projects like Tourist trains, Cruise vessels, Cruise Terminals, Convention Centres, Golf Courses etc. would qualify for assistance. However, this is only an illustrative list.

Hotel & Restaurant component will not be eligible for assistance under the scheme either on a stand-alone basis or as an integral part of some other project. Besides hotel & restaurants, procurement of vehicles and sports facilities like stadiums will also not be eligible for assistance under the scheme.

Promoters of Project: While considering projects for Grant-in-aid under this scheme, priority will be given to projects promoted by private sector and the projects with public private partnership. However, in some cases where private sector participation is not possible or is not forthcoming, then the proposals/projects promoted by State Govts. State PSUs, Central Govt, Ministries/Departments like Railways, ASI and Central agencies like Port Trust and CPSEs will be eligible.

Eligibility for Assistance: Justification for providing assistance/subsidy would be ascertained on the basis of feasibility study/DPR at the stage of consideration of the project by the Competent Authority. While selecting projects, priority would be given to projects which have strong private sector participation and involve least subsidy outgo. The projects selected for assistance under this scheme would not be eligible for subsidy from other schemes of Central Government or State Governments. Similarly, the projects which have already availed subsidy/financial assistance from any other scheme of the Central or State Govt., would not be eligible for Government of India assistance under this scheme.

Requirement of a Special Purpose Vehicle (SPV): A SPV would have to be set up by the implementing partners in case a private party is promoting the project, prior to the consideration of their project under this scheme. However, where the promoter of the project is a State Govt., State PSU or Central Agencies like Port trust or Central PSU, a separate SPV need not be required. In both the cases, a separate Project Management Group would be required and separate accounts would be maintained for the project.

The Project Management Group, where SPV has to be set up will consist of (i) MD/CEO of the SPV (ii) Project Director/ Manager (iii) Finance Director (iv) A representative of the State Govt. to be nominated by them. In the other cases, the Project Management Group will consist of (i) MD/CEO of State PSUs/ Central PSUs/Statutory Body, (ii) State Tourism Secretary (where State Govt. is directly involved), (iii) Project Director/Manager (iv) Finance Director of the Central/State PSU/Statutory Body or the Director-Finance Department of State Government.

Appraisal/Feasibility Report: All project proposals under this scheme must be accompanied by project appraisal carried out by an independent public financial institution. Grant-in-aid for preparation of DPR would be admissible at 50% of the actual cost subject to a maximum of Rs.25 lakh per project. No Grant-in-aid would be admissible for preparation of Feasibility Report.

Public financial institutions, in this case, will include a public financial institution under Section 4A of the Companies Act, 1956 and any institution notified by the Government as authorized to discharge the functions of a public financial institution under this Scheme. Anyone of these institutions could also fund the large revenue generating projects admissible under the scheme.

Norms for Funding: The amount of assistance under the scheme would be released to Government agencies or PSUs, if the project is promoted by them. In case a private party is promoting the project, the assistance would be released to SPV through the financial institutions. The quantum of subsidy for the projects will normally be determined through a competitive bidding process, with a cap of Rs.50 Cr. subject to a maximum of 25% of total project cost or 50% of equity contribution of the private promoter, whichever is lower. Specific reasons will be required to be brought on record in case competitive bidding process is not adopted for determining the quantum of subsidy. The minimum equity stake of the private promoter would be 51%, wherever the private sector participation is envisaged in the projects.

The total project cost in this case will mean the total of:

i. Capital cost of the project, including cost of land, material, labour, transport, consumables, testing, commissioning, overheads, contingencies, interest during construction, insurance and supervision (including any taxes and levies);

ii. Pre-operative cost such as formulation, development, design and engineering; and

Expenses related to fund mobilization if required, such as fees for financial services and brokerage.

The assistance would preferably be credit linked and back ended and would be released in three installments. The first installment, limited to 25% of the assistance to be provided by the Ministry, will be released only after 25% of the total cost of the project has been contributed by the promoters. The second installment, limited to 50% of the assistance to be provided by the Ministry, would be disbursed only after 50% of the promoter's amount is contributed. The last installment of balance 25% of the assistance, to be provided by the Ministry, will be released after the project is fully functional.

Recovery of Government Grant: In case the project does not succeed, and there is any default by the promotees, the Financial Institution can recover its loan component and also recover the Grant-in-aid component on behalf of Ministry of Tourism.

Approval Procedures: The project proposals will be appraised by SFC/EFC depending upon the cost of the project before obtaining approval of the competent expenditure sanctioning authority.

Monitoring and Evaluation: The financial institution, which is funding the project, will be responsible for regular monitoring and periodic evaluation of project compliance with agreed milestones and performance levels. In case there is no financial institution involved in the project then an agency will be designated while sanctioning the project for regular monitoring and evaluation as stated above and the cost for the same will be met out of the scheme. Ministry of Tourism will have a separate Monitoring Group consisting of the concerned Joint Secretary & Director in charge of the scheme alongwith Financial Controller to regularly monitor and review the sanctioned projects.

Scheme for Support to Public Private Partnerships in Infrastructure (Viability Gap Funding)

Development of infrastructure require large investments that cannot be undertaken out of public financing alone. Thus, in order to attract private capital as well as techno-managerial efficiencies associated with it, the government is committed to promoting Public-Private Partnerships (PPPs) in infrastructure development. This scheme has been put into effect for providing financial support to bridge the viability gap of infrastructure projects undertaken through Public Private Partnerships.

Scheme for Support to Public Private Partnerships in Infrastructure (Viability Gap Funding)

Whereas the Government of India recognizes that there is significant deficit in the availability of physical infrastructure across different sectors and that this is hindering economic development;

Whereas the development of infrastructure requires large investments that cannot be undertaken out of public financing alone, and that in order to attract private capital as well as the techno-managerial efficiencies associated with it, the Government is committed to promoting Public Private Partnerships (PPPs) in infrastructure development; and Whereas the Government of India recognizes that infrastructure projects may not always be financially viable because of long gestation periods and limited financial returns, and that financial viability of such projects can be improved through Government support. Now, therefore, the Government of India has decided to put into effect the following scheme for providing financial support to bridge the viability gap of infrastructure projects undertaken through Public Private Partnerships.

Short Title and Extent

(i) This scheme will be called the Scheme for Financial Support to Public Private Partnerships (PPPs) in Infrastructure. It will be a Plan Scheme to be administered by the Ministry of Finance. Suitable budgetary provisions will be made in the Annual Plans on a year-to year basis.

(ii) The scheme shall come into force with immediate effect.

In this scheme, unless the context otherwise requires: Empowered Committee means a Committee under the Chairmanship of Secretary (Economic Affairs) and including Secretary Planning Commission, Secretary (Expenditure) and the Secretary of the line Ministry dealing with the subject.

Empowered Institution means an institution, company or inter-ministerial group designated by the Government for the purposes of this scheme.

Lead Financial Institution means the financial institution (FI) that is funding the PPP project, and in case there is a consortium of FIs, the FI designated as such by the consortium;

Private Sector Company means a company in which 51% or more of the subscribed and paid up equity is owned and controlled by a private entity;

Project Term means the duration of the contract or concession agreement for the PPP project;

Public Private Partnership (PPP) Project means a project based on a contract or concession agreement, between a Government or statutory entity on the one side and a private sector company on the other side, for delivering an infrastructure service on payment of user charges;

Total Project Cost means the lower of the total capital cost of the PPP Project: (a) as estimated by the government/statutory entity that owns the project, (b) as sanctioned by the Lead Financial Institution, and (c) as actually expended; but does not in any case include the cost of land incurred by the government/ statutory entity; and

Viability Gap Funding or Grant means a grant one-time or deferred, provided under this Scheme with the objective of making a project commercially viable.

Eligibility

1. In order to be eligible for funding under this Scheme, a PPP project shall meet the following criteria:
   (a) The project shall be implemented i.e. developed, financed, constructed, maintained and operated for the Project Term by a Private Sector Company to be selected by the Government or a statutory entity through a process of open competitive bidding; provided that in case of railway projects that are not amenable to operation by a Private Sector Company, the Empowered Committee may relax this eligibility criterion.
   (b) The PPP Project should be from one of the following sectors:
      (i) Roads and bridges, railways, seaports, airports, inland waterways;
      (ii) Power;
      (iii) Urban transport, water supply, sewerage, solid waste management and other physical infrastructure in urban areas;
      (iv) Infrastructure projects in Special Economic Zones; and
      (v) International convention centres and other tourism infrastructure projects;

      Provided that the Empowered Committee may, with approval of the Finance Minister, add or delete sectors/sub-sectors from the aforesaid list.
   (c) The project should provide a service against payment of a predetermined tariff or user charge.
   (d) The concerned Government/statutory entity should certify, with reasons;

(i) that the tariff/user charge cannot be increased to eliminate or reduce the viability gap of the PPP;

(ii) that the Project Term cannot be increased for reducing the viability gap; and

(iii) that the capital costs are reasonable and based on the standards and specifications normally applicable to such projects and that the capital costs cannot be further restricted for reducing the viability gap.

Government Support

(1) The total Viability Gap Funding under this scheme shall not exceed twenty percent of the Total Project Cost; provided that the Government or statutory entity that owns the project may, if it so decides, provide additional grants out of its budget, but not exceeding a further twenty percent of the Total Project Cost.

(2) Viability Gap Funding under this scheme will normally be in the form of a capital grant at the stage of project construction. Proposals for any other form of assistance may be considered by the Empowered Committee and sanctioned with the approval of Finance Minister on a case-by-case basis.

(3) Viability Gap Funding up to Rs. 100 crore (Rs. One hundred crore) for each project may be sanctioned by the Empowered Institution subject to the budgetary ceilings indicated by the Finance Ministry. Proposals up to Rs. 200 crore (Rs. Two hundred crore) may be sanctioned by the Empowered Committee, and amounts exceeding Rs. 200 crore may be sanctioned by the Empowered Committee with the approval of Finance Minister.

(4) Unless otherwise directed by the Ministry of Finance, the Empowered Institutions may approve project proposals with a cumulative capital outlay equivalent to ten times the budget provisions in the respective Annual Plan.

(5) In the first two years of operation of the Scheme, projects meeting the eligibility criteria will be funded on a first-come, first served basis. In later years, if need arises,

funding may be provided based on an appropriate formula, to be determined by the Empowered Committee, that balances needs across sectors in a manner that would make broad base the sectoral coverage and avoid pre-empting of funds by a few large projects.

Approval of Project Proposals

(1) Project proposals may be posed by a Government or statutory entity which owns the underlying assets. The proposals shall include the requisite information necessary for satisfying the eligibility criteria specified in paragraph 3 above.

(2) Projects based on standardized/model documents duly approved by the respective Government would be preferred. Stand-alone documents may be subjected to detailed scrutiny by the Empowered Institution.

(3) The Empowered Institution will consider the project proposals for Viability Gap Funding and may seek the required details for satisfying the eligibility criteria.

(4) Within 30 days of receipt of a project proposal, duly completed as aforesaid, the Empowered Institution shall inform the sponsoring Government/statutory entity whether the project is eligible for financial assistance under this Scheme. In case the project is based on standalone documents (not being duly approved model/ standard documents), the approval process may require an additional 60 (sixty) days.

(5) In the event that the Empowered Institution needs any clarifications or instructions relating to the eligibility of a project, it may refer the case to the Empowered Committee for appropriate directions.

(6) Notwithstanding the approvals granted under this scheme, projects promoted by the Central Government or its statutory entities shall be approved and implemented in accordance with the procedures specified from time to time.

(7) In cases where viability gap funding is budgeted under any on-going Plan scheme of the Central Government, the inter-se allocation Between such on-going scheme and

this scheme shall be determined by the Empowered Committee.

Procurement Process for PPP Projects

(1) The Private Sector Company shall be selected through a transparent and open competitive bidding process. The criterion for bidding shall be the amount of Viability Gap Funding required by a Private Sector Company for implementing the project where all other parameters are comparable.

(2) The Government or statutory entity proposing the project shall certify that the bidding process conforms to the provisions of this Scheme and convey the same to the Empowered Institution prior to disbursement of the Grant.

Appraisal and Monitoring by Lead Financial Institution

(1) Within four months from the date on which eligibility of the project is conveyed by the Empowered Institution to the concerned Government/ statutory entity, the PPP project shall be awarded in accordance with paragraph 6 above; provided that upon application made to it by the concerned Government/statutory entity, the Empowered Institution may extend this period by not more that two months at a time.

(2) The Lead Financial Institution shall, within three months from the date of bid award, present its appraisal of the project for the consideration and approval of the Empowered Institution; provided that upon application made to it by the concerned Government/statutory entity, the Empowered Institution may extend this period by not more than one month at a time.

(3) The Lead Financial Institution shall be responsible for regular monitoring and periodic evaluation of project compliance with agreed milestones and performance levels, particularly for the purpose of disbursement of Viability Gap Funding. It shall send quarterly progress reports to the Empowered Institution which will make a consolidated progress report once every quarter for review by the Empowered Committee.

Disbursement of Grant

(1) A Grant under this scheme shall be disbursed only after the Private Sector Company has subscribed and expended the equity contribution required for the project and will be released in proportion to debt disbursements remaining to be disbursed thereafter.

(2) The Empowered Institution will release the Grant to the Lead Financial Institution as and when due, and obtain reimbursement thereof from the Finance Ministry.

(3) The Empowered Institution, the Lead Financial Institution and the Private Sector Company shall enter into a Tripartite Agreement for the purposes of this scheme. The format of such Tripartite Agreement shall be prescribed by the Empowered Committee from time to time.

Revolving Fund

A revolving fund of Rs. 200 crore (Rs. Two hundred crore) shall be provided by the Finance Ministry to the Empowered Institution. The Empowered Institution shall disburse funds to the respective lead financial Institutions and claim reimbursement thereof from the Ministry of Finance.

Guidelines

The Guidelines issued vide Ministry of Finance Press Release as well as OM of F. No. 2/10/04-Inf. dated 19th August 2004 stands withdrawn with immediate effect.

MARKET DEVELOPMENT ASSISTANCE SCHEME

The Marketing Development Assistance Scheme (MDA), administered by the Ministry of Tourism, Government of India, provides financial support to approved tourism service providers (i.e. hoteliers, travel agents, tour operators, tourist transport operators etc., whose turnover include foreign exchange earnings also) for undertaking the following tourism promotional activities abroad:

(A) Sales-cum-study tour

(B) Participation in fairs/exhibitions

(C) Publicity through printed material

The Marketing Development Assistance Scheme (MDA), administered by the Ministry of Tourism, Government of India, provides financial support to approved tourism service providers (i.e. hoteliers, travel agents, tour operators, tourist transport operators etc., whose turnover include foreign exchange earnings also) for undertaking the following tourism promotional activities abroad:

Sale-cum-Study Tour

In order to encourage the small and medium level service providers to go and promote Indian tourism products abroad, Ministry of Tourism, Government of India provides financial assistance to approved tourism service providers for undertaking sale-cum-study tours to foreign countries.

Terms and Conditions

1. Financial Assistance would be permissible on travel expenses by air from India to any other country and/or by air/eurorail from one country to another country abroad, in economy excursion class fare @ 75% of the fare. This would, however be subject to an upper ceiling to Rs.75,000/-(Rupees seventy five thousands only) per tour. No financial assistance is provided for travel within India.
2. One sale-cum-study tour by the tourism service provider to a particular country in one financial year is eligible for MDA assistance.
3. The tour to single country or a group of countries shall be for a minimum of two-nights stay abroad excluding journey period.
4. Assistance shall be permissible to one regular employee/ Director/ partner/ proprietor of the company.
5. The assistance would be available to tourism service providers with foreign exchange earnings up to Rs.10.00 crores (Rupees ten crores only) during the preceding financial year.
6. The company shall not be under investigation or charged/ prosecuted/ debarred/ black listed by Ministry of Tourism, Govt. of India or any other Government Agency. The service provider should furnish a declaration to this effect.

7. The applicant would furnish a declaration in the prescribed format as " I hereby declare that I have not claimed/ received any financial assistance for this sale-cum-study tour from Government/Government Agency."
8. In case of more applications, priority would be given to those service providers who have not availed financial assistance in the past under MDA Scheme.

Procedure for Submission of Application

(i) The eligible tourism service provider shall obtain prior approval of the Department of Tourism, Government of India, before undertaking the tourism promotional activity/ tour abroad. The application shall be submitted direct to the Additional Director-General (Tourism), Department of Tourism, Transport Bhawan, Sansad Marg, New Delhi, in the prescribed format at least 14 days in advance, along with following documents:

1. Proof of approval of the company by Department of Tourism (Copy of approval letter is to be attached)
2. Certificate of Foreign Exchange Earnings duly certified by Chartered Accountant.
3. Details of financial assistance availed during the last three years from the Government including Ministry of Commerce/FIEO and Department of Tourism.

(ii) After undertaking the tourism promotional activity/tour abroad for which prior approval had been accorded by the DOT, tourism service provider would submit the application for MDA claim, in the prescribed format, to the Ministry of

Tourism, Government of India, immediately on return to India but positively within one month of his/her return to India, along with the following documents:

(a) Details of financial assistance availed during the last three years from the Government including Ministry of Commerce/FIEO & Department of Tourism.

(b) Certificate of Foreign Exchange Earnings duly certified by Chartered Accountant.

(c) Self-certified copy of approval certificate issued by the Ministry of Tourism.

(d) Legible photocopy of passport highlighting the entries about departure from India and arrival in India and also the countries visited. In case passport does not have arrival/departure dates regarding visits to various countries, documentary evidence such as Hotel Bills, Boarding pass, lodging pass, etc. may be submitted.

(e) Original air ticket/jacket used during the journey along with three self-certified photocopies. The following details should be given separately in a statement:

i) Name of the Traveller

ii) Ticket number

iii) Flight No.

iv) Date of Departure from India

v) Sectors/countries visited

vi) Class in which travelled

vii) Economy excursion class fare for sectors/countries visited.

(f) Brief Report about the tour and achievements.

(g) Claim form received after one month of return to India or wherein the deficiencies in the claim as intimated are not fully completed within 30 days of the date of information given, would not be entertained and would be rejected.

The Ministry of Tourism, Government of India provides financial assistance to approved tourism service providers for participation in tourism related trade fairs and exhibitions abroad.

1) Financial Assistance would be permissible on travel expenses by air from India to any other country & by air/eurorail from one country to another country abroad, in economy excursion class fair and/or charges of the built up furnished stall, electricity and water charges etc. @75% to the service providing companies. This would, however, be subject to an upper ceiling of Rs.1,10,000/- (Rupees One Lakh and Ten Thousand only) per participation. No financial assistance is provided for travel within India.

2) A maximum of only five participations in a particular trade fair/exhibition by a tourism service provider would be eligible for MDA assistance.
3) Assistance for travel expenses would be permissible to one regular employee/ Director/partner/proprietor of the company.
4) The assistance would be available to companies with foreign exchange earnings up to Rs.10.00 crores (Rupees Ten Crores only) during the preceding financial year.
5) The company shall not be under investigation or charged/ prosecuted/ debarred/ black-listed by Ministry of Tourism, Government of India or any other Government Agency. The service provider should furnish a declaration to this effect.
6) The applicant would furnish a declaration in the prescribed format as " I hereby declare that I have not claimed/ received any financial assistance for participation in this fair/exhibition from Government/Government Agency."
7) In case of more applications, priority would be given to those service providers who have not availed financial assistance in the past under MDA Scheme.

Procedure for Submission of Application

(i) The eligible tourism service provider shall obtain prior approval of the Ministry of Tourism, Government of India, before proceeding abroad to participate in trade fair/ exhibition. The application shall be submitted direct to the Additional Director-General (Tourism), Ministry of Tourism, Transport Bhawan, Sansad Marg, New Delhi, in the prescribed format at least 14 days in advance, along with following documents:

   1. Proof of approval of the company by Department of Tourism (Copy of approval letter may be attached).
   2. Certificate of Foreign Exchange Earnings duly certified by Chartered Accountant.
   3. Details of financial assistance availed during the last three years from the Government including Ministry of Commerce/FIEO & Department of Tourism.

Procedure for Submission of Application

(i) The eligible tourism service provider shall obtain prior approval of the Department of Tourism, Government of India, before printing of publicity material for distribution abroad. The application shall be submitted direct to the Additional Director-General (Tourism), Ministry of Tourism, Transport Bhawan, Sansad Marg, New Delhi, in the prescribed format at least 14 days in advance, along with following documents:

1. Proof of approval of the company by Department of Tourism (Copy of approval letter may be attached)
2. Certificate of Foreign Exchange Earnings duly certified by Chartered Accountant.
3. Details of financial assistance availed during the last three years from the Government including Ministry of Commerce/FIEO & Ministry of Tourism.

ii) After distribution of the publicity material abroad for which prior approval had been accorded by the DOT, tourism service provider would submit the application for MDA claim, in the prescribed format along with necessary documents as indicated in the claim form, direct to the Ministry of Tourism, Government of India, immediately on return to India but positively within one month of his/her return to India, along with the necessary documents.

General Conditions Governing the MDA Scheme

1. For sale-cum-study tour, a tourism service provider is eligible for financial assistance under MDA Scheme for a maximum of two trips in one financial year.
2. For participation in fairs/exhibitions abroad, a tourism service provider is eligible for financial assistance under MDA Scheme to participate in two exhibitions/fairs abroad in one financial year.
3. For production/printing of publicity material, MDA would be available once in a financial year.
4. The financial benefit under MDA Scheme would be given up to a maximum of only two times to the same person in one financial year, irrespective of the number of tourism service providing companies he/she is associated with.

5. These revised MDA guidelines are in supercession to guidelines issued vide this Department's letter No. 15-TP(58)/2001 dated 21.8.2003.
6. These Revised Guidelines will come in force with effect from 16th March, 2004 and till further orders.

PROMOTION SOCIETY

It has been felt for a long time that marketing of India's tourism should be highly focussed, highly professional and highly innovative. Whilethe Govt. of India Tourist Offices in 18 destinations overseas have been promoting India tourism product, it is generally believed that it has fallen short of expectations. Being an extension of the Governmental activity, the Govt. of India Tourist Offices do not have the type of freedom nor the type of resources that are essential for high level publicity and promotion through electronic media and otherwise. The Ministry of Tourism, therefore, took the initiative of having a dialogue with the industry with a view of set up an organisation fully funded and driven by the leaders of hospitality and travel industry with a set of marketing professionals who could meet the objectives and take the marketing efforts much beyond the activities of the Govt. of India Tourist Offices.

After almost 6 months of consultations amongst the industry leaders facilitated by the Govt. of India, Ministry of Tourism, a society has been formed under the Societies's Registration Act to which the industry would provide funds for start up and subsequent operations.

It is a great day for the tourism in this country when all the players in the tourism sector have come together on one platform to promote and build * equity for India's Tourism overseas.

The Society will work for the following objectives:

1. To create brand equity for Indian Tourism product and related services.
2. To promote and market India overseas as a tourist destination.
3. To increase coorperation and unanimity amongst entities involved in tourism related activities in India and abroad.

4. To communicate with Central and State Government and other public bodies within or outside India to achieve the above objectives.
5. To make representations to local and Central Authorities on any matter connected with promotion of tourism.
6. To invest the money and the property of the society not immediately required for the purpose of its objects in such securities or in such manners as may from time to time be determined and subject to the approved modes of investments under the Income Tax Act, 1961.
7. To raise any moneys required for the purposes of the society upon such terms and such manner as may be determined.
8. To affiliate, aid, end to receive aid from international organisations, Govts, any other society, society, company, corporation, firm or person promoting or intending to promote any of the objects of the society and to subscribe to or aid any such society, society, company, corporation, firm or person with a view to obtain any advantage or benefit for the purpose of society and to subscribe to any fund or society as may be considered deserving from time to time.
9. To subscribe, to become a member of and cooperate with any other society, whether incorporated or not, whose objects are all together or in part similar to those of this society and to procure from and to communicate to any such society, such information as may be likely to forward the objects of the society.
10. To do all such things as may be conducive to development of tourism related trade or incidental to attainment of the above objects or any of them.

The following have signed the Articles of Association as the founding members:

1. ITC Hotels Ltd.
2. Asian Hotels Ltd.
3. Indian Hotels Ltd.
4. East India Hotels

5. C&MD (ITDC)
6. Travel Corpn. of India
7. SITA World Travel (India) Ltd.
8. Thomos Cook
9. Director General of Tourism (Honorary Member)

Each founding member of the Society will make a contribution of Rs. 15.00 Lakhs as seed money and a membership fee of Rs. 25000/-per annum. The office of the Society will be located in Ashok Hotel, New Delhi.

Membership

Anybody, corporate, firm, partnership or person who is engaged in the business of hospitality, travel and tourism or tourism related activities and approved, where applicable by the Ministry of Tourism in this regard shall be eligible for membership of the society on payment of prescribed membership fee as per the Rules and Regulations of the Society.

Bibliography

Abram, Simone: *Tourists and Tourism: Identifying with People and Places*, New York, Berg, 1997.

Andronicou, Antonios: *Tourism in Cyprus*, New York, Oxford University Press, 1979.

Apostolopulos, Y., S. Lewadi: *The Sociology of Tourism*, New York, Routledge, 1996.

Ashworth, Gregory J.: *Marketing Tourism Places*, London, Routledge, 1990.

Baldacchino, G.: *'Global Tourism and Informal Labour Relations: The Small-scale Syndrome at Work'*, Mansell, UK, 1997.

Baum, T.: *'Human Resource Issues in International Tourism'*, Butterworth Heinemann, UK, 1993.

Bennett, O.: *Financing for Tourism Projects in Developing Countries*, England, Wiley, 1994.

Boniface, B.G. and Cooper, C.: *Geography of Travel and Tourism*, Butterworth Heinemann, UK, 1994.

Bruce, David : *Tourism Strategies for Rural Development*, Sackville, New Brunswick, 1993.

Bruner, Edward M.: *In International Tourism: Identity and Change*, London, Sage, 1995.

Brunt, P.: *Market Research in Travel & Tourism*, Butterworth Heinemann, UK, 1997.

Butler, R., Hall, R. and Jenkins, M.: *Tourism and Recreation in Rural Areas*, Wiley, UK, 1998.

Chambers, Erve: *Tourism and Culture: An Applied Perspective*, Albany, State University of New York Press, 1997.

Conlin, M. and Baum, T.: *Island Tourism: Management Principles and Practice*, Wiley, UK, 1995.

Cooper, C.: *Tourism: Principles and Practice*, London, Pitman, 1993.

Creque, Darwin: *A Study of the Tourist Industry in the U.S. Virgin Islands*, North Carolina, Amalie, 1964.

Daniel, R.: *Recent Advances in Tourism Marketing Research*, New York, Hawthorne Press, 1996.

David W.: *Tourism Planning*, Chicago, Council of Planning Librarians, 1995.

Davidson, R.: *European Business Travel and Tourism*, England, Wiley, 1994.

Edward, M.: *In International Tourism: Identity and Change*, London, Sage, 1995.

Glenn Kreag, and John Sem: *A Training Guide for Rural Tourism Development*, Minnesota: Rural Tourism Center, 1995.

Harrison, David: *Tourism and the Less Developed Countries*, London, Belhaven, 1992.

Hudman, Lloyd E.: *Tourism: A Shrinking World*, Columbus, Grid, 1980.

Hunter, Colin, and Howard Green: *Tourism and the Environment: A Sustainable Relationship*, New York, Routledge, 1995.

Ireland, Lewis: *Quality Management for Projects and Programs*, Upper Darby, PMI, 1991.

James, Valentine Udoh: *Tourism Development: A Research Note on Africa*, Connecticut, Praeger, 1996.

Jenkins, J.: *Tourism and Recreation in Rural Areas*, Chichester, U.K., 1998.

John Sem: *A Training Guide for Rural Tourism Development*, Minnesota: Rural Tourism Center, 1995.

Julia, Sharpley: *Rural Tourism: An Introduction*, London, International Thomson Business Press, 1997.

Knox, J.: *Tourism Research Priorities in Hawaii and the Pacific*, Honolulu, University of Hawaii, 1979.

Kotler, Philip: *Marketing for Hospitality and Tourism*: New Jersey, Prentice-Hall, 1998.

Leonard J.: *An Introduction to Tourism*, New York, Butterworth-Heinemann, 1997.

Lloyd, E.: *Tourism: A Shrinking World*, Columbus, Grid, 1980.

Marcouiller, David W.: *Tourism Planning*, Chicago, Council of Planning Librarians, 1995.

Margaret Whitla: *Tourism Strategies for Rural Development*, Sackville, New Brunswick, 1993.

Martinus J.: *Tourism by Train: Its Role in Alternative Tourism*, Philadelphia, University of Pennsylvania Press, 1992.

Mary, E.: *A Heritage Tourism Tool: National Register of Historic Places*, Radnor, Pennsylvania, 1993.

McConnell II, D. W.: *Nature-Based Tourism and Rural Coastal Development: Observations, Options, and Trends*, South Carolina, Clemson University, 1990.

Mieczkowski, Zbigniew: *Environmental Issues of Tourism and Recreation*, Lanham, University Press of America, 1995.

Muzaffer Uysal: *Recent Advances in Tourism Marketing Research*, New York, Hawthorne Press, 1996.

Nelson, Bob and Economy, Peter: *Managing for Dummies*, Foster City, IDG Books, 1996.

Purcell, Douglas C.: *Heritage Tourism is in the Future of Many Alabama Communities*, Auburn Univ., Auburn, 1991.

Richard, W.: *Tourism and Recreation in Rural Areas*, Chichester, U.K., 1998.

Ryan, Chris: *Recreational Tourism: A Social Science Perspective*, London, Routledge, 1991.

Sharpley, Richard: *Rural Tourism: An Introduction*, London, International Thomson Business Press, 1997.

Soskice, D.W.: *Appraising Tourist Development in a Small Economy*, London, Heinemann, 1976.

Stephen F.: *Linking Tourism, the Environment, and Sustainability*, Ogden, Utah, 1995.

Stephen, C.: *Tourism in the Navajo Country: Resources and Planning*, Winslow Rock, Navajo Tribe, 1967.

Suggs, C.: *Tourism Research Priorities in Hawaii and the Pacific*, Honolulu, University of Hawaii, 1979.

Valentine, Udoh: *Tourism Development: A Research Note on Africa*, Connecticut, Praeger, 1996.

Victor T. C.: *Sustainable Tourism: A Marketing Perspective*, Woburn, Massachusetts: Butterworth-Heinemann, 1998.

William W. Swart: *Planning for Tourism Development: Quantitative Approaches*, New York, Praeger, 1976.

INDEX

T

V

W

□□□